34.95

Robert Hauptman
Susan Hubbs Motin
Editors

The Holocaust: Memories, Research, References

The Holocaust: Memories, Research, Reference has been co-published simultaneously as *The Reference Librarian*, Numbers 61/62 1998.

Pre-publication
REVIEWS,
COMMENTARIES,
EVALUATIONS . . .

"**A**t a time when the Holocaust is being integrated as a course or unit in the K-12 curriculum, teachers will find this edited work of immense value. Educators will especially find interesting articles about use of the Internet and World Wide Web for investigating the Holocaust, an important feature, as this realm of technology is especially prone to misuse. Most significantly, this volume suggests how professionals must get the story right and also be sensitive not only to the Jewish story during the Holocaust, but other groups such as Roma and Sinti, and other forms of genocide which continue today."

Stephen Feinstein, PhD
Professor of History
Acting Director
Center for Holocaust
and Genocide Studies
University of Minnesota, Minneapolis

"We live in a time when the international Red Cross publicly acknowledges their "moral failure" to respond aggressively to the Holocaust. We live in a time where much is written denying that these tragic and unbelievable events ever occurred. This is not easy stuff, nor should it be. It is painful–no way around it. This is not a typical volume of *The Reference Librarian*, nor can it be. We are dealing with the unthinkable. We are trying to cope with the concept of more than six million "vanished lives." One author termed it "understanding the un-understandable." We are addressing past events that many say cannot happen now, but they do. Edited by Hauptman and Motin, the diverse contributions to "The Holocaust: Memories, Research, Reference" paint a provocative picture of the events of the Holocaust as well as explore educational, library, research and pedagogical perspectives and strategies for these tragic events in our history. Articles includes discussions of the U.S. Memorial Holocaust Museum, approaches for teaching about the Holocaust, the development and use of Holocaust research centers, the silence of churches, perspectives from Congressional Source Materials, qualitative versus quantitative research analyses, biomedical ethical issues (e.g., scientific information obtained by Nazi doctors who violated the Hippocratic Oath), the roles of Holocaust historians, Canadian perspectives, Holocaust autobiographies, examination of the Holocaust through survivor lives and literary works, denial literature, oral histories, Library of Congress cataloging perspectives, extensive Internet resources, and other related research and reference analyses. This is a vital and important work that should be available in every academic institution."

Fred Batt, MLS
Associate Dean, Library
California State University
Sacramento

The Holocaust:
Memories, Research, Reference

The Holocaust: Memories, Research, Reference has been simultaneously co-published as *The Reference Librarian*, Numbers 61 and 62 1998.

Forthcoming topics in *The Reference Librarian* series:

• Four Views of Document Delivery Service, Number 63

Published:

The Holocaust: Memories, Research, Reference has been co-published simultaneously as *The Reference Librarian*, Numbers 61/62 1998.

The development, preparation, and publication of this work has been undertaken with great care. However, the publisher, employees, editors, and agents of The Haworth Press and all imprints of The Haworth Press, Inc., including The Haworth Medical Press and The Pharmaceutical Products Press, are not responsible for any errors contained herein or for consequences that may ensue from use of materials or information contained in this work. Opinions expressed by the author(s) are not necessarily those of The Haworth Press, Inc.

The Haworth Press, Inc., 10 Alice Street, Binghamton, NY 13904-1580 USA

Cover art (a woodcut entitled "Shin/Fire") by Terry Hauptman

Cover design by Thomas J. Mayshock Jr.

Library of Congress Cataloging-in-Publication Data

The Holocaust : memories, research, reference / Robert Hauptman, Susan Hubbs Motin, editors.
     p. cm.
     "Simultaneously co-published as The reference librarian, numbers 61 and 62, 1998."
     Includes bibliographical references and index.
     ISBN 0-7890-0379-1 (alk. paper)
     1. Holocaust, Jewish (1939-1945)–Historiography. 2. Holocaust, Jewish (1939-1945)–Study and teaching. 3. Holocaust, Jewish (1939-1945)–Research. I. Hauptman, Robert, 1941- . II. Motin, Susan Hubbs.
D804.348.H65 1998
940.53′18′072–dc21
                                          97-49165
                                             CIP

The Holocaust: Memories, Research, Reference

Robert Hauptman
Susan Hubbs Motin
Editors

The Holocaust: Memories, Research, Reference has been simultaneously co-published as *The Reference Librarian,* Numbers 61 and 62 1998.

The Haworth Press, Inc.
New York • London

INDEXING & ABSTRACTING

Contributions to this publication are selectively indexed or abstracted in print, electronic, online, or CD-ROM version(s) of the reference tools and information services listed below. This list is current as of the copyright date of this publication. See the end of this section for additional notes.

- *Academic Abstracts/CD-ROM,* EBSCO Publishing Editorial Department, P.O. Box 590, Ipswich, MA 01938-0590

- *Academic Search: data base of 2,000 selected academic serials, updated monthly:* EBSCO Publishing, 83 Pine Street, Peabody, MA 01960

- *CNPIEC Reference Guide: Chinese National Directory of Foreign Periodicals,* P.O. Box 88, Beijing, People's Republic of China

- *Current Awareness Abstracts,* Association for Information Management, Information House, 20-24 Old Street, London EC1V 9AP, England

- *Current Index to Journals in Education,* Syracuse University, 4-194 Center for Science and Technology, Syracuse, NY 13244-4100

- *Educational Administration Abstracts (EAA),* Sage Publications, Inc., 2455 Teller Road, Newbury Park, CA 91320

- *IBZ International Bibliography of Periodical Literature,* Zeller Verlag GmbH & Co., P.O.B. 1949, d-49009 Osnabruck, Germany

- *Index to Periodical Articles Related to Law,* University of Texas, 727 East 26th Street, Austin, TX 78705

- *Information Science Abstracts,* Plenum Publishing Company, 233 Spring Street, New York, NY 10013-1578

- *Informed Librarian, The,* Infosources Publishing, 140 Norma Road, Teaneck, NJ 07666

- *INSPEC Information Services,* Institution of Electrical Engineers, Michael Faraday House, Six Hills Way, Stevenage, Herts SG1 2AY, England

(continued)

- *INTERNET ACCESS (& additional networks) Bulletin Board for Libraries ("BUBL") coverage of information resources on INTERNET, JANET, and other networks.*
  - <URL:http://bubl.ac.uk/>
  - The new locations will be found under <URL:http://bubl.ac.uk/link/>.
  - Any existing BUBL users who have problems finding information on the new service should contact the BUBL help line by sending e-mail to <bubl@bubl.ac.uk>.

  The Andersonian Library, Curran Building, 101 St. James Road, Glasgow G4 0NS, Scotland

- *Journal of Academic Librarianship: Guide to Professional Literature, The*, Grad School of Library & Information Science/Simmons College, 300 The Fenway, Boston, MA 02115-5898

- *Konyvtari Figyelo-Library Review,* National Szechenyi Library, Centre for Library and Information Science, H-1827 Budapest, Hungary

- *Library & Information Science Abstracts (LISA),* Bowker-Saur Limited, Maypole House, Maypole Road, East Grinstead, West Sussex, RH19 1HH England

- *Library Literature,* The H.W. Wilson Company, 950 University Avenue, Bronx, NY 10452

- *MasterFILE: updated database from EBSCO Publishing,* EBSCO Publishing, 83 Pine Street, Peabody, MA 01960

- *Newsletter of Library and Information Services,* China Sci-Tech Book Review, Library of Academia Sinica, 8 Kexueyuan Nanlu, Zhongguancun, Beijing 100080, People's Republic of China

- *OT BibSys,* American Occupational Therapy Foundation, P.O. Box 31220, Bethesda, MD 20824-1220

- *Referativnyi Zhurnal (Abstracts Journal of the All-Russian Institute of Scientific and Technical Information),* 20 Usievich Street, Moscow 125219, Russia

- *Sage Public Administration Abstracts (SPAA),* Sage Publications, Inc., 2455 Teller Road, Newbury Park, CA 91320

(continued)

SPECIAL BIBLIOGRAPHIC NOTES

related to special journal issues (separates)
and indexing/abstracting

- ☐ indexing/abstracting services in this list will also cover material in any "separate" that is co-published simultaneously with Haworth's special thematic journal issue or DocuSerial. Indexing/abstracting usually covers material at the article/chapter level.

- ☐ monographic co-editions are intended for either non-subscribers or libraries which intend to purchase a second copy for their circulating collections.

- ☐ monographic co-editions are reported to all jobbers/wholesalers/approval plans. The source journal is listed as the "series" to assist the prevention of duplicate purchasing in the same manner utilized for books-in-series.

- ☐ to facilitate user/access services all indexing/abstracting services are encouraged to utilize the co-indexing entry note indicated at the bottom of the first page of each article/chapter/contribution.

- ☐ this is intended to assist a library user of any reference tool (whether print, electronic, online, or CD-ROM) to locate the monographic version if the library has purchased this version but not a subscription to the source journal.

- ☐ individual articles/chapters in any Haworth publication are also available through the Haworth Document Delivery Service (HDDS).

This volume is dedicated to
The victims of the Holocaust, both living and gone,
And the memory of Derora Bernstein (1943-1974), friend and scholar

No Paper Bird

Terry Hauptman

You cry out from the box car:
'Shayna Madelah'
One shriek for
Treblinka Auschwitz Dachau Birkenau
O night is dragging its corpses
This hole at the center of sound

No paper bird Beloved
The nightwind knows your number
Your violin leading us onward
You cry out from the mass grave
You kiss earth's colors back to ash
You gaze in the afterglow of hounds
O night is dragging its corpses
This hole at the center of six million

Mad Prowess and Testimony
I Remember I Bear Witness

The Holocaust:
Memories, Research, Reference

CONTENTS

ABOUT THE EDITORS

Robert Hauptman, PhD, is Professor of Learning Resource Services at St. Cloud State University in St. Cloud, Minnesota, where he teaches graduate courses in librarianship and undergraduate courses in the honors program. He is the editor of *Journal of Information Ethics*, and his nearly five hundred publications include *Ethical Challenges in Librarianship* (Oryx, 1988) and *Technology and Information Services* (Ablex, 1993), which he co-authored with Carol Anderson.

Susan Hubbs Motin, MLS, formerly a medical reference librarian at Loyola University in Chicago, Illinois, is Assistant Professor at St. Cloud State University in St. Cloud, Minnesota, where she is the coordinator of the Reference Team. She manages Holocaust material and library sessions and is a member of the Holocaust Advisory Committee for the St. Cloud State University Center for Holocaust Studies. She is also an interviewer for the Spielberg Foundation's Visual History of the Shoah project.

Introduction

We don't have the murder weapon, the fingerprints. We depend
on documents (and) the Nazis documented almost everything.

–Eli Rosenbaum

The Holocaust is an historical event and as such it continues to
exist in memory, landmarks, artifacts, museums, archives, documents, studies, interviews, literary works, and films. Many survivors, scholars and concerned people insist that we must never forget
what happened so that we may continue to affirm the collective
memory and also to avoid a repetition. At the same time, it is
equally important to refuse to popularize the Holocaust by turning it
into an icon for visual or verbal articulation through gratuitous
overviews, studies, commercial films and museum displays. The
Holocaust and its continuing impact is, of course, not to be considered merely as material for just another dissertation, academic
promotion or cinematic epic. It is an event that researchers need to
plumb deeply in order to explain aspects of western culture that we
often choose to keep hidden from ourselves. Herbert Hirsch insists
that applying strict "scientific" methodologies to the study of genocide trivializes human memory: method replaces substance, the
empirical replaces the emotional, and quantification replaces qualitative discussion (74, 77).

This volume is rather different in structure and content. It is
realized that a study of the Holocaust requires a diversity of articu-

[Haworth co-indexing entry note]: "Introduction." Hauptman, Robert, and Susan Hubbs Motin.
Co-published simultaneously in *The Reference Librarian* (The Haworth Press, Inc.) No. 61/62, 1998,
pp. 1-3; and: *The Holocaust: Memories, Research, Reference* (ed: Robert Hauptman, and Susan Hubbs
Motin) The Haworth Press, Inc., 1998, pp. 1-3. Single or multiple copies of this article are available for a
fee from The Haworth Document Delivery Service [1-800-342-9678, 9:00 a.m. - 5:00 p.m. (EST). E-mail
address: getinfo@haworth.com].

lations and therefore a wider breadth of scholarly materials was allowed. The primary emphasis has been placed upon research and the research process. The importance of this may be seen by two revelations. First, in the recent release of World War II files, it was discovered that the Red Cross was aware of the plight of the Jews in concentration camps but was unable to inform anyone. The 25,000 pages of microfilm concerning this issue are now located in the United States Holocaust Memorial Museum (Molotsky). Second, the British Military intercepts from Belarus and the Ukraine that were just made public also show that British Intelligence was aware at an early date of what was occurring. William J. Vanden Heuvel, however, insists that even in 1941, the early murders were public knowledge. Thus, it becomes more evident that when documented material is made available, the complex realities of the Holocaust present multiple painful realities of 20th century western civilization.

Not only should librarians stay abreast of current research and documentation that is continually being released, but as reference librarians working with students learning about the Holocaust or assisting Holocaust scholars in their research, it is also our responsibility to be sensitive and to understand the multitude of issues surrounding the Holocaust. One such issue is language. As in other areas of study, the language used in researching the Holocaust can greatly affect our retrieval of information. For example, historians often use the term revisionism in an acceptable scholarly fashion, but when discussing revisionism in the Holocaust it can become terminology that is used by those whose intent is to obfuscate the reality of the Holocaust. The Internet has also had an impact on the study of the Holocaust. There are many Holocaust sites available via the web and the number continues to grow. Sites such as the United States Holocaust Memorial Museum (http://www.ushmm.org./) and Yad Vashem (http://www.yad-vashem.org.il/) along with many others have added to the electronic resources available. The librarian also must be knowledgeable and employ his or her training and expertise to critically evaluate the abuses that can occur with web sites. Finally, by creating guides that include both print and electronic resources, librarians can greatly assist their patrons in both accessing and assessing materials including those covering the Holocaust. To meet this goal, the reference librarians at St. Cloud State University have created a number of webliographies including one on the Holocaust (http:lrs.stcloud.msus.edu/guides/web/holocaust.html).

Robert Hauptman
Susan Hubbs Motin

REFERENCES

Molotsky, Irvin. "Red Cross Admits Knowing of the Holocaust During the War." *The New York Times*, December 19, 1996: B17.

Heuvel, William J. Vanden. "The Holocaust Was No Secret." *The New York Times Magazine*, December 22, 1996: 30-31.

Hirsch, Herbert. *Genocide and the Politics of Memory*. Chapel Hill: University of North Carolina Press, 1995.

PART I:
MEMORIES

Auschwitz-Birkenau

Arnost Lustig

To write of Auschwitz-Birkenau as it was–no one will do. There were written ten thousand books on Auschwitz-Birkenau till today and we still do not understand. Three writers, who survived it and wrote down what they had seen, committed suicide: Tadeusz Borowski, the greatest talent of Polish literature in our century, almost immediately after he had completed his description of that inferno. Jean Amery, the Austrian humanist and essayist, when he found that the experience would remain the source of explanation for much that was still to come. And Primo Levi, the best one of many, tried to deliver the message only to find out the impossibility to communicate it. Many people who survived Auschwitz-Birkenau went

Arnost Lustig is affiliated with the Department of Literature, The American University, Massachusetts and Nebraska Avenues, NW, Washington, DC 20016.

[Haworth co-indexing entry note]: "Auschwitz-Birkenau." Lustig, Arnost. Co-published simultaneously in *The Reference Librarian* (The Haworth Press, Inc.) No. 61/62, 1998, pp. 5-14; and: *The Holocaust: Memories, Research, Reference* (ed: Robert Hauptman, and Susan Hubbs Motin) The Haworth Press, Inc., 1998, pp. 5-14. Single or multiple copies of this article are available for a fee from The Haworth Document Delivery Service [1-800-342-9678, 9:00 a.m. - 5:00 p.m. (EST). E-mail address: getinfo@haworth.com].

insane as soon as the war was over. Some survivors gave birth to insane children.

Nine out of ten survivors of Auschwitz-Birkenau gain safe distance from it during the day, but at night, when the will is suspended, they inevitably return to it. The American commander of one of the postwar camps for displaced persons is unable to forget the panic that took hold of the people from Auschwitz-Birkenau. Their panic was that the Nazis would come back. Auschwitz-Birkenau was not behind them, but with them. In them.

When I returned to Auschwitz-Birkenau recently a new horror possessed me. Auschwitz-Birkenau as a museum commemorating human brutality does not evoke in one's imagination even a shadow of the fear, anxiety and hopelessness that a single moment of this death factory induced while in full operation. Auschwitz-Birkenau, this empty, silenced camp, the largest one ever built for man, today seems like a calm burial ground. The dead do not talk. The land is almost beautiful, whether grassy or covered with snow, the rivers, Sola and Vistula, lovely. Memory that serves the living betrays the dead. I have been sick to my stomach while writing these words. It is not in one's power, even if one thought of nothing else since leaving Auschwitz-Birkenau, to recall more that a fraction of what was, what happened, how four million innocents died here.

The town of Auschwitz, Poland, connected with the village of Birkenau, near Katowice, and a step from Cracow, is 800 years old. It hosted a garrison of cavalry in Austro-Hungarian times. The time of the gas, the fire, the human ashes, the time of the crematory is now past. I rage at my impotence to express in words the weakness of memory. Balzac is supposed to have said that evil that is too great can never be punished. How to bring this to terms with the four million dead who saw their sun, stars and moon here, with the mothers who saw the last of their children? How at least to breathe afterlife into them?

Once I was a prisoner here. Why do I now feel the same as those who were never here, who never saw Auschwitz-Birkenau? How can I call back to life the feeling of the dead?

Was I really at the camp gate when the orchestra, made up of the finest musicians of occupied Europe, played the French hit "J'attendriai" for the workers going to the chemical plant, Buna Werke, or to the Auto Union? Once we overheard a trio that sang the German version of that hit for those who had attempted to escape and were caught and escorted back to the camp. A piece of paper was pinned to their chest, on which was written: "*Ich bin schon wieder da*" (I am here again). The trio sang: "*Komm zuruck, denn ich warte auf dich, denn du bist fur mich all mein Gluck.*" Come back to me, I am waiting for you—for you who are my happiness.

Did I really stand here in the wind when two friends of mine, the older T. and the younger T., were told to play as best they could but not to win in a soccer game against eleven S.S. men, and to remember that any injury they might inflict on the Germans, or even on themselves, would send them into the chimney? Surviving, they received a loaf of German commissary bread and a half-pound of blood pork pate. I watched the older T.'s clothes and shoes until they were through playing. It was almost like home—two teams, dressing rooms, lines, a field, goals and a round ball. But, as Tadeusz Borowski later wrote, between the starting and final whistle of the referee, a stone's throw from the soccer field, 3,000 people went to the gas.

Did I really talk with twins Pavel and Peter on whom a German doctor experimented and whom he castrated? Back in Theresienstadt at the Home for Youth, the twins gave me three ounces of sugar in exchange for a collection of poems by the Catholic poet Otakar Brezina. When I asked where their parents were, they replied that they had flown through the chimney in Crematorium No. 2 as if telling me they had taken the Orient Express to Istanbul.

But these are only details. The main purpose of the camp was to kill millions of people in a world where conscience meant weakness or crime.

I remember how in September 1944 we were brought through the gate onto the ramp in Auschwitz-Birkenau. We felt what animals feel before a solar eclipse or a forest fire or an earthquake.

Within several minutes, children under fifteen, women and men above forty, the sick and the ones with glasses or grey hair, were in showers where Cyclon B came through the roof and out of the ceiling instead of water. In half an hour, a greasy fire was flashing from Chimneys No. 2 and No. 3, followed by smoke that gave off the pungent smell of human bones. On the bathroom was written

"ZUM BAD", "ZUM DESINFEKTION" (to the bath, to disinfection).

All those who could not work, or looked as if they would not last, went to the gas, walking through the gate with the inscription "ARBEIT MACHT FREI"–Work liberates.

I understand how difficult it is to write about this in primers and textbooks for children who were born years after the time when the swastika flag fluttered above Auschwitz-Birkenau headquarters. Sometimes I wish that all men and women, wherever they live on earth, would have to visit Auschwitz-Birkenau for a day, an hour, or even a single second during the time when Hitler, Himmler, Eichmann or Baldur von Schirach, the Hitler Youth leader, swelled with pride at what they had commissioned German architects, planners and builders to do. This visit would be a test of maturity, before they could receive a driver's license or be allowed to vote or get married–with a guarantee, of course, that nothing would happen to them. I believe that this peek into hell would ripen their image of the world, for only those who have seen how little is needed to peel what is human from us, to turn us again into animals, can understand the world into which we are born.

Auschwitz-Birkenau is at the beginning of all question that torment us, and instead of providing answers it can only lead to further questions.

I remember an afternoon in September 1944 when I stood in the Gypsy camp by the high-voltage wires, surrounded by bare Polish plains and forests. A thin transparent fog enveloped the ground, the people. It penetrated the soul. We could see Crematory No. 2 and No. 3, where our relatives were burning. A purple fire flashed from the chimneys, glowing a deeper purple before turning into evil-reeking black smoke. Everything stank. The smoke became a cloud, and slowly a black rain–ashes–dropped down. Like everyone else I wished the wind would lift or the earth reverse its direction. The ashes had a bitter taste. They were not from coal or burnt wood, rags or paper.

They fell on us–mute, deaf, relentless ashes, in which human breath, shrieks and tears could be felt. I stood at a concrete fence post with white porcelain insulators, taking it all in like a hallucination. A tune from Johann Strauss's "Die Fledermaus" ran through my mind.

A couple of days earlier I had heard the tune at the cabaret with my father, in the attic of the fire station in Theresienstadt. Now my father was only material for soap. Ashes. Smoke tasting of bones. The fog, as white as swan's wings, turned black, and song, sky and ashes fused into one. The curve of the Strauss melody and the plait of the lyrics suddenly acquired a new meaning: *Glucklich ist, wer vergisst, was doch nicht an Andernist.* Happy the one who forgets what cannot be changed. I was singing. My friends dragged me into the barracks before prisoner count so I would live at least unto the next day.

It was exactly what the men of the S.S. wanted for those who still lived in Auschwitz-Birkenau: to feel as insane and lonely, as lost and helpless, as in a nightmare; to regard the absurd as normal and the normal as absurd. But the loneliness among the dead is still better than the loneliness of the living. Sometimes I would go to the concrete fence post and wires just as one might visit a cemetery, save that our dead did not have graves. I could only catch the ashes in the palm of my hand or watch the chimney smoke day and night.

Once, standing by the wires again, I saw a little herd of naked women. It was October and cold wind blew on them as they each carried shoes and a bundle of effects under their arms. Their heads were shaven bare. The last twenty wore transparent skirts. All were barefoot.

Since my father had become soap and ashes, and since hearing the echo of Strauss's "Fledermaus," I could not get rid of the thought that it would perhaps be better if my mother were to join him. Then I would not have to watch her walk barefoot on the muddy October ground, through wet patches of snow. I watched the chilled women one after another to see if my mother was among them. I saw that she was not walking among the naked ones, nor the ones in shirts. Only when the last two came into view did I see that the next to last was my mother.

I was glad she did not notice me. She did not even watch where she was going. I was sad that she had not been sent to the Bath of Eternal Forgetting. Before they stole her clothes, shoes and underwear, and shaved her head, she had been beautiful. I was unable to call to her. I did not want to imagine what was in store for my mother apart from torture, gas, fire. I watched until she disappeared into the fog. I woke up the next day with the consoling thought that she must have frozen before she reached the end of the road between the wires. In my mind, I buried my mother with that song in which one is happy when one forgets what cannot be changed.

I thought of her when the Jewish women were hanged who had smuggled firing powder from the Krupp-Union-Werke and had helped the Jewish men from the Sonderkommando, a special group of Jewish prisoners responsible for herding prisoners into the showers, then cremating their bodies, to make grenades. Lather, while I was still in Auschwitz-Birkenau, these men set fire to Crematorium No. 4 in Birkenau.

As the rabbi who took a piece of my bread when he thought I was dead told me later, everyone in Auschwitz-Birkenau lived and died alone, as if the world was only a sinking ship where everyone hears the echo: Get away if you can, each on his own, after us the deluge!

We were lying on the concrete in barrack No. 21 as my friend Jiri Fischl, who would die a few weeks after the war in a Prague hospital, consoled me by saying that my father might still be alive. There were no crematory, he said, only tunnels, and the thousands of people who entered them every day exited somewhere on the other side. Fire came from the chimneys because the Germans were burning old rags. The next day, his ten year-old brother, Milan, went into the chimney. His father was a Jew, his mother a Christian. He asked me what I thought. I replied as he had to me the day before. Was I to believe the Germans were killing children like soldiers? Could those buildings be factories? The Germans were burning some junk to scare us.

The Nazis considered Jewish men, women and children as star dust that had no business on planet Earth. But they stowed away every gram of gold from dental bridges and manufactured the tons of shorn hair into blankets, nets and protective suits for German submarine crews. From our bones they made soap in an experimental factory in Danzig and perfumes to beautify German women in the Reich.

Nothing in Auschwitz-Birkenau went to waste except human lives. The men of the S.S. were rewarded for harshness and reproached for the slightest indication of compassion. In Auschwitz-Birkenau, Germany elevated sadism to a state philosophy, robbery to a branch of its national economy. Everything was carefully registered, counted, checked, paid and accounted for, by legions of scribblers, clerks, accountants and auditors in Auschwitz-Birkenau and the Third Reich's control centers.

The Nazis created a system in which Jewish men had to herd their own families into underground baths and then burn their dead bodies, although only the men of the S.S. had the privilege of throwing Cyclon B into the Bath of Eternal Forgetting. I know two of the Jewish helpers who survived by some incredible oversight. What they saw is silenced by the limits of language.

Meilech Buki, now in Jerusalem, worked in the Sonderkommando and listened daily to the men of the S.S. telling the newcomers to undress and not to worry, they would only be taking showers. The arrows pointed "To Disinfection." The S.S. told them they would be working. Germany needed workers. ARBEIT MACHT FREI. Then the S.S. would collect in their caps wedding rings from the poor, jewels from victims better off and watches from everyone.

One day Buki heard his name in the washroom. He saw his younger brother, Joseph, begging for water and asking what was to come. Buki could not tell him. He ran to a man of the S.S. on duty and told him his little brother was to be gassed and cremated in five minutes. Could he give him a little bit of water before he went in? Buki got permission to take a small cup of water from the Jewish cook in the S.S. kitchen. His brother was already in the gas chamber when he returned, so he handed the water to the nearest man and asked him to pass it on to his brother. Buki yelled to Joseph that the same fate awaited him, too, and all of them. Who knows if Joseph heard?

Nothing in the washrooms scared the men of the S.S. as much as panic. It would be evident–as it was many times–that even at the peak of their glory they were not as strong as they perceive themselves to be and as they wanted the world to perceive them. For when hopelessness became clearer than hope to the sacrificial sheep, the sacrificial sheep were transformed into wild tigers–the Jewish men–and wild tigresses–the Jewish mothers. Every Jew did as much as he could—when he knew his fate—to defend himself, to fight. Everyone in his own way.

I spoke to Imrich Gonczi, who came to Auschwitz-Birkenau with his father in July, 1942 from Maidanek, where the Nazis selected agriculture laborers. He convinced his father that where there are horses and cows they will eat. On Saturday in the morning came a young S.S. guard to his father who was working, took his hat, threw it away, then ordered him to run and pick it up. The father ran and the S.S. shot and killed him. Imrich Gonczi jumped at the guard. The S. S. guard hit him with the butt of his rifle and ordered him to pick up his father and to carry him to the camp. He felt his father's blood on his hands. They murdered out all of his family. The mother, sister, aunts, and grandparents but he didn't see it.

Later Imrich Gonczi worked in the *Hygiene Institut der S.S.* in Auschwitz, in the bacteriological laboratory, so that the S.S. doctors would have material for research. When doctors found out that prisoners ate the boiled beef meat, they were ordered to use only the human flesh. They boiled for the S.S. doctors, Jewish men, women, children and old people.

In Auschwitz-Birkenau the Nazis killed the human idea, thousands of years old, that the world is a place where good is rewarded and evil punished. Hitler dismissed conscience as a Jewish invention that cripples the mind just as circumcision cripples the body. If he was able to sacrifice the best German blood, he said, why hesitate to spill the blood of the enemy?

I remember a day that seemed to me like a miracle. I was then a slave leaving Auschwitz-Birkenau to work for one meal a day at what used to be the Hugo Schneider Aktiengesellschaft, making kitchen utensils, but was now the Hassag munitions factory. We produced ammunition for airplane machine guns. It was October 28, 1944, a sunny day. The young S.S. guard with steely blue eyes and blond hair on duty in the train, who went with us to our destination, had a clear expression of disgust against us since he had been brought up to regard us as "the clean vermin." But the disgust of the young S.S. soldier was for the camp, which he was as glad to leave as we were. He told me to sit next to him and then asked me how long I had been there. Without waiting for an answer, he told me that compared to him I knew only a fraction of what Auschwitz-

Birkenau was like. His face expressed many kinds of exhaustion. The fatigue of a man who worked a lot, which in Auschwitz-Birkenau meant killed a lot; the fatigue of a man who had not slept for many nights and even lying in a bed could not fall asleep; and finally, the fatigue of a man for whom life was a burden, a disgust, because it had lost sense and beauty, value and balance. I would be lying if I said I pitied him. Most men of the S.S. were cold-blooded killers, good at their trade. The word compassion was as rare in their vocabulary as were blanks in their firearms. The guard had no one to talk to. Talking to me was not a trick, or a caprice, maybe a spur of the moment. Both of us were leaving hell, he told me, and as soon as the transport arrived, he would ask the S.S. command for a transfer. That meant the Eastern Front and, for a man of the S.S. in the retreating German Army, almost certain death. If his transfer request was rejected, he would kill himself. At no price would he return to serve at Auschwitz-Birkenau.

His face haunts me to this day, as our freight car passed through the gate. ARBEIT MACHT FREI was behind us. We knew we were leaving hell. He confided to me in German, which I had learned to understand, that if he told his father what he did for the S.S. in Auschwitz-Birkenau, his father would never talk to him as a German again; if he told his mother she would kill herself; and if he told his grandmother or grandfather, they would die of shame.

He was not much older than I. I was 17 going on 18, and I had seen what a man living for a thousand years could not have seen. I told him how to commit suicide. You pour water in the gun barrel, put the nozzle in your mouth, and pull the trigger.

I think of that young German in his clean S.S. uniform on the way from Auschwitz-Birkenau as if he were the conscience of Germany. Saying this, I do not want to insult any German who was anti-fascist. I know that during the war Germans existed who could have been brothers of mine. In the munitions factory the foreman would pat my head when no one could see us and say I was going to be his son. He had lost one son in a Stuka raid on London, another in Russia at the Volga; the third, gravely wounded during a retreat from Russia, had died in his homeland. Any Germans who reached out to me I thought mad, or I suspected, or I wondered what had happened to soften them and make them human. I reacted like an animal that an unknown human hand wanted to pet, an animal deaf to human motives. It was this mistrust that Germany bred into me. The bathroom inscriptions—*zum disinfektion, zum bad*—were etched into me, as were the assurances of the men of the S.S. that we were only going to take showers and that we should undress quickly and tie our shoes together by their laces so we could retrieve our things more easily. The foreman used to bring me bread. Sometimes, when he saw that I shared it with my friends, he would bring me more. But that young man of the S.S. I think about differently, almost as I sometimes think about myself, about what has had and will have meaning in my life. I would be glad if he were alive. I would like to hear what he told his wife, his parents, his children. If it was his destiny to die, I would like to know how he died.

In the middle of a clear day I can close my eyes and see shadows. They are not specters but the hunched figures of men and women, children and old people. It is the ramp in Auschwitz-Birkenau, the baths where "Disinfection" is written in German. They are going to the gas. This is the Germany I carry within me. This is the Germany I carry within me even though I wish I could be more like my mother who spoke its language, before Auschwitz-Birkenau became the measure of everything German for her just as well as for me.

In the two thousand years of their existence, the Germans have imprinted their traces on the history and map of Europe. They spread the spirit of their culture throughout the space we all inhabit, as a bee pollinates a blossom before it becomes a flower, an apple, a tree. But twelve years of Nazism submerged that past so fully that it will take another two thousand years at least for the scale to return to where it was before Germany accepted Hitler, Hitler became Germany, and Germany became Auschwitz-Birkenau.

Translated by: Josef Lustig

Viewing the Impossible:
The U.S. Holocaust Memorial Museum

Linda M. Belau

The belief that some things are not possible allows humankind to proceed historically, to comprehend a presumed totality, and to imagine events as they happen. Insofar as there are things that are not possible, the things which we do understand as possible make perfect, rational sense. What, then, of the sudden appearance of the impossible *as possibility*? This is the essence of catastrophe: a catastrophe that radically interrupts and disrupts the historical plane that we often simply presume as stable. It is precisely such a catastrophe that confronts our collective consciousness, shattering our ability–as individuals and as a society–to comprehend the impossibility that is the Holocaust.

More than fifty years after the end of World War II, the last of the Holocaust survivors continue to disappear. With their passing emerges an urgent concern: who will bear witness to the atrocities of the Third Reich? Who will stand in as representative and historian? Who will help us remember the events as they actually took place? Without the materiality of a first-hand account, how will we ever be assured that history will represent this event as it occurred? What, if anything, will be left of the particulars of the Holocaust once the possibility for a material, first-hand witness account is no

Linda M. Belau is affiliated with the Department of Comparative Literature, Binghamton University, State University of New York, POB 6000, Binghamton, NY 13902-6000.

[Haworth co-indexing entry note]: "Viewing the Impossible: The U.S. Holocaust Memorial Museum." Belau, Linda M. Co-published simultaneously in *The Reference Librarian* (The Haworth Press, Inc.) No. 61/62, 1998, pp. 15-22; and: *The Holocaust: Memories, Research, Reference* (ed: Robert Hauptman, and Susan Hubbs Motin) The Haworth Press, Inc., 1998, pp. 15-22. Single or multiple copies of this article are available for a fee from The Haworth Document Delivery Service [1-800-342-9678, 9:00 a.m. - 5:00 p.m. (EST). E-mail address: getinfo@haworth.com].

15

longer available? Not surprisingly, these were among the many questions asked around and about the opening of the United States Memorial Holocaust Museum in Washington DC. With this memorial, the ambition seems, once and for all—and, perhaps, just in time—to set the record straight. There are other Holocaust Museums, and this is precisely why the issues that have erupted around this one are so curious. For some reason, this is the museum that tops them all—the largest collection of artifacts, a prestigious place on the famous Mall, nestled in comfortably with the Washington Monument and the Smithsonian. Amidst the clamor to do something *right*, there is an undeniable impulse to so something *measured*, as if the recording of a catastrophic event demands a certain type of pretension. As if visibility—and the more, the better—were the basis for a viable memory. Does all this necessarily evoke a truer representation of the Event? Does it help us remember better? Or is something essential forgotten in this material contest of memory?

In *The Life of the Mind*, Hannah Arendt insists on the significance what she calls "the unquestioned priority of vision for mental activities."[1] There is just something about *seeing* an event that makes it tenable. This, it seems, is the idea behind this Holocaust memorial: show the nightmare so that visitors will be faced with the reality of it. How any memorial successfully represents the Holocaust or that one can ever adequately do so is questionable, however, especially since it is, in many ways, difficult, if not impossible, to conceptualize the brutal murder of six million (or more) individuals. In the face of such staggering numbers, one is left with the inadequate impression of statistics. Stalin had a compelling point, indeed, with his cynical dictum that one death is a tragedy, while a million deaths is merely a statistic. One moves into a realm of excess which cannot be known in the same way that readily measurable events are understood. Thus, the statistic itself functions as an anonym, marking, in its place, that which is utterly incomprehensible, traumatically exposing the collapse of meaning into the impossibility of understanding.

Any attempt to represent the events of the Holocaust will necessarily be fraught with difficulties, for as Arendt points out, "we attempt to understand elements in present or recollected experience that simply surpass our powers of understanding."[2] These difficulties are especially evident for the writers of survivor accounts who attempt to truthfully recount the events they have witnessed. What is the truth, after all, when one is witness to an unrepresentable and incomprehensible event? How can truth even *begin* to become a player in the realm of the impossible? According to Arendt, victims of the concentration camp experience are often unable to believe even their own memories, especially as they aspire to remember events "truthfully":

> The more authentic they are, the less they attempt to communicate things that evade human understanding and human experience. . . . None of these reports inspires those passions of outrage and sympathy through which men have always been mobilized for justice. On the contrary, anyone speaking or writing about concentration camps is still regarded as suspect; and if the speaker has resolutely returned to the world of the living, he himself is often assailed by doubts with regard to his own truthfulness, as though he had mistaken a nightmare for reality.[3]

Having witnessed the abyss of atrocity, survivors often find themselves reclaiming memories that resist the rigidity of the truth. Lawrence Langer calls this impossibility to reclaim what one could comfortably posit as true "a disconcerting uncertainty about the process of recollection itself."[4] This is not to say that witnesses are less than truthful, of course. The truly devastating point is that they *cannot* be truthful, simply because truth–something we rely on so heavily to order our lives in convenient and comfortable ways–is no longer possible.

To the extent that the concentration camp experience is an impossible and incomprehensible (unimaginable) one, it is impossible for one to think of both its existence as well as its consequences adequately. If one proceeds as a utilitarian thinker, insisting on the usual tools of rationality, then the experience of the concentration camp will remain unthinkable, hopelessly forgotten within the impossibility of memory. Arendt argues that "if we assume that most of our actions are of a utilitarian nature . . . then we are forced to conclude that this particular institution of totalitarianism is beyond human understanding."[5] This is surely a dangerous conclusion, for the concentration camp experience must not be dismissed or ignored as one resigns oneself to the impossibility of representation. At the same time, however, Arendt argues that "the greatest danger for a proper understanding of our recent history is the only too comprehensible tendency of the historian to draw analogies."[6] Thus, one cannot too easily presume to comprehend and explain this experience. If, like Arendt, one is unwilling either to give in to the impossibility of it all or to resort to easy explanations, then one's task is to attempt to think beyond the constraints of rational or utilitarian thought. How is it, then, that one goes about representing and/or memorializing this event? How do we, as a society, take the responsibility to remember such an event while, at the same time, refusing the temptation to reduce it to a knowable and potentially solvable problem? It would seem that, in the attempt to memorialize what I consider the radically unknowable reality of this disaster, one should recognize the tension between the impossibility of an individual memory and the necessity for a historical memory, a historical memory that might, perhaps, emerge out of the kind of memorial that James Ingo Freed, the architect responsible for the design of the Holocaust museum, has built.

In his 1993 editorial in the *Washington Post*, Melvin Jules Bukiet charges that the Holocaust Museum creates a universal symbol of suffering which may serve to distort the reality of the Holocaust and turn it into a reasonably palatable concept that soothes and comforts rather than disturbs. Bukiet maintains that this "tainted gift" jeopardizes the memory of the Holocaust:

> I believe it is because the Shoah has become domesticated, and the War Against the Jews has become safe enough for every suburban synagogue to build its own mini-museum with a few blown-up photographs and a scrap of charred Torah in a display case.
>
> But history and theology are not safe. The Holocaust is a black hole that swallows all light intended to illumine it and threatens to swallow anyone audacious enough to hold the lantern. . . .
>
> Unfortunately the museum will not spur the remembrance the donors seek, but will finally permit this country to forget.[7]

Insofar as it attempts to represent what he considers unrepresentable, Bukiet fears the building of the Holocaust Museum will do more harm than good. Because there is something untouchable and unknowable that characterizes the abyss that is the Holocaust, Bukiet perceives a kind of irresponsibility and, perhaps, disrespect when one attempts to reify the horror and (un)reality that is the Holocaust. In this sense, it seems, the Holocaust must remain radically ahistorical since any attempt to historcize it somehow negates its significance, denying the unbearable fact that no stable memory of it will ever be possible.

There is a fundamental problem with this position, however. Despite the impossibility and incomprehensibility of this event, there remains the unfortunate fact that it actually happened, and some sort of memory must be forged. The Holocaust Museum is responding to this demand. And not without a strong sense of the danger of doing so, one might argue. Embracing so much more than the architect's usual responsibility for a project, James Ingo Freed constantly worried over the complexities of the task as he proceeded. Freed has taken great pains (both literal and figurative pains in the physiological and emotional sense) to embrace the impossibility or ahistoricity of the event as he places it concretely back into history with the monument he was asked to build. Freed understands all too well the ungraspability of what he presumes to represent. Comparing the Holocaust Museum with another project, Freed says,

> the problem with that project [the remarkably abstract Danteum Museum] is that unless you have very specialized knowledge, you don't understand it. It is very cerebral. And I don't believe that you could ever understand the Holocaust with the mind. You have to feel it. Feeling may be a better way of getting at it because horror is not an intellectual category as far as I can tell.[8]

Freed's position clearly embraces the difficulty (if not the impossibility) of his undertaking. He in no way seems to be attempting to domesticate or reify the horror that is the Holocaust by forcing a rigid rationality onto the event that can invoke nothing other than a dishonest memory.

In meeting the challenge to represent the unrepresentable, Freed also does not force absolute expectations onto the act of memory. Memory is polysemic and open-ended, he maintains, and every engagement with the (un)reality of the Holocaust must also necessarily avoid forcing memory onto any kind of established framework. There are no correct memories or interpretations, nor are there undisputed recollections. According to Freed:

> We wanted an evocation of the incomplete. . . . Things call for interpretation but remain insufficient in themselves. The more you know, the greater the difficulty. This kind of distancing with ambiguity was also important because every survivor has his or her own story that is so personal, so stripping. It is essential that people are left with what separates them more than with what joins them together. We created differences, so that memory must play a part.
>
> Perception, or memory, is the most important thing. Because memory is a charlatan. Everybody I talked to has reconstructed a different memory of the event. I as the architect reconstruct yet another memory that never was, but it can act as a resonator for the memories of others.[9]

This multiplicity of memory is where any historicization of the Holocaust can again become a possibility, it seems, and despite the concrete, fixed nature of Freed's building, as well as the suggestion of stability and completion that a concept such as a "permanent collection" evokes, it is precisely during the process of one's engagement with Freed's structure that this possibility emerges out of its utter impossibility. According to James E. Young, "memorials depend completely on the visitor."[10] Young goes on to argue that visitors to memorial sites create a kind of dialogue with the memorial itself, animating the memorial and giving it its power to signify remembrance. In this exchange, there are no common, stable memories, only a shared site of memory where each individual is able to remember. In all of this, Young says,

> we recognize that the art of memory neither begins with a monument's ground-breaking nor ends with the ceremonies conducted at its base. Rather, this art consists in the ongoing activity of memory, in the debates surrounding these memorials, in our own participation in the memorial's performance.[11]

Thus, the possibility for memory emerges out of an open-ended engagement with the impossibility of representation, marked in and through the various debates and controversies that accompany the reception of any attempt to memorialize a catastrophic and incomprehensible event.

Finding a way toward understanding the incomprehensibility of the concentration camp experience is of the most urgent importance if we expect to keep the Holocaust from becoming an absolutely meaningless event. At the same time, we must also be wary of any characterization of events that places them outside the possibility of representation, lest we find ourselves caught up in a too easy avoidance. We must realize that the inadequacies of our language do not necessarily banish representations of the Holocaust and the possibility of its historicization from the sphere of civilized consciousness and normal sociality. Langer argues that, rather than transporting us beyond the limits of understanding, the impossibility of memory drives us to the *periphery* of comprehension. Consequently, Langer insists, "we need to search for the inner principles of *in*coherence that make these representations accessible to us."[12] Incoherence does not mean inaccessibility; in fact, within an expanded notion of representation, it is the *very* thing that yields accessibility, meaning, and history. In order, then, to historicize the impossible event, we must not attempt to fix it in place, to define it completely, as if we have finally, once and for all, learned to know it. We must push beyond the parameters of traditional history and understanding in order to do right by the impossibility of remembrance, for it is precisely this (im)possibility of memory that allows for the historicization of the Holocaust and keeps one from forgetting what cannot be remembered.

NOTES

1. Hannah Arendt, *The Life of the Mind: Thinking* (New York: Harcourt Brace, 1971), p.101.

2. Hannah Arendt, *Origins of Totalitarianism* (New York: Harcourt Brace, 1973), p.441.

3. Ibid., p.439.

4. Lawrence Langer, *Versions of Survival: The Holocaust and the Human Spirit* (Albany, NY: State University of New York Press, 1982), p.xi.

5. Hannah Arendt, "Social Science Techniques and the Study of Concentration Camps," *Jewish Social Studies* 12/1 (1950): p.51.

6. Ibid., p.64.

7. Melvin Jules Bukiet, "The Museum vs. Memory: The Taming of the Holocaust," *Washington Post*, April 18, 1993.

8. James Ingo Freed, "The United States Holocaust Memorial Museum," in *The Art of Memory: Holocaust Memorials in History*, James E. Young, ed. (Munich: Prestel Verlag, 1994), p.96.

9. Ibid., p.96.

10. James E. Young, "The Art of Memory: Holocaust Memorials in History," in *The Art of Memory: Holocaust Memorials in History*, James E. Young, ed. (Munich: Prestel Verlag, 1994), p.37.

11. Ibid., p.38.

12. Lawrence Langer, *Holocaust Testimonies: The Ruins of Memory* (New Haven: Yale University Press, 1991), pp.16-17.

Blue Tattoo:
The Creative Process

Lyn Lifshin

*Lyn Lifshin's **Blue Tattoo** presents chilling graphic images of the Holocaust experience. Yet Ms. Lifshin is neither a Holocaust survivor nor is she the child of survivors. She was, in fact, born in Burlington, Vermont–a decade after the horrors which resulted in World War II.*

***Blue Tattoo** is a collection of poems dealing with the various stages of anti-Jewish sentiment in Europe during the 1930's, culminating in the Holocaust. Often written from a first-person point of view, like letters or diaries, the poems are immediate, intense and accessible. Their presentation in **Blue Tattoo**, with its narrow columns set in type faces from the era, reads like fragments of war news transmitted from the front lines.*

Event Horizon Press recently asked Ms. Lifshin to describe how she became involved in writing about the Holocaust, what her relationship is to the Holocaust, and how she has undertaken writing poetry about it.

As many know, I am not a survivor, nor am I a child of survivors. Growing up Jewish, I heard my mother's accounts of roommates in the mostly non-Jewish college from which she graduated. The roommates would say such things as, "Hitler is right, Frieda, but *you* are different."

The summer I was six, a baby sitter told me tales of what happened in tunnels to Jewish children during World War II. She told

---

Lyn Lifshin, 2719 Baronhurst Drive, Vienna, VA 22181-6158.
Reprinted with permission from The Event Horizon Group.

[Haworth co-indexing entry note]: "Blue Tattoo: The Creative Process." Lifshin, Lyn. Co-published simultaneously in *The Reference Librarian* (The Haworth Press, Inc.) No. 61/62, 1998, pp. 23-26; and: *The Holocaust: Memories, Research, Reference* (ed: Robert Hauptman, and Susan Hubbs Motin) The Haworth Press, Inc., 1998, pp. 23-26.

me of the torture, the ovens. I slept fitfully for that whole year, and often woke up screaming. The stories had entered my dreams, my nightmares, and kept me dreaming of fire over and over. From that time on, I have been haunted and fascinated by the many narratives I heard from those who were actually involved. I was stunned when I first saw the film *Night and Fog* in the '60s, and since then have absorbed as many anecdotes as I could—reports from survivors, stories in films, diaries, and journals, interviews, radio discussions, books, magazine and newspaper articles. I went to museums and exhibits, viewed countless films, and took notes for years, filling my own journals with the chronicles, and trying to capture the speaking voices, just as they told their incredible histories.

Over the years, people have called to tell me their long, long narratives, have asked me to retell their parents' tales, and begged me to write down what they were telling, in order to keep their words and lives alive.

As a poet who writes about diverse subjects I'm often asked to lead writing workshops on many things: feelings about war, mothers and daughters, feelings about women's sexuality and sensuality. I do workshops about writing the story of one's life, the urban ghetto, about diaries and journals, and about writing from the inside out and the outside in—with an emphasis on using museums, exhibits and the lives of others as creative impetus.

When I was asked to do a workshop about Writing Through the Holocaust, in combination with an exhibit and with Holocaust survivors involved, I felt inadequate knowing only the stories of others. But I wanted to bring the reality of the Holocaust—the actual words and feelings and experiences of those who had gone through what they had gone through—to my students, many of whom were not Jewish, many of whom were young. My main aim was one I feel is the same as that most desired by those who perished and those who survived the Holocaust: that their words and experiences not be forgotten. I wanted my students to be close—to get as deeply as possible into the lives and feelings of those who underwent the atrocities and told of them in their own words. I stressed these words to my students through the voluminous notes I had taken.

Over time these words became part of my poems: not with the intention of using the lives and deaths as art for its own sake, but to use art as a means of keeping the reality of the words alive. When planning a workshop, I would take armfuls of books from the library, fifty books at a time, and then go back for more. Friends sighed that I talked and thought of nothing else. I jotted down passages to share with my students, passages to trigger their own poems. These were writing workshops, not history workshops, and it was the passion and feeling, the life experiences, I fervently wanted the students to comprehend.

When Event Horizon Press contacted me about doing a book of Holocaust poems to be published on the fiftieth anniversary of Victory in Europe Day, I sent the editors over a thousand poems. These were derived from readings, interviews, dreams, museum visits. telephone calls, photographs, films, videos, fantasies, surrealistic free-flow, panel discussions, conversations with survivors, stories others told me of their discussions with survivors, letters. exhibits, writing with students in workshops, discussions with soldiers who liberated the camps, African American soldiers, Jewish American soldiers, news reports, radio accounts, children born to survivors in Israel . . .

The process of creativity is one of things merging, being telescoped and braided together with–hopefully–proficiency, imagination, and devices of the craft. Since I am only an *observer* of the Holocaust, the feelings, words and impressions I have set down in the poems must, by their very nature, be ultimately attributed to others.

It would be impossible to pinpoint attributions for each poem in **Blue Tattoo**. A historian recently told me that some of the passages and images are derived from accounts in *Lodz Ghetto: Inside a Community Under Siege*, edited by Alan Adelson and Robert Lapides. She also noted sources such as Robert Azbug's *Inside The Vicious Heart* and *The Art of the Holocaust*, as well as the films *Shoah* and *Hotel Terminus*.

So–the voices in **Blue Tattoo** are based on the voices of those who were involved in the Holocaust. I know some people believe that one who has not participated directly in the Holocaust should not write about it. Others feel that poetry and fiction should not come from these experiences. But I feel that keeping the memory alive, relating the experiences and the suffering, and drawing upon the real words of real people who knew the Holocaust firsthand, is a legitimate way to remember and honor those who were its victims.

This collection of poetry is assembled in the spirit of countless survivors who intoned. "Lest they forget," as they painfully told of their experiences. As a member of the surviving Jewish culture, though not literally a Holocaust survivor, for me their anthem translates "Lest *we* forget." I will continue to do workshops to assure that we do not.

Five Poems from *Blue Tattoo*

Lyn Lifshin

Irena's Story

All week, distant barking
of dogs, guns, shouts
in German: *Alle Juden raus!*
All Jews out. Thousands
of people brought on wagon
to the hospital, taken
in trucks to the unknown.
The last day of deportations
we get up at 6.a.m., drink
boiled water with saccharine.
Luckily, our street has
already been gone through.
But suddenly, gunshots!
Orders are shouted for
all Jews to come out.
Rifle butts bang the door,
Mother grabs my arm—
Maybe we can hide.
Father tries to calm us:
Rub your cheeks,
bite your lips, straighten up
and walk with a smile.

Lyn Lifshin, 2719 Baronhurst Drive, Vienna, VA 22181-6158.
Reprinted with permission from The Event Horizon Group.

[Haworth co-indexing entry note]: "Five Poems from *Blue Tattoo*." Lifshin, Lyn. Co-published simultaneously in *The Reference Librarian* (The Haworth Press, Inc.) No. 61/62, 1998, pp. 27-31; and: *The Holocaust: Memories, Research, Reference* (ed: Robert Hauptman, and Susan Hubbs Motin) The Haworth Press, Inc., 1998, pp. 27-31.

Father is 56 but looks fine.
His face swollen with hunger
looks round and full.
His well-rubbed cheeks,
normal color; no grey hairs.
Mother is thin, her face drawn,
her hair white.
But she is only 42
and her shy eyes
have a beautiful young smile.
We move slowly
through selection.
I am told to go to the right.
I wait, feel my body
a petrified bundle
of muscles and nerves.
Others come,
but not my parents.
I elbow my way through
the crowd of people,
start running
toward the Germans,
see a hand raised,
recognize a neighbor's face.
When I reopen my eyes
I'm standing near the same
people who tried to hide me.
When I get home
I see a classmate, Fryda,
on the stairway, like a mute,
her parents also
never returned.

The Song

Overlooking a quarry
where hundreds of Dutch Jews
have been forced to jump
from a high cliff

to their death.
an SS officer orchestrates
a blasting operation
that makes even
jaded prisoners tremble:
he orders an Italian Jew
known to have a beautiful voice
to stand on a rock mound
and sing the *Ave Maria*.
As he sings, charges
are laid around the rocks.
In mid-song the officer
presses the plunger
and blasts the rocks
and the Jew
with dynamite.

The Red Trillium

Red Trillium
poking up
through thick leaves
dark as menstrual blood
pooling at the bottom
when they open
the gas chambers,
the bodies frozen,
merging,
leaning toward an
imagined light:
a family fused
in the claws of each other,
a daughter climbing
her mother's side,
up past her shoulders
as she did as a baby,
as if the little air left
would help her
hold on.

After The Selection

Old people who had
hidden themselves
come back weak–
some haven't eaten for days–
held by relatives
so they don't fall over.
In the courtyard
a woman bewails.
What do I have in life?
My twelve year old boy
shot today,
my girls six and fourteen
taken away.

Auschwitz

There is an electrical fence.
You can't climb it
but can speak through it.
Families are taken together.
They take their luggage
into the camp.
Their hair isn't cut.
They are treated differently
than anyone here has seen.
These people have
special cards that say
gassing and quarantine.
They're to be kept six months.
There is a school for their
children, a theatre.
They are told to write letters
to relatives in the ghetto
to say they are working,
together.
The SS take the children
to play at Heidi Branch.
At midnight the parents

receive a note.
The *Lake of Ashes* is where
the cremated are dumped.
There is no Heidi;
the train runs right to
the crematorium.

PART II:
RESEARCH

Preparing a Holocaust Unit
for High School Students

Roselle K. Chartock

SUMMARY. This article focuses on how teachers in the Social Studies Department at Monument Mountain Regional High School in Great Barrington, MA constructed, in 1972, a six-week curriculum on the Nazi Holocaust. The unit is considered to be the first formal curriculum on that subject for secondary students. The author of the article, who was a member of the department at that time, explains how she and her colleagues chose the material to be included, which resources were particularly useful and how two of the teachers updated the anthology of readings that had become the basis of the curriculum.

The anthology was published initially by Bantam Books in conjunction with the Anti-Defamation League of B'nai B'rith as a trade book in soft cover and was entitled *The Holocaust Years: Society on Trial* (Chartock and Spencer, eds., 1978). After being out of print for

Roselle K. Chartock is Professor of Education, North Adams State College, North Adams, MA 01247.

[Haworth co-indexing entry note]: "Preparing a Holocaust Unit for High School Students." Chartock, Roselle K. Co-published simultaneously in *The Reference Librarian* (The Haworth Press, Inc.) No. 61/62, 1998, pp. 33-40; and: *The Holocaust: Memories, Research, Reference* (ed: Robert Hauptman, and Susan Hubbs Motin) The Haworth Press, Inc., 1998, pp. 33-40. Single or multiple copies of this article are available for a fee from The Haworth Document Delivery Service [1-800-342-9678, 9:00 a.m. - 5:00 p.m. (EST). E-mail address: getinfo@haworth.com].

nearly ten years, it was republished in hardcover in 1995, with a new title, *Can It Happen Again? Chronicles of the Holocaust* (Black Dog and Leventhal) with nineteen additional entries. Since the 1970s the anthology has served as a springboard for other educators interested in developing their own interdisciplinary curriculum on the Holocaust. *[Article copies available for a fee from The Haworth Document Delivery Service: 1-800-342-9678. E-mail address: getinfo@ haworth.com]*

"When we get to World War II in the textbook, there's always just one line about the Holocaust, just one line!" It was with such frustration voiced by the chairperson of the Social Studies Department at Monument Mountain Regional High School in Great Barrington, Massachusetts, that the creation of a six-week unit of instruction on the Nazi Holocaust began.

After explaining some of the background related to the development of the unit, the author will focus on how its creators chose the material to be included, which resources were particularly useful, and how two of the creators updated the anthology of readings that had become the basis of the curriculum.

The unit, considered to be the first formal curriculum for secondary students on the subject of the Holocaust, was born during the summer of 1972, during which time the social studies department, of which the author of this article was then a member, hunted for and gathered interdisciplinary sources that would fit into a curriculum framework based on the tried and true five Ws. For example, the first question to be addressed was, What happened? But ultimately the major criterion that these sources had to satisfy was to shed light on the question, Why did the Holocaust happen? Their research was facilitated by a small grant from the National Conference of Christians and Jews.

The unit—or at least the readings that comprised the core of the unit—was distributed nationally and internationally in 1978, when Bantam Books in conjunction with the Anti-Defamation League of B'nai B'rith published the anthology entitled *The Holocaust Years: Society on Trial* (Chartock and Spencer, eds., 1978). The paperback trade book was purchased by both high school and college instructors who had been looking for a comprehensive resource on the subject as well as by lay readers interested in this complex and painful phenomenon.

The book went through three editions ending in 1984. During its travels to book shows here and abroad, the book's major claim to fame was to be among the sixteen or so titles banned at the 1981 Moscow Book Fair. In 1995, after being out of print for eleven years, the anthology was republished in hardcover by Black Dog and Leventhal with nineteen additional readings, a new title, *Can It Happen Again? Chronicles of the Holocaust,* and a new chapter sub-section, "Other Voices, Other Victims."

The editors have, over the years, received a number of letters and calls from teachers and school systems indicating that they used this material in order to create their own original units as well as whole courses on the Nazi Holocaust and related subjects.

HOW THE READINGS WERE CHOSEN

As indicated earlier, the readings had to satisfy two objectives. First they had to help answer each of the questions that had become the framework for the unit including What Happened? Who Were the Victims and Victimizers? How and Why? What Does the Holocaust Reveal About the Individual and Society? What Was the Aftermath? and Could It Happen Again? Under each of these broad questions there were additional questions. For example, the last section included What Are Parallels in Literature and Life? and What Are Ominous Signs?

The members of the social studies department had customarily used primary sources in their teaching and usually addressed subjects from interdisciplinary perspectives. So the second objective that needed to be met was to locate materials with historical, political, sociological, philosophical, literary, scientific and psychological frames of reference. The teachers began their search first by looking on their shelves and the shelves of the school library for historical materials related to World War II, Nazism, prejudice and Jewish history. They found, among other books *The Shaping of Western Society: An Inquiry Approach* (Fenton and Goode, 1968) and *The Rise and Fall of the Third Reich* (Shirer, 1960), which fitted the criteria. From Fenton and Goode came "Seven Case Studies," vignettes that reveal the lives and feelings of a cross-section of Germans in the year 1930 and reflect the mood of increasing frustration. These vignettes helped to explain how the Holocaust began. The excerpt the teachers took from Shirer detailed "What Happened?" and included quotations from the testimony of Rudolf Hoess, the commanding officer of Auschwitz.

The teachers referred to publishers' catalogues they regularly received, such as the *Social Studies School Service* and one issued by the Anti-Defamation League in which the teachers found materials related to the nature and causes of prejudice, anti-Semitism in particular. On the shelf was also the classic text, *The Nature of Prejudice* (Allport, 1979) with pertinent explanations of the origins of anti-Semitism and prejudice from a psychological perspective, and *Prejudice: The Invisible Wall* (Goodykoontz, ed., 1968) published by Scholastic, Inc., whose materials the department had been using on a regular basis. From these materials which the teachers already had at their fingertips, they went on to sources in local bookstores, as they awaited the arrival of books they had ordered from catalogs with the assistance of the school librarian.

At the time that the unit was being prepared, 1972, the teachers did not face the kind of overwhelming decisions they would have faced if preparing the unit today. The proliferation of Holocaust-related books had not yet occurred and there were far fewer personal accounts and primary sources to choose from. Elie Wiesel and other survivors of the Holocaust had, however, published either historical novels or autobiographies about their experiences. Besides Wiesel's works (*Night*, 1960 and *Legends of Our Time*, 1968), the teachers tapped Catherine Noren's "We Escaped From Hitler's Germany" (Scholastic, 1974) and Viktor Frankl's *Man's Search for Meaning* (Beacon Press, 1962) among other eyewitness accounts.

Besides the two criteria cited above for selecting excerpts, i.e., fit the framework of questions established and conveyed an interdisciplinary perspective, there were other criteria. The excerpts from Goodykoontz, for example, and one from *Hey, White Girl* (Gregory, 1970) were chosen because of their simplicity of language *and* their power in relating the complex issue of prejudice directly to the students' own lives. It was this power of language and the use of metaphor and allegory that led the teachers to integrate excerpts from literature in their "Parallels in Literature and Life" section. For example, there were clearly indirect relationships to the Holocaust between Huxley's *Brave New World* (Harper Collins, 1960) and Orwell's *Nineteen Eighty-Four* (Harcourt Brace & Co., 1949) and black poet Claude McKay's "If We Must Die" (Harcourt Brace, 1959).

Other selections were chosen for their historical data that provided students with the story of the earliest seeds of the Holocaust. For example, Uriel Tal's *Christians and Jews in Germany* (Magnes Press) contained facts about Christians and Jews in Europe between 1870 and 1914, and Richard Grundberger's *Hitler's SS* (Delacorte Press, 1970) detailed the breeding and euthanasia programs planned and carried out by the Nazis. Although the language of some of *these* excerpts was quite challenging, particularly in the case of the Tal book, the teachers decided to use them for their historical richness and assumed that the less skilled readers could gain this information either with the help of their teachers or through the discussion of the material in class. They also believed that there were a sufficient number of very readable excerpts from which students could gain the knowledge needed to answer certain questions on their own.

It was in part because of the desire to reach all students and because of the power of film that the department decided to supplement the readings with several brilliant films which were readily available, including "The Diary of Anne Frank," "Judgement at Nuremberg," and "Playing for Time," based on the true story of Fania Fenelon who survived Auschwitz because of her membership in the women's orchestra in the concentration camp.

Several useful shorter films were available from the Anti-Defamation League including "Night and Fog," made by French director Alain Resnais who superimposed black and with film footage taken by the Nazis themselves with color scenes of the barren and seemingly innocent camps today.

The teachers also supplemented the anthology with appropriate sources that kept appearing subsequent to their publication in 1978, of *The Holocaust Years: Society on Trial*. For example, they ordered copies of Keneally's *Schindler's List* (Hemisphere Publ., Ltd., 1982) when it first came out and *Maus I* by Art Spiegelman (Pantheon, 1986). But the real core of the unit was the collection of ninety-five readings in their anthology taken from the work of historians, philosophers, psychologists, scientists and poets, all chosen for their usefulness in addressing–though not, perhaps, in fully answering–several basic questions, the main one being, "Why did the Holocaust happen?" The anthology went through three editions, and then Bantam ceased publishing it in 1984.

HOW WE UPDATED AND WHY

The author of this article went on to teach education courses at a small college not far from the high school, but she and her co-editor continued to collect articles and books related to the Holocaust that were appearing almost on a daily basis along with other phenomena both positive and negative in nature. On the positive side was the opening of the Holocaust Memorial Museum in Washington, D.C. in April 1993, and in 1994 the Steven Spielberg film based on Keneally's book about Schindler, the German businessman who helped hundreds of Jews survive. At the same time, however, there was the rise of Neo-Nazis in Germany and the Holocaust denial movement in America as well as the reappearance of genocidal behavior in Rwanda that paralleled the Holocaust in many ways. Clippings from the *New York Times Book Review* section and many newspaper articles related to the above events accumulated, and, by 1992, this author saw the need to include them in the anthology that had been out of print for nearly ten years and to seek another publisher for the updated version.

With co-editor Jack Spencer, who was still teaching in the social studies department at the high school where the unit had been launched, she selected nineteen additional readings that would not only reflect the Holocaust-related events and publications of the last ten years but would also supply important data that had inadvertently been left out of the first editions of the book. In particular, they found material that conveyed the history of other groups targeted for extermination by the Nazis, including gypsies (Fein, Free Press, 1979 and Ramati, 1985) and homosexuals (Sherman, *New York Times*, April 23, 1993) and a book review of Deborah E. Lipstadt's book, *Denying the Holocaust: The Growing Assault on Truth and Memory* (Free Press, 1993). They also relied on the newspaper for the human interest story of one town's response to skinheads in their midst (*New York Times*, February 19, 1994), a story which subsequently went on to be dramatized in a made-for-television movie. Clearly the newspaper was a major reference and source for these anthologists, in addition to interesting new publications such as Sichrovsky's *Born Guilty: Children of Nazi Families* (Basic Books, 1988). Also in keeping with the interdisciplinary approach, a piece entitled "Politics and Music: Wagnerian Music and Thought in the Third Reich" (Chartock, 1988) was among those added.

In all, nineteen readings were added to the anthology and Black Dog and Leventhal, Inc. published the updated version in 1995 in hardcover with a new title, *Can It Happen Again? Chronicles of the Holocaust*. Because of its interdisciplinary approach and its simple framework around basic questions, this anthology represents a useful resource for teachers of different subjects, as well as for the average reader interested in a subject that continues to challenge our ability to fully comprehend. But like any resource, it is limited and thus needs to not only be consistently updated but also supplemented by new research like *Hitler's Willing Executioners: Ordinary Germans and the Holocaust* by Daniel Goldhagen (Knopf, 1996), *and* data that appears on the many Internet web sites, now a rich source of information. Indeed, teachers need not be frustrated any longer when textbooks provide only one line about such major historical phenomena!

REFERENCES AND CENTERS OF INFORMATION

- Center for Studies on the Holocaust

  Anti-Defamation League of B'nai B'rith
  823 United Nations Plaza
  New York, NY 10017
  1-212-490-2525

(One of the best sources for Holocaust-related films and a major reference for this unit.)

- Chartock, Roselle K. and Jack Spencer, eds. (1995)

  Can It Happen Again? Chronicles of the Holocaust
  New York: Black Dog and Leventhal

(Contains the references referred to in this article and several more.)

- Jewish Welfare Board Lecture Bureau

  15 East 26th Street
  New York, NY 10010

(Another excellent source of films including "Judgement at Nuremberg" and "The Diary of Anne Frank," "The Pawnbroker," and "The Shop on Main Street." The video store, however, is the closest source for such films.)

- Social Studies School Service Catalog

  10200 Jefferson Boulevard, Room 151
  P.O. Box 802
  Culver City, CA 90230-0802
  1-800-421-4246

(This is the social studies teacher's major resource "bible!")

- U.S. Holocaust Memorial Council

  2000 L Street, N.W., Suite 588
  Washington, D.C. 20036

(With the arrival of the Holocaust Museum, teachers have a vital central clearinghouse.)

- Yad Vashem Martyr's and Hero's Remembrance Authority, Jerusalem, Israel

- Yiddish Institute of Scientific Research (YIVO)

  1048 Fifth Avenue
  New York, NY 10028

A Holocaust Resource Center Becomes a Beehive: The Case of the Richard Stockton College of New Jersey

G. Jan Colijn
William Bearden
Gail Rosenthal

SUMMARY. This contribution describes the beginning years of a Holocaust Resource Center and its collection development in a four-year public institution, the Richard Stockton College of New Jersey. The authors argue that, with such preconditions as strong institutional leadership and commitment and with good "town-gown" relationships, Holocaust and Genocide Studies can be placed central to the liberal arts experience. Such centrality is particularly important given the repeated occurrence of genocide in this century. In view of uncertain fiscal support for public higher education, multiple ways must but can be found to develop Holocaust and Genocide book and media collections. *[Article copies available for a fee from The Haworth Document Delivery Service: 1-800-342-9678. E-mail address: getinfo@haworth.com]*

G. Jan Colijn is Dean of General Studies and Professor of Political Science. William Bearden is the College Library's Assistant Director of Technical Services, and Gail Rosenthal is Supervisor of the College's Holocaust Resource Center and she also coordinates the College Outreach (Hillel) program, all at The Richard Stockton College of New Jersey, Jim Leeds Road, Pomona, NJ 08240.

[Haworth co-indexing entry note]: "A Holocaust Resource Center Becomes a Beehive: The Case of the Richard Stockton College of New Jersey." Colijn, G. Jan, William Bearden, and Gail Rosenthal. Co-published simultaneously in *The Reference Librarian* (The Haworth Press, Inc.) No. 61/62, 1998, pp. 41-50; and: *The Holocaust: Memories, Research, Reference* (ed: Robert Hauptman, and Susan Hubbs Motin) The Haworth Press, Inc., 1998, pp. 41-50. Single or multiple copies of this article are available for a fee from The Haworth Document Delivery Service [1-800-342-9678, 9:00 a.m. - 5:00 p.m. (EST). E-mail address: getinfo@haworth.com].

Many strands of Holocaust awareness in the United States lead in one way or another to Elie Wiesel. So it was when the daughter of two South Jersey notables returned home in 1985 after the semester from Boston University and told her parents about Wiesel's lamentation in his final lecture that in fifty years—without him or other survivors alive—the Holocaust would recede in history and human consciousness. He had urged students to go back to their communities and to make sure that survivor stories were recorded.

The student's parents—prominent community leaders who had both served as president of Atlantic County's Federation of Jewish Agencies—were intrigued. They knew that there were several dozen survivors among the Jewish community of some 15,000 in the immediate region, and they solicited the cooperation of Stockton College's then and current president Vera King Farris to find a suitable storage facility at the College once the survivor histories were recorded. Stockton had become attractive under Farris' leadership because of its rapidly growing academic reputation as a very selective public four-year institution and because the college was creating an institutional climate of racial harmony and diversity while gaining national attention for its retention rates among minority students.

President Farris had a long standing interest in Holocaust education. She had, for example, provided the impetus for a Holocaust Center at Kean College of New Jersey and at several other institutions. Farris' interest was not only remarkable because she was African-American but because it was inspired by her legally blind mother, Ida E. King and her response to the Holocaust. Her mother had cried when, several decades earlier, Farris had told her what she had learned about the Holocaust in Atlantic City High School that day—the only day in her life Farris remembers her mother crying.[1] Farris has stated that her mother was " . . . most deeply moved by the Holocaust and taught me the meaning of the tragedy that had fallen upon the Jewish people (. . .) as a way to understand the suffering of all human beings." Moreover, Farris holds succinct views on the responsibility of education: "I want each student graduating from Stockton to be a total human being."[2]

A local oral history project began in 1986-87, with the provision of background and training to the interviewers led by Joanne Rudolf, from Yale's Fortunoff Video Archive for Holocaust Testimonies[3] and a local rabbi-survivor, and with video taping facilities donated and coordinated by the local NBC affiliate, WMGM-TV-40. By 1989, the first fifteen histories had been recorded.

However, the community and the College were by then already forging ahead with a substantially enlarged vision of the "storage facility" originally requested: President Farris had offered the construction of a full-fledged Holocaust Resource Center which would operate as part of the College library but would be separately funded as a joint "town-gown" project, with the Federation of Jewish Agencies of Atlantic County. Construction on the $90,000 Center was begun in December 1989. The solemn but superb design was donated by the architect Gary Mednick, and the Center was eventually equipped with $12,500 worth of furnishings, audio and video recording equipment, and display cases. The Center opened during the week Germany reunified, on October 2, 1990, with a poignant address by Yaffa Eliach.

A mission statement was completed in September 1990, with five objectives:

I. To commemorate the Holocaust and develop sensitivity and understanding by combating anti-Semitism, racism, hatred and oppression.
II. Memorialize the victims of the Holocaust, pay tribute to the survivors, liberators, and eyewitnesses and participate in educating future generations.
III. Focus on the study of the Holocaust. Foster academic research and serve as a repository for Holocaust materials, including oral history.
IV. Sponsor awareness programs, provide internships to train those teaching the Holocaust and make available printed and audiovisual material to students, educators and scholars.
V. Serve to enhance greater awareness of Holocaust through special activities such as exhibits, seminars and symposiums.

Perhaps most remarkable, the first of these objectives clearly provides legitimacy for linking the Holocaust with current and future issues such as racism, genocide, and totalitarianism.

Concurrent with the Center's opening, President Farris upgraded an adjunct position in Holocaust Studies to a half-time faculty line and secured funding for the first named chair in Holocaust Studies in a US public institution, the Ida E. King Distinguished Chair of Holocaust Studies. The chair would be occupied by internationally prominent Holocaust scholars of various faiths on a rotating basis. This arrangement would provide a constantly fresh and inherently interdisciplinary approach. Moreover, the position was linked clearly with the Holocaust Resource Center, as opposed to the more typical research focus of endowed chairs.[4] Franklin Littell became the first holder of the chair.

The Littell appointment was a very important choice. It signaled the notion that Holocaust Studies should be an interdisciplinary and interfaith affair and not marginalized under the rubric of Jewish Studies. With Littell's leadership, the final version of the Center's mission clearly centered on pro-active pedagogy, noting that

> The Center's purpose is to facilitate teaching the lessons of the Holocaust. Especially, the Center will help to fix the understanding of genocide as a crime and to create the public mind that will support future structures and laws to reduce its incidence.

Spun-off from this mission statement were five specific functions, i.e.,

- the Center's projected service as a *library/depository* (including the oral history project);
- the Center's projected role in *education* on-and-off campus, through outreach programs, exhibits, co-curricular programming and teacher training;
- The Center's projected role as an incubator of faculty and student *research*;
- the Center's role in linking the Holocaust to current and future issues in *society*, e.g., racism, totalitarianism and genocide;
- the Center's projected role, as a joint project with the Federation of Jewish Agencies, in building *college-community* relations.

THE CENTER'S ACTIVITIES AND USE

It has been the College's position that, in this genocidal age, it is critical to put the issues raised by the Holocaust central in liberal arts education. Holocaust and genocide courses, therefore, are part of the College's interdisciplinary "commons" which is required of all students. Although this curriculum does not constitute a traditional core curriculum (students have a broad choice of interdisciplinary offerings in the arts and humanities, the social sciences, and the natural sciences, and mathematics) today some thousand students (out of an FTE of 4,700) take these courses every year, a figure unique in American higher education.

To underscore the currency of education as a bridge between issues of morality, values, meaning and such broad societal issues as prejudice, racism, hatred, genocide, the Center has since its inception also offered workshops, seminars, and in-service training for K-12 teachers. In fact, the New Jersey Commission on Holocaust Education, an early supporter, designated the Holocaust Resource Center as a teacher training "demonstration site" and has continually underwritten a number of these activities each year. The Center's main external partner, the Federation of Jewish Agencies of Atlantic County (now Atlantic and Cape May Counties) not only subvents the salary of the Center's director, first part-time, now full-time, but its Foundation generously helped with the development of the collection in Jewish and Holocaust studies at the College well before the Center came into being.

Since its inception, the Center has organized several major events:

- It hosted the 21st Annual Scholars Conference on the Holocaust and Churches (1991)
- It hosted the "Anne Frank in the World" exhibit which was seen by more than 7,000 visitors (1991)
- Center associates were involved with the large, international "Remembering the Future II" conference in Berlin (1994)

Modest revenues of the first two events were plowed back into collection development.

In the first full year of operation, 925 students and 50 teachers were reached through presentations and workshops; in 1993 the number of in-service workshops reached some 1,875 high school teachers while 1,260 school children visited the Center or were involved in its presentations; the Annual Holocaust Awareness Contest brought 1,400 entries.

In the last two years, the Center's activities have involved over 10,000 teachers and students, and the 1997 Annual Holocaust Awareness Contest brought 3,000 entries from four states. Each of the rotating visiting scholars have augmented the Center's activities by providing public lectures from their particular area of expertise. Hubert Locke, for example, co-founder of the aforementioned scholars conference, provided a three part public lecture series "An African-American Looks at the Holocaust" to standing-room-only audiences in Atlantic City during the time that Nation of Islam lecturers had brought their centrifugal message to several campuses. Another example: Henry Huttenbach, an expert not only on the Holocaust but also on ethno-nationalism, dedicated the annual Kristallnacht lecture to the issue of ethnic cleansing.

COLLECTION DEVELOPMENT

It should be noted that the Center is part of the College's library and that the College's general collection includes Judaica and Holocaust related books and journals whose arrival, in many cases, predates the Center's establishment. Similarly, videos and films are housed in a Media Center which is housed in the library but operates as a separate budget unit. The Holocaust Resource Center has its own collection as well. Generally, reference works and irreplaceable texts are placed in the Holocaust Resource Center but the collection development of the Center and library follows no detailed and prescribed patterns: the collection has been developed as opportunities arose.

The current collection configuration (Holocaust material only, not Judaica) is as follows:

	Holocaust Resource Center		Library		Media
Oral History Videotapes		60	N/A		N/A
Other Video/Films		196	N/A		178
Books	By title	760	By title	711	N/A
	By volume	940	By volume	830	
Journals		5		15	N/A

In addition, the Center contains hundreds of "vertical files" of pamphlets, arranged by subject matter (e.g., "Anne Frank," the "deniers"), innumerable sample lesson plans, curriculum guides, posters, and all papers from the conferences with which the Center has been involved. In addition, the Center contains a young adult book collection.

In retrospect one can identify some ten avenues whereby the collection has grown. These avenues were not necessarily planned; often, opportunities simply offered themselves.

- Foundation grants by the local Federation of Jewish Agencies were absolutely critical as this "early money" allowed us to build a skeletal collection as early as 1991.
- The New Jersey Holocaust Commission supplied the Center with a so-called "green box" which contained books, media and lesson plan suggestions easily taken 'on the road' to in-service teacher training sites. An updated version, again worth several thousands of dollars, was donated in 1996.
- The 1991 Annual Scholars Conference on the Holocaust and the Churches and its associated book sales led to the donation of several dozen scholarly books by various publishers.
- Collateral sales during the Anne Frank exhibit were such that several thousands of dollars in net revenue could be earmarked for the purchase of material related to Anne Frank and for the general collection in the Center.
- The Jewish Chautauqua Society has, throughout the 1990s, contributed books in Judaica and Holocaust Studies to the institution. The former are typically placed in the library general collection, the latter in the Center.
- The Center continually runs a number of workshops, seminars, and presentations under contract. The net revenue of such contracts is used for collection development.
- The College bookstore, run by Follett, on occasion has donated volumes, especially children and young adult books, after a book sale related to such Center activities as an on-campus teachers' workshop.

- Donations have been received from individuals liquidating private libraries. We have developed a bookplate that goes into each donated book in recognition of the donor.
- Book reviews in scholarly journals by faculty and staff associated with the Center have brought us dozens of books, as publishers now send us books for possible review.
- Unsolicited books arrive from publishers, e.g., *Hitler's Willing Executioners*, and also from survivors, and others[5] who are very keen to have their stories not only recorded, but actively used in the work we do.

In addition, the library's general collection continues to be developed under the Jewish Studies/Holocaust profile from Blackwell's approval plan which we adjust from time to time, with faculty input on subsequent selections. That service adds from 100-150 copies to the collection annually.

THE USERS

As usual with special collections, the central location of the Center, with most Holocaust material in one place, is a great convenience to users. Those users consist, first of all, of college students. However, they are not limited to those taking Holocaust and Genocide courses, or even those taking Jewish Studies courses–a minor at Stockton. Other interdisciplinary courses focus at least partially on the Holocaust so that the Center becomes a resource to students in, say, a general social science course entitled "Violence in America," a course on bioethics, even a writing course. The use of student interns in the Center is especially useful in this context because it provides a non-threatening, facilitative environment for research strategies, through peer-to-peer help.

The second major group of users are K-12 teachers, many of whom under mandate to attend to Holocaust and genocide studies as New Jersey is now one of five states where such a mandate exists. Teachers use the Center for research in class preparation but also seek help from the Center's supervisor (who has training in early childhood development) on questions of pedagogy and in the development of lesson plans.

In addition, as the Center has developed, we have seen M.A. and Ph.D. students who are working on Holocaust related theses and dissertations, and just as students from courses other than Holocaust and genocide studies now frequent the Center we are seeing an increase of faculty use, e.g., faculty in public health who are interested in the euthanasia issue.

Finally, the collection is, as is not unusual these days, not only used *in situ*. The Center receives questions via its homepage on the College's Web site, and questions are submitted from teachers and students by phone, mail, and email; the Atlantic County Library Reference desks use our Center for answering questions on the Holocaust. Although the collection does not fully exist in cyberspace, it certainly exists in a virtual reality beyond the Center's doors.

CONCLUSIONS

What conclusions can be drawn from the Stockton experience? The necessary pre-condition for the Center's success is clearly the pro-active, visible and personal leadership from the college president: in the face of hate speech, racialist tensions and intolerance such leadership is a *conditio sine qua non* for any campus that hopes to be, to borrow from Walter Lippman, civilization's court of last resort. A corollary to such leadership is the assertion that Holocaust education is everyone's affair and should not be relegated to the margins of liberal arts (i.e., to Jewish Studies) but everywhere where it makes people uncomfortable: Holocaust and Genocide studies must be central to any liberal arts education worth its grain of salt in this virulently genocidal age. The issue here is as Jeffersonian as it is Parsonian: liberal learning remains the key to democratic society, and democracy is our last best hope.

Higher education is under considerable stress in the late twentieth century. George Will once lamented that students knew little about the Holocaust and were very vulnerable to disinformation, as they

> passed through college unmarked by the information about even the largest events of the century, but acquired the conventional skepticism of the empty headed: when in doubt, doubt.[6]

Empty-headedness, the denier industry, the postmodern notion that nothing is really fixed and the ahistorical nature of our society all conspire to make truth circumspect. We believe, however, that the Stockton experience shows that, with good leadership, creativity, dedication and community assistance, today's campus does not have to be a hollow vessel of moral abdication or an ethical wasteland; and if a small, public four-year institution, without an endowment but with a bit of determination, can begin to address the thundering silence that often surrounds xenophobia, racism and genocide, then other institutions can find the will to do so as well.

REFERENCES

1. For the full story, see Sally Friedman, "Righting a Wrong on the Holocaust," New York Times, January 5, 1992; the early days of Stockton College's Holocaust Resource Center are also chronicled in G. Jan Colijn and Gail Rosenthal, "The Holocaust at the Center of Liberal Arts Education: The case of Richard Stockton College of New Jersey," paper presented at the Remembering for the Future II International Conference March 13-17, Berlin and available on Marcia S. Littell et al., The Holocaust–Remembering for the Future II CD-Rom, Geneva/Stamford, CT: Vista InterMedia Corporation, 1996.

2. Interview in the Jerusalem Post, August 14, 1990.

3. The Stockton project has an "affiliate relationship" with the Yale project.

4. For example, after Franklin Littell, the 'father' of US Holocaust education, had been selected as the inaugural chair, his contract specified that he was expected to lend his " . . . considerable experience and scholarly insights (to the Center's Executive Committee) in such areas as future programming, the development of the Center as a depository for Holocaust materials, and the establishment of the Center as a research facility." It was also expected that the scholar would " . . . enhance the College's understanding in the academic world and in the community at large by offering some public lectures" in addition to teaching courses at the College itself, the actual core of the appointment.

5. Irmtrud Wojak and Lore Hepner, "Geliebte Kinder . . . :" Briefe Aus dem Amsterdamer Exil in Die Neue Welt 1939-1943, Essen: Klartext Verlag, 1995.

6. George Will, "Modern Culture Abets Those Who Deny the Holocaust," The Press, Atlantic City, August 30, 1993, p.A9.

Remainders of Vanished Lives: Teaching the Painful Legacy of the Holocaust

Patricia M. Gantt
with David A. Meier

But I am trying to remember. I must. More than my honor is at stake; my right to survive is at stake. I must not take this essential thing to my grave with me. It must stay on here, in this world, as an offering or a sign, all that remains of a vanished life.

–Elie Wiesel, *The Forgotten* (314)

The image of an individual emerging from a library with fresh reading material in hand is so tacitly accepted in this country that it seems difficult for Americans to imagine a society where smoke from burning books darkens the skies and intellectuals are persecuted in order to stifle independent thought. Yet Nazi Germany in 1933 was such a place, with books being burned in "huge public rallies" held all across the country (*Teaching* 111). As the decade proceeded, destruction turned into attempts at annihilation, persecution turned into murder, and murder into genocide of such proportions that the mind still struggles to take it in.

But take it in we must, for as scholars such as Gerhard Schön-

---

Patricia M. Gantt and David A. Meier are affiliated with Dickinson State University, Dickinson, ND 58601-4896.

[Haworth co-indexing entry note]: "Remainders of Vanished Lives: Teaching the Painful Legacy of the Holocaust." Gantt, Patricia M. and David A. Meier. Co-published simultaneously in *The Reference Librarian* (The Haworth Press, Inc.) No. 61/62, 1998, pp. 51-57; and: *The Holocaust: Memories, Research, Reference* (ed: Robert Hauptman and Susan Hubbs Motin) The Haworth Press, Inc., 1998, pp. 51-57. Single or multiple copies of this article are available for a fee from The Haworth Document Delivery Service [1-800-342-9678, 9:00 a.m. - 5:00 p.m. (EST). E-mail address: getinfo@haworth.com].

berner remind us, "The historical facts must be made known, the social causes that made them possible must be understood, and we must become aware of our own responsibility for what goes on around us" (USHMM On-line). If we do not remember the painful history of the Holocaust, we not only undermine our collective responsibility to honor the more than six million "vanished lives" that were lost to its horrors, we abrogate our opportunity to counter further assaults on freedom of thought, thus making it easier for a climate in which human rights violations occur to flourish.

It is for these purposes of remembering, of collecting, and of disseminating information useful in teaching the Holocaust that Dickinson State University in Dickinson, North Dakota, has developed a Holocaust Resource Center within its Department of Teacher Education's West River Teacher Center. The University, an institution of approximately seventeen hundred students, serves the Dakotas and eastern Montana, and is historically committed to providing pre-service and in-service teacher training throughout the region. Capitalizing on the enthusiastic public reaction to Holocaust courses recently instituted at Dickinson State, in 1996 the West River Teacher Center affiliated with the United States Holocaust Memorial Museum. The Holocaust Resource Center established at the WRTC is now the provider of Holocaust-related materials and instruction for teachers and other researchers throughout the region. According to the University President, Dr. Philip W. Conn, "We are pleased to be able to offer this important new resource to teachers. We are convinced that having the Holocaust Resource Center located within our West River Teacher Center not only strengthens the cause of Holocaust education, but the University's teacher training programs and its mission to serve our region" (6 May 1996). The HRC has much to offer teachers doing research not only on the Shoah, but on a variety of human rights issues pertinent to diversity or justice.

The West River Teacher Center is one of ten such facilities providing materials and continuing education to teachers throughout North Dakota, although it is the only one systemically linked to a university-level teacher training program, as well as the only one housing a Holocaust resource collection within its Teacher Center library. Center constituents are area teachers in public, parochial, or home-school learning environments; university education majors on the elementary or secondary level; and interested community members. As director, I am also a teaching member of the Department of Teacher Education and supervise pre-service experiences for university seniors working in North Dakota and Montana schools. Collaborating with me in coordinating the offerings of our Holocaust Resource Center is Dickinson State history professor Dr. David A. Meier, who has an established record of teaching and scholarship on the Shoah. Dr. Meier's access to materials–particularly his connections with an international network of incredibly generous contributors–has literally made the University's Holocaust Resource Center possible. Working together to build our holdings and to plan workshops and other teacher training opportunities, we have been able to add a small, yet vital, link to the growing chain of research libraries with a Holocaust focus.

Admittedly, the collection of Holocaust materials housed in the West River Center is quite modest, and our budget for acquiring them is even more so. Most of what we have is available to interested facilities at minimal or zero cost, just by contacting the many generous scholars and institutions eager to be helpful, such as Dr. William L. Shulman of the Queensborough, New York, Holocaust Resource Center and Archives; the Holocaust Remembrance Committee, UJA Federation of Greater Toronto; the Holocaust Educational Foundation; Yad Vashem; or the Holocaust Memorial Museum in Washington. Periodicals like the Southern Poverty Law Center's free magazine, *Teaching Tolerance*, make excellent instructional additions. These materials are simple to attain, but pay high educational dividends, since all are of very solid instructional quality. The humble beginnings our HRC exemplifies should be an encouragement to other libraries, which can easily start a Resource Center of their own, even on today's extremely tight budgets. It by no means takes lavish funding to set up a dynamic program of Holocaust education–just the willingness to do so and the time necessary to write, e-mail, or telephone educators with comparable interests in such an enterprise. In short, anyone who wishes to establish a Holocaust Resource Center can.

For North Dakota to be home to a Holocaust Center may be surprising to some, but it should not be. Many of the Center's origins can be traced back to southwest North Dakota's long-term commitments to public education and to exploring and honoring its history, which includes varied heritages. Proud of the state's ethnic patchwork, including Native Americans, Germans, Jews, Ukrainians, Bohemians, and Scandinavians, North Dakotans place tremendous value on the contributions each of these groups has made to its diverse culture.

In fact, European Jewry played a unique and distinct role in the development of the Dakota territories. European-born Jews moved in and established new towns, often going into agriculture by taking advantage of the Homestead Act of the 1820s. As they settled across the High Plains, they built synagogues in virtually every city in which they resided–including Dickinson. They labored to preserve their cultural heritage, dietary habits, and social customs. When economic and climatic conditions proved particularly difficult for inhabitants of the Dakotas (as last winter's harsh weather attests they still do), Dakota Jewry divided between those moving on to the west coast and others favoring the more climatically hospitable life to be found in Minnesota. By the mid-twentieth century, their impact appeared to have lessened considerably. Nevertheless, these Dakotans continued to make their presence felt. One example is Herman Stern, a successful businessman and Jewish emigrant from Germany, who worked with the American consulate in Stuttgart to negotiate the emigration of over one hundred German Jews from Hitler's Third Reich to North Dakota.

Since the 1970s, North Dakota has been part of the resurgence of interest in the Holocaust that has occurred nationwide, with increasing numbers of Holocaust awareness programs spreading across the state. Many new publications have emerged, exploring the contributions of Dakota's Jewry to the state's growth and stressing commonalities among plains settlers, regardless of their origins. One pioneer memoir, *Rachel Calof's Story: Jewish Homesteader on the Northern Plains*, has proved especially germane, and its impact has been notable. People throughout the state can empathize with the Calofs, wheat farmers who survived the rough winters at the turn of the late century with a combination of youthful enthusiasm and hard work that Dakotans still prize. Meanwhile, the continuing popularity of studying *The Diary of Anne Frank* formed another nexus between schools across the state and requests for increased Holocaust instruction. When North Dakota's Girl Scouts brought an Anne Frank exhibit to the state capital in Bismarck, thousands of interested visitors crowded to see it. The popularity of films like *Schindler's List*; the proliferation of books, on-line or other multimedia sources, and public television programs about the Holocaust; and an abundance of documentaries televised through cable formats like Arts & Entertainment or the History Channel also contribute to the local demand for information. Each of these steps led the University closer to establishing a Holocaust Resource Center.

An especially gratifying aspect of our HRC's origin is that it came at the impetus of classroom teachers who contacted Dickinson State University, seeking materials that they could use in planning to teach *The Diary of Anne Frank*, twentieth-century United States history, or other units touching on the Holocaust and Holocaust-related themes. "In that respect," says Dr. Meier, "our Resource Center is an outgrowth of requests by those whom it serves, actual elementary, middle-level, and secondary teachers and the students in their classes. We are not superimposing Holocaust studies on them; rather, we are responding to their expressed needs" (26 April 1997). As they learn more through researching the books, periodicals, teacher guides, student study helps, and additional articles that are in the collection, area teachers are extending the applications they make of these items, including them in their students' work with film study, oral histories, diaries, and a number of comparative inquiry projects.

From their initial search for materials useful in teaching Anne Frank or Adolf Hitler, teachers have expanded their interest in Holocaust research by taking new university course offerings or WRTC Holocaust workshops, each taught by Dr. Meier. Often educators come to the Teacher Center looking for specific materials to follow up on what they or their students have seen on television, wanting to know more—for example—about Nazi persecution of homosexuals or the reaction of average German citizens to concentration camps. When area students travel to Washington, D.C., to participate in national programs like Close Up, they often visit the Holocaust Memorial Museum; these visits are sure to create a flurry of requests at our Resource Center upon the students' return to Dickinson. Teacher Center researchers can also access the growing number of Internet Holocaust connections, including those originating here at Dickinson State University. Even the current celebration of the thirty-fifth anniversary of the publication of Harper Lee's *To*

Kill a Mockingbird has caused secondary teachers to reach out for historically-based materials that can help them create classroom opportunities to discuss larger issues of tolerance and understanding. By providing an abundance of specific information, both in the subject and the pedagogy of the Holocaust, our Center can contribute to improving instruction at the individual classroom level.

In housing materials within the Center library, I have chosen to put them into a unified location, both on the shelves and in our WRTC catalog, where they are itemized, with cross-listings to appropriate subjects. Although some may feel this procedure creates a self-imposed intellectual ghetto, I would argue instead that it showcases Holocaust materials. Patrons can locate them by using a system that invites more thorough investigations than would occur if items were subsumed into categories as generic as *social studies*, *history*, *literature*, or even *human rights*. Direct access is easy, and the organization of materials grants the collection its merited prominence.

To publicize acquisitions, we utilize our Teacher Center newsletter, the *WRTC News*. The *News* goes out to approximately sixty schools and one thousand pre-service or in-service teachers and other members eight times a year. It is the primary means we have of informing teachers about upcoming classes, workshops, conferences, or other items of professional interest. In addition, the newsletter contains teacher tips, book reviews, and information about Internet and other resources advantageous to instructional planning. The *News* has at times been a vehicle for announcing the formation of our Holocaust Resource center or updates to its holdings; for recommending children's books relating to the Shoah, like Carol Matas' *Lisa's War*; for reviewing texts like *Rachel Calof's Story* or *Abe's Story: A Holocaust Memoir*; and for publicizing free Holocaust workshops for educators.

Dr. William L. Schulman underscores the significance of the West River Teacher Center's Holocaust Resource Center and others similar to it, calling them

> an essential part of the network of educational institutions that are being established across the United States. It is especially important that such centers be set up outside the major urban areas, because there is a great need to bring this information to teachers who cannot get the training provided by such institu-

tions as the United States Holocaust Museum in Washington, D.C. It is also essential that there is a center within reaching distance to which teachers can go to obtain materials and exchange information with colleagues. (16 May 1997)

Holocaust instruction can only benefit from all these professional linkages, as instructional need goes on to create further instructional need, affirming both the place of HRC resources in present curricula and the necessity for continued growth in our holdings and outreach.

Each Holocaust Resource Center, regardless of its size or location, has much the same function as the West River Teacher Center's Holocaust Resource Center–to educate. Kurt Jonassohn articulates this instructional purpose as a charge "to counteract all forms of denial and to keep the memories alive" (5). He goes on to emphasize that it is imperative, as well, "to educate a generation of citizens who will not be prepared to be passive bystanders to the violation of human rights, but who will actively criticize and/or oppose their governments when they want to engage in such violations" (6). Holocaust Resource Centers and their libraries therefore have a Janus-like function: to look backward at what has been, making sure the painful memories of "vanished lives" do not fade away, and to look forward to what is to come–all the while contributing to the vital task of assuring that our common future is one where books are not burned and freedom of thought is encouraged, rather than silenced.

WORKS CITED

Conn, Philip W. Personal interview. Dickinson, North Dakota. 6 May 1996.

Jonassohn, Kurt. "Prevention without Prediction." *Holocaust and Genocide Studies* 7.1 (Spring 1993): 1-13.

Meier, David Aaron. Personal interview. Dickinson, North Dakota. 26 April 1997.

Schönberner, Gerhard. Quoted in "Educational Projects and Resources." United States Holocaust Memorial Museum. On-line site. Gc.apc.org/ddickerson. html. 20 April 1997.

Schulman, William L. Letter to Patricia Gantt. 15 May 1997.

Teaching about the Holocaust: A Resource Book for Educators. Washington, D.C.: United States Holocaust Memorial Museum, n. d.

Wiesel, Elie. *The Forgotten.* New York: Schocken Books, 1992.

Incorporating Contemporaneous Newspaper Articles About the Holocaust into a Study of the Holocaust

Samuel Totten

INTRODUCTION

It is completely understandable as to why so many have described the Holocaust as "indescribable," "unbelievable," "beyond comprehension," "unfathomable," and "a mystery." Both the Nazis' plan to exterminate every Jew residing in Europe as well as its systematic, thorough, and horrifyingly brutal execution of the plan nearly defies the human imagination. But it did happen. It was planned by human beings, carried out by human beings, and perpetrated against human beings. And because of that, humanity living in the aftermath of that horrendous event–one that has been deemed by some to be a watershed in the annals of humanity–must be studied. Put another way, it is absolutely imperative that educators and others work together to assist the young of today and those of future generations to gain an "understanding [of] the un-understandable" (Cargas, 1981, p. 203).

Due to the "unreal" nature of the Holocaust, it is little wonder that many people (and particularly students at the secondary level) have an excruciatingly difficult time coming to grips with the "un-

Samuel Totten is affiliated with the University of Arkansas, Fayetteville, College of Education, 107A Peabody Hall, Fayetteville, AR 72701.

[Haworth co-indexing entry note]: "Incorporating Contemporaneous Newspaper Articles About the Holocaust into a Study of the Holocaust." Totten, Samuel. Co-published simultaneously in The Reference Librarian (The Haworth Press, Inc.) No. 61/62, 1998, pp. 59-81; and: The Holocaust: Memories, Research, Reference (ed: Robert Hauptman and Susan Hubbs Motin) The Haworth Press, Inc., 1998, pp. 59-81. Single or multiple copies of this article are available for a fee from The Haworth Document Delivery Service [1-800-342-9678, 9:00 a.m. - 5:00 p.m. (EST). E-mail address: getinfo@haworth.com].

real reality" of that horrendous tragedy. In light of that difficulty, I have made, over the past several years, a concerted attempt to develop pedagogical strategies that are effective in breaking through the barriers and difficulties teachers and students face when coming face to face with such a horrendously horrible subject as the Holocaust. At one and the same time, during my presentations of these methods at workshops (including those offered by the U.S. Holocaust Memorial Museum) and seminars (at statewide conferences on the Holocaust as well as at national educational conferences such as the National Council for the Social Studies) I have collected ideas from other educators along these lines and then attempted to synthesize and weave them into a meaningful fabric that play off, complement and supplement one another.

The aforementioned efforts have resulted in two earlier papers: "The Use of First-Person Accounts in Teaching About the Holocaust" and "Using Literature to Teach About the Holocaust." The express purpose of the former paper was to discuss the value, limitations, purposes and methods of using of first-person accounts of Holocaust survivors and others to teach about the Holocaust. Therein, made the assertion that "by supplementing the study of the Holocaust with such accounts, it moves the study from what is often a welter of statistics, remote places and events, to one that is immersed in the 'particular'" (Totten, 1989, p. 63). At the very least, the use of first-person accounts by a teacher with his/her students places a human face on the facts and events that led up to and culminated in genocide. In "Using Literature to Teach About the Holocaust," the aim was to delineate the various types of literature available on the Holocaust (e.g., poetry, short stories novels, drama, young adolescent literature), and discuss the strengths, limitations, purposes, and methods of using such literature in the classroom. In that paper I quoted Glenn (1973) who asserted that "Art captures the terrible reality of the fact, which the objective statement simply fails to convey" (p. 71).

The objectives of this piece are basically the same as those in the other pieces. That is, I plan to discuss the purpose of using newspapers in a secondary classroom to teach about the Holocaust, the strengths and limitations of such a resource, and effective methods for doing so.

RATIONALE FOR INCORPORATING CONTEMPORANEOUS NEWSPAPER ARTICLES INTO A STUDY OF THE HOLOCAUST

> Flimsy newspaper clippings, nearly crumbling, document history when it was fresh . . . Paper–tangible, tactile paper in its dusty, brittle, workaday glory–connects time and place not only cause of the data it bears but because of the medium itself.
> (The Associated Press, June 30, 1996, p. AS)

As Mary Lynn Ritzenthaler, who supervises document conservation at the National Archives, has pointed out: "People have a strong connection and reaction to paper. It's something that is extremely common and everyday, and that makes it a real link to history" (The Associated Press, June 30, 1996, p. AS). The latter point concerning "a real link to history" is true whether one searches for articles by actually paging through old newspapers themselves or through microfiche.

There are numerous reasons for incorporating contemporaneous newspaper articles into a study of the Holocaust. Historically speaking, it provides students with the opportunity to attempt to ascertain all of the following: whether or not the press actually covered various issues relating to Nazi Germany and its ill-treatment of the Jews and others; the depth of coverage accorded the events unfolding in Nazi Germany; the actual page placement of articles on key topics relating to Nazi Germany, and the possible significance of that; the tone of the articles (e.g., concern or alarm, skepticism or disbelief, a certain nonchalance, masked or euphemistic language) about various events in Nazi Germany, especially in regard to the ill-treatment of the Jews; any hint of censorship suffered by the press (either at the hands of the Nazis, the United States government or by a newspaper publisher); how the press may have helped to form or influence U.S. citizens' attitudes in regard to what was taking place in Nazi Germany and/or Nazi-occupied Europe; the amount and/or lack of information that the average citizen could know about the events in Nazi Germany and Nazi-occupied Europe should he/she have solely relied on obtaining information from certain newspapers; the responsibility (or lack thereof) of the press in covering such a major series of events; the possible reasons why the press covered the events unfolding in Nazi Germany the way it did (including the other events that were taking place at the time in the U.S. and around the globe, and the impact that those had on press coverage of Nazi Germany); what sort of statements and responses the U.S. government, private and public organizations, and individual citizens were making, if any, in regard to the events in Nazi Germany; and the extent of first-hand accounts that were included in the press reports versus second-hand reports and/or rumors; etc.

On a different note, another key reason for incorporating contemporaneous newspaper accounts of the Holocaust into a lesson or unit is that the inclusion of such materials/resources helps to bring the history alive for students. That is, instead of reading staid, watered-down and lifeless prose in a typical history or social studies textbook, students are availed of key historical events in a resource that was actually written as the incidents and events exploded and unfolded on the world scene. Concomitantly, newspaper writing is generally more engaging, lively, and informative than typical social studies or history texts used in the secondary classroom. certainly one reason as to why the writing of newspaper articles is generally a cut, or more, above textbook writing is due to the fact that journalists are professional writers who write for a living, and thus their words, images and expressions must, by their very nature, be capable of catching an audience's attention. In fact, studies have shown that students learn and retain more from lively writing, and newspapers—at least the better newspapers—are generally more likely to include such writing than typical textbooks. (For a telling and fascinating study vis-à-vis the latter concern, see Bruce DeSilva "Schoolbooks: A Question of Quality. A *Hartford Courant* Special Report." Hartford, CT: The Hartford Courant, 1986, p. 5.)

It is also true that newspapers often present information from the perspective of someone who is seeing, experiencing or witnessing a situation unfold in front of their eyes. This could involve the journalist him/herself and/or stories about individuals who have been involved in an event and are thus quoted. If the reporting is accurate, unbiased, and uncensored then such "first-person perspectives" are capable of providing students with unique and powerful insights (and facts) into key historical situations.

It should go without saying, of course, that such newspaper accounts should only constitute one of many sources that are brought to bear in such a study. This is particularly important when one begins to examine and understand how the newspapers of the period often provided inadequate, sometimes inaccurate and, in many cases, slanted information (sometimes the result of censorship either imposed by the journalist him/herself, the Nazi regime, or even the publisher of a U.S. paper and/or anti-Semitism by the journalist or publisher) vis-à-vis the intentions and actions of the Nazis and the fate of the Jews.

Finally, using alternative resources such as newspaper articles also provides a unique change of pace for students; that, in and of itself, makes learning, at least for some, more engaging.

OVERVIEW OF U.S. NEWSPAPER COVERAGE OF THE HOLOCAUST DURING THE 1930s AND 1940s

In *The Age of Atrocity: Death in Modern Literature*, Lawrence Langer (1978) states that "The sudden, violent, irrational extinction of vast numbers of people is part of the personal and historical consciousness of the twentieth century" (p. 40). That may be the case today, but it has not always been so. More specifically, *despite* the horrors of World War I, the Turks' slaughter of the Armenians and the Soviet man-made famine in the Ukraine in 1932-1933, the "sudden, violent irrational extinction of vast numbers of people" had not *yet* become, by the early 1940s, "part of the personal and historical consciousness of the twentieth century"; and thus, many people–including those in position of power–were skeptical when they heard and read about "millions of people being slaughtered" by the Nazis. A point in fact is that "[i]n a January 1943 Gallup poll nearly 30 percent of those asked dismissed the news that 2 million Jews had been killed in Europe as just a rumor. Another 24 percent had no opinion on the question. In formal polls taken by the *Detroit Free Press* and the *New York Post* in 1943 found that a broad range of Americans did not believe the atrocity reports" (Lipstadt, 1986, pp. 240-241). In 1945, author William Ebenstein asserted that "if a few hundred or even a few thousand people had been killed by the Germans, people would have easily believed, but told that 'many millions of Jews and Christians . . . have been systematically burned and slaughtered' . . . people naturally refuse to believe it" (quoted in Lipstadt, 1986, p. 356). Skepticism, then, kept many journalists and/or publishers from writing and printing articles about the Nazi extermination of the Jews and others, and/or toning down what they wrote. What is important to keep in mind is that "an astonishing amount of information was available long before the end of the war. There was practically no aspect of the Nazi honors which was not publicly known in some detail long before the camps were opened in 1945" (Lipstadt, 1986, p. 2).

Skepticism, however, was not the only reason why newspapers either refused to publish articles about the fate of the of Jews (including the early and treacherous discrimination instituted against them by the Nazis) and/or downplayed or printed articles tucked away in the back pages. There were many other reasons–some understandable, some contemptible.

The many other reasons, as Lipstadt (1986) painstakingly shows, included but were not limited to the following[*]: early on some reporters feared being expelled from Germany for reporting the complete and brutal truth, particularly those who had had colleagues suffer such an action; many Americans thought the early reports of the Nazis' actions to be exaggerated for they couldn't believe that such a cultured people as the Germans could act in such a despicable manner; various reporters contradicted one another, some claiming, incorrectly, that things were not as bad in Germany as some reporters were reporting, and thus, the general public wasn't sure what to believe; "during the first months of Nazi rule, American reporters in Germany were urged by United States diplomats to moderate the tenor of their dispatches, lest public opinion against Germany be so inflamed that relations between the two countries would be irrevocably harmed" (Lipstadt, 1986, p. 7); in the early years, journalists had to contend with "reports" by both

---

[*] It must be understood that the actions and reactions of the press (writers, editors and publishers) were not of a single voice, and was contingent upon a number of factors, including a reporter's own experiences in Nazi Germany, the political views of the parties, the courage or lack of courage of the players involved, etc. Concomitantly, it must also be understood that the actions and reactions of the press fluctuated over the years, and in certain situations, such as the incident of Kristallnacht (or the Night of Broken Glass) that took place on November 9-10, 1938, the press actually became bolder in its condemnation of the Nazis. However, as Lipstadt (1986) points out, " . . . the press did not only condemn; once gain it sought rational explanations for this [Kristallnacht] apparently senseless course of events" (p. 99).

tourists and business people who claimed that all was well in Germany, and thus contradicted articles about the ever-increasing discrimination and tenor of the Nazis; early on the Nazis, themselves, decried even the most even-handed reporting by U.S. journalists, repeatedly "denied the veracity" of the reporting (Lipstadt, 1986, p. 21), which, in turn, made some reporters somewhat tentative in their reporting of the facts; in certain cases, "[t]he Nazis would 'punish' reporters they deemed guilty of sending 'atrocity stories' by banning their papers from Germany and preventing them from using the German mails, as was done with the *Manchester Guardian* in April 1933" (Lipstadt, 1986, pp. 21-22); the Nazis sometimes harassed reporters by spying on them and/or stationing SS men outside their homes; after being repeatedly questioned about the veracity, accuracy and/or tone of their reporting, some journalists chose to "censor" themselves and actually "downplayed the German terror" (Lipstadt, 1986, p. 25); some journalists toned down their reports out of fear of causing the victims (the Jews) even more grief should the Nazis react to the reporting in a negative or punitive fashion, and still others "feared that if they told too much, they might reveal their sources, who then might be arrested, sent to concentration camps, or even killed" (Lipstadt, 1986, p. 30); certain information written up in articles by reporters were considered "unreliable or unbelievable" (Lipstadt, 1986, p. 7) by editors, and thus the articles were not printed; in certain instances, reporters misconstrued the nature of the Nazis' anti-Semitism and goals, and thus underestimated the role that the Nazi government played in discriminating against the Jews; the reports of actual occurrences were so horrendous that certain editors and publishers, along with many members of the general public, found them too astounding to believe; some journalists and others believed that the rumors of the mass destruction of the Jews were propaganda ploys ("to sway neutral opinion" to a particular position, Lipstadt, 1986, p. 137) similar to the ones issued about the Germans' use of poison gas, the brutal killings of babies, and mutilations of defenseless women in during World War I that proved to be false; the anti-Semitism on the behalf of journalists, publishers and people in power within the U.S. government; the use of public relations and propaganda by governments and governmental agencies contributed to reporters becoming even more skeptical and cynical than they previously had, and thus made them question any and all information they were receiving from such bodies; "[i]f doubt about the trustworthiness of this news was one prism through which the American view of Germany was refracted, the fear of being drawn into Europe's internecine affairs was another. During the 1930s a deep rooted isolationist sentiment permeated American public opinion" (Lipstadt, 1986, p. 9); when World War II exploded, and particularly when the U.S. became engaged in the fight, a vast majority of the press' attention began to focus on that event as opposed to the fate of the Jews; and, the locations in Poland where the Jews were being gassed and burned were made inaccessible to foreign reporters by the Nazis.

Quite obviously, the aforementioned situations were complex than delineated herein; and many of the situations were the result of various and complex factors that it would behoove students to study during the course of their examination of how and why the U.S. press covered the Holocaust years in the way that they did. At the same time, it also needs to be noted that certain journalists and publishers did, in fact, forge ahead and attempt to provide their readership with the truth. (For a thorough, detailed and scholarly discussion of these issues and others, one should consult Deborah Lipstadt's *Beyond Belief: The American Press and the Coming of the Holocaust 1933-1945*.)

As Deborah Lipstadt (1986) has perspicaciously noted: "The press may not determine what the public thinks, but it does influence what it thinks about. If the media pays particular attention to an issue, its importance is enhanced in the public's eyes, and if the media ignores something, public reaction will be nil, for as Gay Talese has observed, news unreported has no impact" (p. 3).

TEACHING ACTIVITIES

There are many ways in which teachers can incorporate newspaper and magazine articles into their lessons and units on the Holocaust. Those highlighted here have either been useful in the author's own pedagogical efforts or are otherwise familiar to him.

1. As the authors of *Guidelines for Teaching About the Holocaust* (Washington, D.C.: United States Holocaust Memorial Museum, 1994) state: "A study of the Holocaust raises difficult questions about human behavior, and it often involves complicated answers as

to why events occurred. Be wary of oversimplifications. Allow students to contemplate the various factors which contributed to the Holocaust" (p. 3). Taking these points into consideration, an ideal activity for teachers interested in teaching their students about the reaction of the free press during the Nazi years is to have the students conduct a study of the various factors that were at play in regard to the press' stance, reporting procedures and actual reports vis-à-vis the ever-increasing discrimination, and ultimately, slaughter faced by the Jews in Nazi-occupied Europe. As the students will readily discover, the issues at play were multi-faceted and complex. In other words, there is no single or simple explanation as to how the reporters and their papers (the two of which, in fact, were often at odds) reported what was taking place in Nazi-occupied Europe vis-à-vis the plight of the Jews.

A good way to conduct such a study would be to have the students do a cooperative learning exercise called "Jigsaw" around certain chapters in Deborah Lipstadt's excellent book entitled *Beyond Belief: The American Press and the Coming of the Holocaust 1933-1945* (New York: The Free Press, 1986). In the course of doing the exercise, each student will become an "expert" on one aspect of the issue of the definition of genocide, and teach that to those fellow students in his/her group. (Note: For directions on developing a Jigsaw exercise in class, see Samuel Totten's (1995) "Jigsaw Synthesis: A Method for Incorporating a Study of Social issues into the Extant Curriculum," pp. 389-424. In Jon E. Pedersen and Annette Digby (Eds.) *Cooperative Learning In Secondary Schools*. New York: Garland Publishers, 1995).

2. The teacher could supply the students with copies of actual newspaper reports on a particular topic (e.g., the Nuremberg Laws; Kristallnacht; the mass murder of the Jews; the immigration of Jews to free countries, including the U.S. and Britain; the plight of the passengers on the "St. Louis") in order to incorporate unique resources into the students' study of the Holocaust period. An excellent resource for locating such articles is Deborah Lipstadt's *Beyond Belief: The American Press and the Coming of the Holocaust 1933-1945* (New York: The Free Press, 1986). Teachers and students can also, of course, use the *Readers Guide to Periodical Literature* and the indexes to such newspapers as the *London Times*, the *Manchester Guardian*, the *New York Times*, etc.

3. Take the students to a library that has a newspaper microfiche collection, and have each student locate several of the earliest articles on information about the Holocaust. Individual students could be assigned different topics (e.g., possible information about the Nazis' anti-Semitism, the earliest recorded discrimination fad by the Jews under Nazi Germany, information on the Nuremberg Laws, the impact of the Nuremberg Laws on Jews, Kristallnacht, the first reports of mass killings). In older to obtain as wide a body of information as possible, students could be asked to cull information from a series of different newspapers (this will be contingent on the microfiche collection of the library that is used, but it would be ideal to make use of at least one major newspaper (e.g., *The London Times, The Manchester Guardian, The New York Times*, the *Washington Post*) and a more regional or local newspaper). Once the students have located 3-5 articles on their topics, they should be required to: (a) Make a photocopy of the article; (b) Mount the article on a piece of paper; (c) Provide the following information underneath the mounted article: name of the newspaper, title of the article, date of the publication, and page number(s) where the article appeared; (d) Write a brief synopsis of the article; (e) Comment on any new information he/she gleaned from the article; (f) Comment on the placement (e.g., page number) where the article appeared and any insights that the student has in regard to the importance (or lack thereof) that an editor/publisher may have given to the information contained in the article; (g) List those lines that provide a sense of the tone/perspective/attitude of the reporter, and discuss the tone; and (h) Discuss how readers not knowing much about the facts of the Holocaust might interpret the information in the article. *NOTE:* In addition to using newspapers for this and the other assignments listed below, students could also use such newsmagazines as *Time* and *Newsweek*.

If the students are able to do a search on a computer, it also might be helpful to provide the students with some key words/terms in older to locate articles. Obviously, the words and terms would have to be those used during the actual period under study (1933-1945). For example, if the students used the term ''Holocaust,'' which was not coined until many years after the events now referred to as the Holocaust, then they would not succeed in locating any articles to study. Thus, they should be advised to use such key terms as Hitler, Nazis, Jews, anti-Jewish laws, Jewish persecution, etc.

4. Once the students have collected their articles for the afore-mentioned activity (#3), have them, as part of a group project, prepare a book/booklet that contains all of their articles (with or without their commentary) arranged in chronological order. Indi-vidual students could be required to write a short introduction to their set of articles (noting at a minimum, the name of the newspa-per, title of the article, date of the publication, and page number(s) where the article appeared and a succinct statement on the unique focus of the article). This book/booklet could be placed in either the classroom library or the school's library to be used as a reference throughout the study as well as by other students who undertake a future study of the Holocaust.

5. Have the students compare and contrast different newspapers' reports from the same period of time on various issues/subjects related to the Holocaust. As the students read these articles (and ideally this will be done throughout their study of the Holocaust and not constitute simply one discrete component of it), they could keep a tally of their findings. An interesting, informative and telling way to do this is to tape a huge sheet of butcher paper on the classroom wall that has several distinct headings, and each time students read, study and discuss a newspaper article, they can, as a group, note the following information under the headings: name of the newspaper, date of publication, title of the news article, page number(s) where the article is located, and key information gleaned from the article. Ideally, each citation should be placed in chronological order so that by the end of the study the students will have completed a rough historical overview of the period as told in the series of newspaper articles they have examined. Periodically, the teacher should direct the students' attention to their findings (e.g., the comparisons and contrasts between articles) and hold a class discussion in which they examine the unique insights gleaned from their findings as well as the ramifications of such information. Teachers may wish to use issues discussed in Deborah Lipstadt's (1986). *Beyond Belief: The American Press and the Coming of the Holocaust 1933-1945* (New York: The Free Press) as a means for establishing the focus of the project.

6. From the outset of a study on the Holocaust (during which the

students are immersed in the history of the period), the class could be divided into small groups of students (3 to 4 students to a group), and each could be given a particular topic to study in depth (that is, in more depth than they would generally be able to study the issue during the regular course of study). Among the topics might be: the rise of the Nazi party, the development of the concentration camps, the Nuremberg Laws, Kristallnacht, the plight of the refugees and how nations responded to their plight, the Einsatzgruppen, the extermination camps, the liberation of the camps. Each group could be required to read three to four key essays on the topic by noted scholars, read a series of first-person accounts that specifically address the topic, and cull through newspapers of the period and develop a booklet comprised of key newspaper articles that address the particular topic under study. In developing their book of articles, the students could mount the article, note the newspaper it is from as well as the date of publication and title of the specific article, and provide a short synopsis of the key and/or most telling or unique points of the article. Once all of the articles have been collected, mounted, written about, the students could write an introductory essay for the booklet in which they provide an overview of their topic by bringing to bear all they have learned about it from the scholarly essays and first-person accounts they have read as well as the articles they have collected and studied. Additionally, they could address within the context of their essay certain points and questions that the teacher has asked all groups to address as part of their study. Such questions might be: (a) Provide a general discussion of the most significant aspects of your topic; (b) What aspects of this history impacted you most, and why; (c) What was/were the major insight(s) you gleaned from your study, and why do you think that is so?; (d) What one point about this history most astonished you and why?; (e) If you wanted other people to learn just one point about this history, what would it be and why?

Students need to be informed that in order to address these questions, there needs to be ample discussion within and between members of their group, and that if there is more than one strong opinion by various members of the group then these should be incorporated into the introduction.

7. The students should be provided with a chronology of the actions and laws directed against the Jews in Nazi Germany be-

tween 1933 and 1945, and then be asked to scan various U.S.-based newspapers of the period for information that addressed such actions and laws. In completing this assignment not only will the students begin to gain a sense as to how newspapers either covered or did not cover such concerns, but they will also likely glean how the Nazis' actions constituted an ever-increasing steam roller that deprived the Jews of their basic rights.

One source for the aforementioned chronology is Roselle K. Chartock and Jack Spencer's (Eds.) *Can It Happen Again: Chronicles of the Holocaust* (New York: Black Dog and Leventhal, 1995, pp. 48-53).

8. A social studies teacher (Paul Wieser) in the state of Arizona has developed a three-part lesson plan on the Holocaust in which one of the parts briefly focuses on the American press and the Holocaust. In the latter lesson he suggests that teachers provide different groups of students with sets of newspaper articles from the *New York Times* and the *New York Herald Tribune*. His directions are as follows: "Once the teacher has identified the make-up of the student groups, each group will be given a set of newspaper articles. The articles from the *New York Times* are from the following editions: July 2, 1942 (pp. 1 & 6); July 23, 1942 (pp. 1 & 6); July 29, 1942 (pp. 1 & 7); November 25, 1942 (pp. 1 & 7). The article from the *Herald Tribune* is from the November 25, 1942 edition, pages 1 and 10. Along with the articles the students will also receive a set of instructions which will guide them through the successful completion of the assignment.

"Upon completion of the assignment, which may take two class periods, each group will report its findings to the entire class. At that time a teacher-led discussion may focus on the following points: Do you think the American people, from simply reading the daily newspaper, had enough information to realize the Holocaust was actually taking place?; Why did news of the Holocaust seldom appear on the front pages?; and How did local coverage differ from national coverage?"

The directions to the students are: "You have received copies of specific pages from a 1942 edition of the *New York Times* and/or the *New York Herald Tribune*. All contain Holocaust-related news items. Follow the directions below and answer the questions as they appear: (1) Read through the pages of the newspapers you have been given and locate any news items that relate to the Holocaust. Briefly summarize these articles; (2) On what pages did you find news of the Holocaust? What other kinds of articles appeared on that page? What sort of message does this convey to you in regard to how newspaper editors/publishers perceived the Holocaust?; (3) For those dealing with the *Times* and *Tribune* editions of November 25, 1942, what differences in coverage did you note? [Who/]What do you think is responsible for such obvious differences?; (4) Locate a copy of your local daily newspaper that corresponds to the date of the edition of the *New York Times* or *Tribune* that you are working with. Was there any news of the Holocaust in your local newspaper? If so, on what page did it appear? Briefly summarize the article. Compare and contrast the coverage in your local newspaper(s) with that of the *New York Times* and *Tribune*. What do you make of the differences?"

9. Have students conduct short interviews of people who were alive during the 1930s and 1940s in regard to what they knew and when about the Holocaust, how they gleaned their information, and where they gleaned their information. Students should be assisted by the teacher to as they prepare questions for the interviews (e.g., the types of questions that need to be asked, how to make sure that one's questions are comprehensive, the need for and the method on how to ask follow-up questions), the proper way to use a tape recorder during an interview (including the need to check that the machine is operating correctly; the placement of the microphone), the methods to be used to accurately transcribe the tape and place the interview in q and a (question/answer) format, and the style and tone needed in a short informative introduction to the interview (complete with names of the interviewee and interviewer, the time and location of the interview, etc.). Subsequently, the students should share their information during a class discussion; and in doing so, discuss the ramifications of their findings.

10. As a follow-up to the interview activity (#9), students could conduct short interviews of their peers, teachers, parents and other adults in regard to a major human rights infraction or genocidal process taking place today and obtain the same information that they attempted to glean in the former activity (e.g., what the interviewee knows about the infraction/process and when he/she gleaned such information, how they gleaned their information, where they

gleaned their information, etc.). Again, the students could share their information during a class discussion; and in doing so, discuss the ramifications of their findings. They could also compare and contrast these findings with their earlier ones vis-à-vis the Holocaust.

11. Numerous polls were conducted during the Holocaust years (1933) that surveyed peoples' views in regard to various issues germane to the Holocaust (e.g., on the plight views of the Jews, views on refugees, etc.). The results of many of these polls were published in newspapers. A teacher (or his/her students) could locate and copy such polls/surveys for the purpose of incorporating them into a study of the Holocaust.

In doing so, polls could be selected that address certain issues that directly pertain to an issue being studied. For example, during the discussion of the extermination camps (during which teachers could have students examine the newspaper reports on the mass deaths of the Jews), the teacher could bring in a Gallup Poll that was conducted in December 1944 that "asked people if they believed the stories that the Germans had murdered many people (the question did not mention Jews) in concentration camps" (Lipstadt, 1986, p. 347).[1] The students could then discuss and debate what people knew when, what their attitudes were to particular sets of situations/questions, and probe (using the history of the period) into why people thought/felt as they did. The key here is to help the students come to the realization that there are no simple answers to this history or any other period of history, and to assist them to make a concerted effort to delve deeply into the history (including the antecedents, the social and political climate of the period, the decision making processes at various levels of society, the various incidents and events, and the motivation of various parties).

For a series of very telling polls on "American Views on the Refugee Question," see Charles Herbert Stember's *Jews in the*

---

1. In that particular poll, a follow-up question "was asked of those who had responded in the affirmative [that] illustrated the depth of confusion even among those who were willing to acknowledge that many had died" (Lipstadt, 1986, pp. 347-348): "Nobody knows, of course, how your best guess? As for the results: 27% guessed 100,000 or less, 5% guessed 100,000 to 500,000, 1% guessed 500,000 to one million, 6% guessed 1 million, 4% guessed 6 million or more, and 25% were unwilling to venture a guess" (Lipstadt, 1986, p. 348).

Mind of America (New York: Basic, 1966). It includes polls from various periods of time (e.g., March 1938, May 1938, November 1938, 1944), and posits such questions as: "Do you think the persecution of Jews in Europe has been their own fault?"; "If you were a member of Congress, would you vote yes or not on a bill to open the doors of the United States to a larger number of European refugees than are now admitted under our immigration quotas?"; "Should we allow a large number of Jewish exiles to come to the United State to live?"; "It has been proposed to bring into this country 10,000 refugee children from Germany, most of them Jewish, to be taken care of in American homes. Should the government permit these children to come in?" The latter poll was taken in 1944 and 30% responded "Yes," 61% responded "No," and 9% responded "No opinion." Excerpts from various polls from the Stember book are also available in *The Holocaust and Genocide: A Search for Conscience: An Anthology for Students* (New York: Anti-Defamation League of B'nai B'rith, 1983, pp. 82-83).

12. As an adjunct assignment, the students could be required to do the same sort of project as in activities two, three, four, five, six, seven and eight above but this time with a focus on editorial/political cartoons. Prior to conducting these activities, the teacher will need to provide students with an overview of the purpose and focus of political cartoons, possibly some background history on political cartooning, and the skills needed to read and comprehend such cartoons, etc.

13. As another adjunct study, the students examine how radio stations (a prime method of obtaining news in the 1930s and 1940s since television had not yet been invented) covered the period of the Holocaust as compared with newspapers. Three useful resources for such an activity are: Edward J. Bliss' *In Search of Light: The Broadcasts of Edward R. Murrow, 1938-1961* (New York: Knopf, 1967); Joyce Fein's "American Radio's Coverage of the Holocaust; 1938-1945," senior thesis, Hampshire College (U.S.), Spring 1984; and William Shirer's *The Nightmare Years, 1930-1940* (Boston: Little, Brown, 1984).

14. At certain periods in time throughout history, there have been (and are) certain events and phenomena that various people simply cannot bring themselves to believe as true. For example, prior to Columbus's "discovery" of the New World, many people believed

that the world was flat and thus could not even begin to fathom that there was a possibility that the earth was a sphere. Following man's first walk on the moon, the press reported that certain individuals (some in the southern part of the United States) refused to believe that the event had actually occurred and instead claimed that the photographs documenting the fact were, in actuality, trick photography.

It is little wonder that people in the latter half of the first part of this century would find it unbelievable that such a cultured people as the Germans would plan and then systematically annihilate a whole group of people numbering in the millions. It was simply beyond people's ken.

Thus, it is no surprise that when " . . . the BBC broadcast some sections from the Protocols [revelations by Jewish escapees from Auschwitz in April-May 1944], such broadcasts were construed by world public opinion basically as horror propaganda material" (Braham, 1981, p. 120). The facts were just too outlandish for many to believe.

The latter is easier to comprehend when one realizes that " . . . the Hungarian Jews living so close to Auschwitz, had no sure knowledge about the gas chambers, or about the mass murders committed further afield by the SS Einsatzgruppen. They discounted what they heard about these horrors as rumors or anti-Nazi propaganda. It was thus even easier for the masses than their leaders to delude themselves about their relative safety. They rationalized their predicament by arguing that whatever was really happening to the Jews of Poland and elsewhere, such horrors could not possibly take place in Hungary, where the destiny of Jews and Christians had been intertwined for over a thousand years" (Braham, 1981, p. 125).

As Lipstadt (1986) has perspicaciously stated: "Ultimately the most formidable obstacle to the spreading and acceptance of news of the Final Solution was the nature of the information itself. People are naturally inclined to doubt the fantastic and the unprecedented, especially when the story told is an atrocity tale. Had the Germans chosen to enslave and oppress the Jews but not to annihilate them, there would have been fewer doubts about what they were doing. Given the German record since 1933 of brutalities and persecution, people might have eventually believed this news. But because the Nazis chose to do the unprecedented, the reports of their actions were most likely to be rejected as inaccurate. The extreme nature of the news fostered doubts in the minds of victims and bystanders. The systematic annihilation of an entire people seemed beyond the realm of the possible" (pp. 141-142).

Students should be asked to take part in a group brainstorming session in which they list on the board all of those events and/or phenomena that people in the past could not bring themselves to believe despite the fact that they (the events and phenomena) actually occurred.

Once that list is on the board and copied, the students should take part in another brainstorming session in which they list those events/phenomena that people–at least some people–can't believe happened, are happening or possibly being discovered or taking place (e.g., that there is life on other planets in space).

At the conclusion of the two brainstorming sessions, the class should briefly discuss what they have come up with.

Next, the students should be required to conduct, in pairs or threes, a short study in which they attempt to ascertain why so many people during the late 1930s and early to mid-1940s could not believe that the Nazis were murdering the Jews in the millions via firing squads, gas vans, and gas chambers. In doing so, the students should locate newspaper accounts, first-person accounts, primary documents, and other resources to undergird their points. At the conclusion of the project, a class discussion should focus on the students' findings.

15. Following a short study of the anti-Semitic newspaper *Der Sturmer* and its editor, the rabid anti-Semite Julius Streicher, the students could, as an adjunct assignment, examine the articles and editorial/political "cartoons" found in the *Sturmer*. In doing so, they could discuss the type of information, tone, the role of propaganda, the distortion of facts, etc., in the articles and cartoons.

Prior to having the students engage in this activity, it would be a good idea to provide them with a solid sense of the Nazis' rabid anti-Semitism and racism, and how that manifested itself in Nazi Germany and beyond. In this way, the students will not approach the study of the *Der Sturmer* in a vacuum; and hopefully, the students will be better prepared to understand why and how Streicher used his lies and skewed views both for propaganda purposes as a means to malign the Jewish people in the nastiest and most brutish of ways.

16. Another worthwhile adjunct activity would be to introduce the students to the controversy over how Walter Durant, reporter for the *New York Times*, covered the man-made famine in the Ukraine during 1932-1933. (See Marco Carynnyk's "Making the News Fit to Print: Walter Durant, *The New York Times* and the Ukraine Famine of 1933." In Roman Serbyn and Bohdan Krawchenko (Eds.) *Famine in Ukraine 1932-1933* (pp. 67-95). Edmonton: Canadian Institute of Ukrainian Studies at the University of Alberta, 1986.) The aforementioned article raises a host of questions in regard to the objectivity of the press and how certain influential reporters may influence the general public and/or their own and other governments as a result of their reporting, accurate or not). The students could be asked to compare and contrast how Britain and the U.S. covered certain aspects of the Ukraine famine in comparison and contrast to certain aspects of the Holocaust. While the two events were totally different in nature, with the major exception that both involved genocide, it could be instructive for the students to ascertain how and why the press covered/covers certain genocidal events.

17. Another worthwhile adjunct activity would be to introduce the students to the controversy over how the United States and Britain press covered the man-made famine in the Ukraine in 1933. (See Marco Carynnyk's "Blind Eye to Murder: Britain, the United States and the Ukrainian Famine of 1933." In Roman Serbyn and Bohdan Krawchenko (Eds.) *Famine in Ukraine 1932-1933* (pp. 67-95) Edmonton: Canadian Institute of Ukrainian Studies at the University of Alberta 1986.) The students could be asked to compare and contrast how Britain and the U.S. covered certain aspects of the Ukraine famine in comparison and contrast to certain aspects of the Holocaust. While the two events were totally different in nature, with the major exception that both involved genocide, it could be instructive for the students to ascertain how and why the press covered/covers certain genocidal events.

18. An interesting and worthwhile activity would involve the students in a study, discussion or debate to ascertain whether (and if so, how) the coverage of the Holocaust period by U.S. newspapers influenced the U.S. government's stance on such issues as the ever-

increasing discrimination against the Jews as well as the annihilatory practices of the Nazis. They should and should also examine whether the U.S. government's stance on such issues influenced the coverage of such events in U.S. newspapers. (Again, an excellent source for information on such a subject would be Lipstadt's *Beyond Belief: The American Press and the Coming of the Holocaust 1933-1945.*)

19. When Elie Wiesel, the noted author and survivor of the Holocaust, taught courses on the Holocaust in the early to mid-1970s at the City College of New York, he would send his students to the index of *The New York Times* for answers to who knew what and when about the Nazi onslaught against the Jews. In doing so, he told them to focus on the years 1942-1943. "Every massacre," he would tell them "was reported in full detail. The press fulfilled its mission but the politicians didn't act. The Allies know more than the victims." As part of their assignment, students could be asked to complete the exact assignment that Wiesel gave his students. The one key difference in the directions, though, would be to have them not only use *The New York Times* but other sources, including weekly magazines. They could also be asked to copy off the articles they find, and then report their findings. If a teacher wishes, he/she could also provide the students with guiding questions that they could respond to in writing.

CONCLUSION

In order to make a study of the Holocaust as engaging and thought-provoking as possible, teachers need to use all of the "tools" at their disposal. This includes both unique pedagogical strategies, learning activities and resources. Certainly the inclusion of contemporaneous newspaper articles is a source that many students will find unique, engaging and, hopefully, revelatory. The latter is particularly true when the students are engaged in thought-provoking exercises that challenge them to view such a resource from a new perspective and through the lens of how and why journalists reported, interpreted and possibly impacted the events of the period.

REFERENCES

Associated Press (June 30, 1996). "Paper tells tales of the past, but what of the digital future?" *Northwest Arkansas Times*, p. A8.

Braham, Randolph L. (1981) "What Did They Know and When?" pp. 109-131. In Yehuda Bauer and Nathan Rotenstreich (Eds.) *The Holocaust as Historical Experience*. New York: Holmes & Meier Publishers.

Cargas, Harry James (1981). *A Christian Response to the Holocaust*. Denver, CO: Stonehenge.

DeSilva, Bruce (1986). "Schoolbooks: A Question of Quality. A *Hartford Courant* Special Report." Hartford, CT: The Hartford Courant.

Glenn, Jerry (1973). *Paul Celan*. New York: Twayne Publishers, Inc.

Langer, Lawrence (1978). *The Age of Atrocity: Death in Modern Literature*. Boston: Beacon Press.

Lipstadt, Deborah E. (1986). *Beyond Belief: The American Press and the Coming of the Holocaust 1933-1945*. New York: The Free Press.

Totten, Samuel (1995) "Jigsaw Synthesis: A Method for Incorporating a Study of Social Issues into the Extant Curriculum," pp. 389-424. In Jon E. Pedersen and Annette Digby (Eds.) *Cooperative Learning in Secondary Schools*. New York: Garland Publishers.

Totten, Samuel (1987). "The Personal Face of Genocide: Words of Witnesses in the Classroom." *Social Science Record: The Journal of the New York State Council for the Social Studies* (Special Issue on "Genocide: Issues, Approaches, Resources" edited by Samuel Totten), *24*(2):63-67.

Totten, Samuel (1994). "The Use of First-Person Accounts in Teaching About the Holocaust." *The British Journal of Holocaust Education*, 3(2):160-183.

Totten, Samuel (in review). "Using Literature to Teach About the Holocaust."

United States Holocaust Memorial Museum (1993). *Guidelines for Teaching About the Holocaust*. Washington, D.C.: Author.

SELECT ANNOTATED BIBLIOGRAPHY

Historical Works:

Feingold, Henry (1980). *The Politics of Rescue: The Roosevelt Administration and the Holocaust, 1938-1945*. New York: Schocken. In this scholarly study, Feingold's purpose is to present an examination of the political climate and context that shaped the U.S. response (or lack thereof) to the events unfolding in Nazi-occupied Europe. A key aspect of the book focuses on the U.S. and international refugee policy as it evolved from the Evian Conference in 1938 to the creation of the U.S. War Refugee Board in 1944.

Gallup, George H. (1972). *The Gallup Poll: Public Opinion, 1935-1948*. New York: Random House. An excellent source for the type of polls conducted (and the sort of information gleaned) around various issues germane to Nazi Germany.

Friedman, Saul (1973). *No Haven for the Oppressed: United States Policy Toward Jewish Refugees, 1938-1945.* Detroit, MI: Wayne State University Press. Friedman examines the various factors that were at play in the U.S. as Jewish refugees sought to emigrate to the U.S. in the face of the Nazi onslaught.

Laqueur, Walter (1980). *The Terrible Secret: Suppression of the Truth About Hitler's "Final Solution."* Boston; Little Brown. "Using sources and documents that [had] only recently been made available, Laqueur examines when and how information about the genocide [of the Jews] became known to millions of Germans, international Jewish organizations, leaders of Jewish communities throughout Europe, and top government officials in neutral and Allied countries."

Lipstadt, Deborah E. (1986). *Beyond Belief: The American Press and the Coming of the Holocaust 1933-1945.* New York: The Free Press. This outstanding book by the noted scholar Deborah Lipstadt presents the most detailed discussion to date vis-à-vis the coverage of the American press on the Holocaust years. Lipstadt also addresses, but to a lesser extent, the British press, particularly articles found in the *London Times* and the *Manchester Guardian.* Also cited are the *Daily Telegraph and Morning Post*, the *London Observer*, the *Spectator*, *London Daily Herald*, *Evening Standard*, and the *Glasgow Evening News.* For those teachers who are going to have their students examine the press' coverage (particularly that of the U.S. and British) then this is a must work for them to read and consult. Its section entitled "Notes" is packed with excellent references, many of which are included in this selected annotated bibliography. Included in the aforementioned lists of references are the names of scores of newspapers across the U.S. and some of the many articles on the Nazis' actions that were included in such newspapers.

Marty, Martin E. (April 10, 1985). "The *Century* and the Holocaust," *Christian Century*, pp. 350-352. In this piece Marty defends the *Christian Century's* editorial position during the Holocaust years. In *Beyond Belief: The American Press and the Coming of the Holocaust 1933-1945* Deborah Lipstadt states: "While Marty correctly cites a number of occasions when the journal did speak out on behalf of persecuted Jews, there were many other occasions when its position was ambivalent at best" (p. 331).

Morse, Arthur (1967). *While Six Million Died: A Chronicle of American Apathy.* New York: Random House. While this book's exclusive focus is not on the American press but rather on the attitudes, perspectives and action/lack of action President Franklin Roosevelt, the U.S. State Department and Congress vis-à-vis the unfolding of the Holocaust, it includes pertinent information for those who are examining how and why the U.S. acted the way it did in regard to the fate of the Jews in Nazi-occupied Europe. As Deborah Lipstadt (1986) notes in *Beyond Belief: The American Press and the Coming of the Holocaust 1933-1945*: "The book which propelled both the discussion of American policy during the war and the question of "When did they know?" into the public arena was Arthur Morse's *While Six Million Died*" (p. 322).

Mosse, George (1981). *Nazi Culture: A Documentary History.* New York: Schocken. This book is primarily an anthology of original source material. Its selections include material taken from newspapers, speeches, diaries, and other sources.

Sanders, Marion K. (1973). *Dorothy Thompson: A Legend in Her Time.* Boston: Houghton Mifflin. Contains information on this reporters perspective on the situation in Nazi Germany following a visit there in March 1933, her expulsion from Germany in 1934 which was ostensibly a result of her interview with Hitler in 1932 and her reports in 1933 castigating the Nazi's anti-Semitic actions.

Shirer, William (1984). *The Nightmare Years, 1930-1940.* Boston: Little, Brown. A fascinating and informative examination of the Nazi rise to power by a reporter who viewed the rise from close-up.

Wyman, David (1984). *The Abandonment of the Jews: America and the Holocaust, 1941-1945.* New York: Pantheon Books. Wyman examines the issue of what was known, when and by whom in the U.S. about the physical annihilation of the Jews by the Nazis. As survivor Elie Wiesel states in the introduction to this book: "Roosevelt's politics was only part of the problem; the rest had to do with the particular mood of the country at that time. David Wyman provides us with a few striking instances of it: the Congress's unequivocal opposition to immigration, the Christian churches' near-silence, the press's burial of news of the death factories in the back pages of their newspapers" (p. ix).

Wyman, David (1985). *Paper Walls: America and the Refugee Crisis, 1938-1941.* New York: Pantheon. In *Paper Walls* Wyman examines the American policy on refugees in the years leading up to World War II. From 1938 through 1941 German Jews attempted to leave their country, but were barred from entering the United States due to restrictive immigration policies. Ultimately, millions were killed while a mere 150,000 were eventually admitted to the U.S. Wyman argues that the basis for the denial to allow the desperate Jews to enter the U.S. were: "unemployment in the U.S., nationalism, anti-Semitism, and, later, fear of fifth columnists disguised as refugees."

Pedagogical Pieces:

Wieser, Paul (October 1995). "An Introduction to Teaching the Holocaust." *Social Education* (Special Issue on the Holocaust edited by Samuel Totten, Stephen Feinberg, and Milton Kleg), *59*(6):C1-C6. The first section of this three part lesson plan is entitled "The American Press and the Holocaust: The Cry That Fell on Deaf Ears." It includes a brief overview of the U.S. press' response, and an accompanying lesson plan. The lesson plan is comprised of a goal, a set of objectives, a set of directions for the teacher, and a set of directions (list of activities for the students).

How Silent Were the Churches?
Canadian Protestantism and the Jewish Plight During the Nazi Era:
Notes on Method

Alan Davies

Professor Marilyn Nefsky of the University of Lethbridge (Lethbridge, Alberta) and I have recently finished a book with the above title. *How Silent Were the Churches?* will be published in 1997 by Wilfrid Laurier University Press. Our study was prompted by the claim that the Christian churches of Canada were either silent or largely silent in the face of the Jewish refugee crisis in Nazi-occupied Europe, as well as the Holocaust itself. This charge appears in a highly influential work entitled *None is Too Many,* written more than a decade ago by two Canadian historians, Irving Abella and Harold Troper: "As long as the churches remained silent–which they did–the government could dismiss the (Canadian National Committee on Refugees and Victims of Political Persecution) members as well meaning but impractical idealists to be patronized but not taken seriously."[1] The government in question was, of course,

Alan Davies is affiliated with the Department of Religion, Victoria College, University of Toronto, 73 Queens Park Crescent, Toronto, Ontario, Canada M5S 1K7.

The material in this essay has been adapted from the book's Introduction.

[Haworth co-indexing entry note]: "How Silent Were the Churches? Canadian Protestantism and the Jewish Plight During the Nazi Era: Notes on Method." Davies, Alan. Co-published simultaneously in *The Reference Librarian* (The Haworth Press, Inc.) No. 61/62, 1998, pp. 83-88; and: *The Holocaust: Memories, Research, Reference* (ed: Robert Hauptman, and Susan Hubbs Motin) The Haworth Press, Inc., 1998, pp. 83-88. Single or multiple copies of this article are available for a fee from The Haworth Document Delivery Service [1-800-342-9678, 9:00 a.m. - 5:00 p.m. (EST). E-mail address: getinfo@haworth.com].

83

the Liberal government of Prime Minister W.L. Mackenzie King. Our volume can be described as an attempt to reconstruct the era and to examine the extant evidence in light of this indictment as far as the Protestant churches of Canada were concerned (because of the size of the subject, we reluctantly decided to omit the Roman Catholic church). One of our models was a similar study of the American churches during the same period by William E. Nawyn.[2] At stake was not only the accuracy of the historical record but also the integrity of Christian Canada and its social conscience. An interesting feature of our enterprise is that it represents the collaboration of a Jew and a Christian. Our conclusions serve to ameliorate the severity of the charge–with certain exceptions, the mainstream Protestant denominations of the day were neither silent about the fate of the European Jews nor indifferent to their plight–but not to annul it entirely. The picture is complex and, like much of history itself, tinted in grey rather than black or white. But it contains some striking splashes of whiteness.

In this essay, however, our methods of research rather than our conclusions are at stage centre. Since our subject was speech, or its alleged absence, the quest was relatively straightforward: what did the churches actually say? Ecclesiastical bodies speak through various organs, notably episcopal and diocesan letters, synodical, presbyterial and conference resolutions, the minutes of meetings, public statements and other official documents of one kind of another: all which collect dust in church archives. They also speak (directly or indirectly) through denominational papers and journals, frequently the best index of contemporary Christian opinion. Because of the centrality of the pulpit in Protestant Christianity, sermons are of paramount importance, but not many sermons find their way into print or even survive in manuscript form, and, unless the preacher is famous, the few that do are difficult to locate. During the thirties and forties, however, especially in large cities such as Toronto, it was a frequent practice among daily newspapers to publish on Monday a brief synopsis of anything topical or noteworthy uttered by popular local ministers (i.e., those in large churches) from their pulpits on the preceding Sunday. We found some relevant material in this fashion. In essence, our research consisted of a vast scavenger hunt through these various domains until we had accumulated sufficient material in order to allow some impressions to develop. Each church or Protestant collectivity–the highly fragmented Baptists, Lutherans and Mennonites did not comprise single churches or denominations–was explored separately, and a profile of each was created on the basis of what was said or not said on the Jewish plight during the Nazi era. The United Church of Canada, the Church of England in Canada (now Anglican Church of Canada), the Presbyterian Church in Canada, the major Baptist conventions together with certain other evangelical churches, and finally the Lutherans, Mennonites and Quakers, comprise the sequence of chapters. Not every religious body of the period that called itself Protestant has been included; Protestantism has too many offspring. Size was a rule of thumb, eliminating some of the smaller holiness groups (e.g., the Standard Church in eastern Ontario), although, for special reasons, the numerically insignificant Salvation Army and the even more numerically insignificant Society of Friends could not be ignored.

This procedure was attended by some difficulties. For one thing, the archives were scattered. Canada is not a small country and its churches do not all possess centralized archival centres. Fortunately for the authors, much of the material of the major denominations could be found in Toronto or its vicinity, but excursions to Waterloo, Ontario (Lutherans and Mennonites), Winnipeg, Manitoba (Mennonites) and Saskatoon, Saskatchewan (Lutherans) and Ottawa (National Archives of Canada) also proved necessary. Because of these complications, the process of research was slow and piecemeal, leaving no assurance that, even after a decade of work, nothing important had been overlooked. Such projects cannot be hurried; however, even when they proceed at a leisurely pace, an uneasy feeling lingers. The uneasiness is prompted not merely by the fear of a serious omission in the evidence, but the deeper fear, when everything has been assembled, of writing what R.G. Collingwood called "scissors-and-paste" history, or history that is not really history at all but only a juggling of texts and testimonies.[3] True history, according to Collingwood, concerns itself with the inside as well as the outside of events.

Since, in our book, we were very much concerned with the inside of events, it was important to interpret our texts with care, and to place them in their proper context. Official documents are not easy to weigh; should they be accepted at face value, or should they be dismissed, as Nawyn has said, as "gratuitous and emotional protests" of a kind that religious institutions love to engage in when their sensibilities are aroused?[4] Making the right noises is a good device for doing nothing, since words are cheap and actions are expensive. Some churches in the United States as well as Canada said much but did little; the Quakers, on the other, said little but did much as far as practical assistance was concerned. Others said little and did little. However, if speech in itself proves nothing, neither does silence, if we are searching for attitudes and underlying motifs: anti-Judaism and antisemitism lurked in the battleground of the great refugee question, and both what the churches said and did not say during the Nazi era cannot be evaluated without reference to these subterranean forces. In varying degrees, the Protestant churches of Canada were captive to uncritical anti-Jewish theological ideas endemic to historical Christianity that post-Holocaust Christian theologians now repudiate: Jewish 'legalism' (usually called Pharisaism), Jewish materialism, Jewish instigation of the execution of Jesus, Jewish displacement as God's people, Jewish punishment for their disbelief through exile and persecution, etc.—the list is long. In varying degrees also, the churches were infected by nativist and antisemitic sentiments present in society at large, especially during the Great Depression when petty fascist movements arose on Canadian soil and when the public was in a xenophobic and anti-immigrant state of mind. Because they were part of Canada themselves, to say anything in favour of the Jews required the churches to struggle against the popular and political streams, a fact that cannot be left out of account. In this sense, the inside as well as the outside of events is of the utmost significance.

Another problem involved the interpretation of editorials and articles in the church journals. Denominational papers do not always speak unequivocally for the churches that sponsor and finance them. Editors are editors, and cherish their independence; they are rarely slavish agents of their employers, who may or may not wish to keep them on a short leash. In certain churches (notably the United Church of Canada), a deliberate hands off policy was adopted towards the 'official' church paper, *The New Outlook* (later renamed *The United Church Observer*). Editorial freedom was both permitted and encouraged. In other churches, the opposite was true. Moreover, the various denominational papers and journals varied greatly in character. The Mennonite press, for example, especially its German-language newspapers *Der Bote* and *Die Mennonitische Rundschau*, allowed a wide range of opinion into its pages, including some quite extreme pro-Nazi views, but their authors usually spoke only for themselves rather than for anyone else, and certainly not for their churches (in any case, the highly fragmented nature of the Mennonite churches made collective statements of any kind virtually impossible). Hence, care must be exercised; how pro-Nazi really were German-speaking Mennonites in Canada during the 1930s? Dare one judge from a few loud-mouthed correspondents? Another problem was that of judging incidental factors. In the case of one church paper, *The Canadian Churchman*, the main publication of the Church of England in Canada, staff infighting during the Nazi era apparently interfered with its reportage on various matters, raising doubts about the degree to which it could be regarded as a reliable reflection of Anglican opinion at the time. For such reasons, facile equations between the churches and their official or semi-official journals had to be avoided. Nevertheless, the church press supplied a unique forum for debate and Christian commentary, and the wide array of editorials, articles, reprinted sermons, columns, letters and book reviews cast indispensable light on the mood of Protestant society in Canada in the thirties and forties. It was a rich vein to mine.

In addition to ransacking archives and reading old newspapers, we also interviewed a few–actually, very few–individuals who were alive at the time and actively engaged in the battle against the Canadian government and its harsh anti-alien policies. Personal memories are invaluable, but must be handled with care; no one is truly objective, and, even with the most noble of intentions, the human mind deletes some things and revises that which it retains. However, without some oral recollections to breathe life into the dust of yellowed documents, our tale would have assumed a more scholastic tone. It was the late James Parkes, for example, who told me that much of the political opposition to the admission of Jewish refugees to wartime Britain came from Herbert Morrison, the Labour home secretary in the war cabinet headed by Winston Churchill.[5] Morrison had nothing to do with Canada, except insofar as Canada and Britain were linked by the ties of throne and empire as well as the allied cause against Hitler, but there were significant parallels between British and Canadian bureaucratic and governmental policies (although the British record is much better[6]) as well as between Anglican responses in both countries. The strongly pro-refugee stand of the English archbishops galvanized the Canadian Anglicans into a similar protest against their own government. Not everything is explained by written sources; even anecdote has its uses, as scholars have long known.

No doubt our work, like all human endeavours, has its flaws. Much data is almost certainly missing, and perhaps someone else will eventually fill in some of the gaps. But the past in its entirety can never be recaptured, however mountainous its annals; if we can depict its light and shadows, we have done well.

ENDNOTES

1. Irving Abella & Harold Troper, *None is Too Many: Canada and the Jews of Europe 1933-1948*, Toronto: Lester & Orpen Dennys, 1982, p. 51.

2. Willan E. Nawyn, *American Protestantism's Response to Germany's Jews and Refugees 1933-1941*, Ann Arbor: UMI Research Press, 1981.

3. R.G. Collingwood, *The Idea of History*, London: Oxford University Press, 1956, p. 257f.

4. Ibid., p. 135.

5. James Parkes, a clergyman of the Church of England, was the author of several extremely important studies of the roots of antisemitism in Christian history and theology, including his seminal book *The Conflict of the Church and the Synagogue*, first published in 1934. In our conversation more than a decade ago, he described Morrison as an "extremely callous man."

6. As in Canada, antisemites walked the corridors of power in Britain, especially in the colonial office. Churchill, however, was a restraining force on behalf of the Jews, preventing more extreme measures advocated by some of his subordinates. Cf. Bernard Wasserstein, *Britain and the Jews of Europe 1939-1945*, Oxford: Clarendon Press, 1979, p. 47.

Comparative Genocide Studies and the Future Directions of Holocaust Research: An Exploration

Henry R. Huttenbach

Initially, Holocaust research had to be *sui generis*. Questions posed by scholars originated from the topic itself. From the moment of confrontation with the event, a tidal wave of problems and dilemmas arose to face those seeking to comprehend the Final Solution and its far-reaching impact. There was no need to refer to other incidents of genocide (assuming there were any of this dimension) to generate research guidelines and establish a prioritized list of themes. This momentum of Holocaust-inspired research ideas and projects continued well into the late '70s and early '80s when the study of the Holocaust began to lose intellectual vitality. An element of déja vu began to creep into Holocaust scholarship.

The symptoms of this malaise was a certain artificiality reflected in the titles of monographs and articles; instead of probing broad questions, scholarship became increasingly micro-focused and macro-irrelevant, over-specialized, often leading to a conceptual *cul-de-sac*. Instead of raising vitally *new* questions, Holocaust scholarship

---

Henry R. Huttenbach is affiliated with the Department of History, The City College of New York, 138th Street and Convent Avenue, New York, NY 10031.

[Haworth co-indexing entry note]: "Comparative Genocide Studies and the Future Directions of Holocaust Research: An Exploration." Huttenbach, Henry R. Co-published simultaneously in *The Reference Librarian* (The Haworth Press, Inc.) No. 61/62, 1998, pp. 89-97; and: *The Holocaust: Memories, Research, Reference* (ed: Robert Hauptman, and Susan Hubbs Motin) The Haworth Press, Inc., 1998, pp. 89-97. Single or multiple copies of this article are available for a fee from The Haworth Document Delivery Service [1-800-342-9678, 9:00 a.m. - 5:00 p.m. (EST). E-mail address: getinfo@haworth.com].

89

tended to veer towards the circular–posing the same (now tiresome) questions and, worse, betraying signs of a theoretical fatigue. In recent years, Holocaust research, still dependent on self-generated horizons, has proven to be increasingly barren, suffering from a form of academic sclerosis, despite the infusion of significant amounts of new materials, thanks largely to the opening of ex-communist archives throughout Eastern Europe. These documents, however, have tended to confirm, corroborate, or modify past research rather than force radical revisions and introduce unexpected, new avenues of inquiry, much to most scholars' understandable disappointment.

Fortunately and fortuitously, since the mid-'70s, a sizable literature on genocide and other related fields (i.e., ethnonationalism) has begun to repair what had become an egregious imbalance, an overfocus on the Holocaust and a neglect of other genocidal events. Past genocides, such as the Armenian tragedy, have at last attracted considerable scholarly attention and, necessarily, opened up the possibility of legitimate comparisons, in hopes of determining both areas of fundamental commonality and of significant difference(s). In the case of the Armenian tragedy, that meant establishing the specificity of each incident of genocide, though it and the Holocaust were separated, in this case, by geography and one generation. Since then, other genocides (such as that of the Aché Indians in Paraguay)[1] have been examined more closely, offering the promise of an even wider field of comparative opportunities, so one can now literally speak of a broad spectrum of genocides, each of which needs to be categorized according to several criteria.[2] Any future work on the Holocaust, to be academically authentic, will have to include a structural comparative component. Indeed, thanks to the growing need for comparison between genocides, a rather complex methodology of comparative genocide has at last become a standard requirement, although it still calls for considerable honing and finetuning before one can claim it to be reliable and of a minimal level of respectable sophistication. In this context, new central questions tend to originate from *outside* the event itself. In short, key questions about the Holocaust have begun to originate increasingly from other genocides. After half a century of Holocaust research, the opportunity for cross-fertilization in a context of comparative genocide studies has come about.

More recently, the raging inter-ethnic genocides in central Africa between Hutus and Tutsis–originally confined to Rwanda and Burundi and now spread to east Zaire–and those in the ex-Yugoslavia (not just Bosnia!)–have forced the attention of scholars and policy makers on a phenomenon that may continue well into the 21st century. The term "ethnic cleansing," implying a kind of genocide, has potentially radically altered the research agenda of scholars of genocide in general and of the Holocaust in particular.

For one thing, less and less of what is known about the Holocaust helps explain contemporary outbreaks of genocidal violence; on the contrary, as knowledge and understanding of other genocides unfold, it seems to shed more light on the Holocaust of half a century ago. More pertinent to this essay, the study of other genocides increasingly raises questions not yet posed by scholars of the Holocaust, challenging some of their fundamental assumptions. To take but one example: a considerable segment of Holocaust research concludes or adopts the conclusion that the Holocaust, i.e., genocide, is a by-product of the modern state and its technology; it is the administrative institutions of the state combined with the destructive powers of science that provide the lethal core and instrumentality of genocide. Without it, one is led to believe, genocide in its contemporary variant is impossible. And yet, for example, what are we to make of the genocidal slaughter in 1994 in the short span of three months of nearly one million Tutsis by machete-wielding Hutus? No bureaucratic round-ups here; no organized deportations by railroad, no census lists, no gas chambers, no "emptying" ghettos by machine gun. Only intense hatred, carefully nurtured and organized, focused on mass death carried out by pre-industrial means, the machete![3]

A second example of what might be termed a loss of imagination is the oft-repeated mantra-like plaint that the essence of the Holocaust–the unlimited brutality it unleashed–is "incomprehensible."[4] That is either an emotive way of stressing the depth of cruelty one is made to witness and which transcended the imaginative capacity of the scholar (and even of the survivor) or it is a form of desperate intellectual capitulation, an admission that the Final Solution defies one's ability to understand it. Some in the latter category go one step further and mystify the inner meaning of the Holocaust as an event that hides its real significance, making it intellectually inaccessible, locating it beyond traditional, rational analysis.

The former is an understandable reaction to the horror of the human capacity to do harm; but that is no proof of mystery. If anything, it tells us more about the person repelled by evil than about the evil itself or the evil doer. At best this is a failure of imagination, at worst a sentimentalized form of psychological escape, a defensive mechanism to avoid further exposure to the stark Holocaust reality, the details of the act of genocide–not in its sterile documentary and conceptual forms, but in its unadulterated naked self. The latter is an anti-intellectual stance, an attempt to upgrade an historic event to the level of a metaphysical phenomenon that cannot, by definition, be grasped by reason alone. This is an untenable dichotomy, a regression to the Romantic notion of the natural and the supra-natural and the pre-Renaissance theocentrism that fought so strenuously against rationalism. Just as one ascribed events to God's intervention into human affairs–be it the outcome of battles or the success or failure of harvests–so, in the case of the Holocaust, one seeks to endow it with meta-human significance instead of treating it as a purely man-willed genocide, indeed a *crime* that violates international law.

The more one studies other instances of genocide, the temptation to treat them as more than a human act tends to weaken. Seen singly, the individual genocide raises the same seemingly unanswerable questions: "How was it possible?" and "What on earth does it mean?" Placed alongside other genocides, the "uniqueness" of the isolated event quickly diminishes as basic commonalties are unearthed. The human capacity to carry out extermination becomes less exceptional and more quotidian. There is less need to fall back on emotive solutions and unsustainable irrational conclusions. Seen collectively, genocides automatically demystify themselves and become all too human, far less pathological (aberrational) and much more "normal" in the course of human history and in the context of the 20th century. Common sense ultimately forces one to admit that there is nothing about genocide in general and the Holocaust in particular that is immune to satisfactory rational interpretation and secular explanation. There is nothing about the incidents of ethnic cleansing in ex-Yugoslavia—itself a form of genocide—that is beyond the range of a scholar's comprehension: the mass expulsions, the mass rapes, the killing of *all* males (a form of gendercide), the sadistic brutalities inflicted collectively on prisoners prior to their execution, none of these cannot be accounted for by academic methodologies. After years of self-perpetuated claims by some researchers of the Holocaust's ultimate unintelligibility, the pendulum is finally swinging in favor of those who accept its overall comprehensibility. What still remains not fully understood, they insist, will, eventually, be clarified. It is a matter of patience and persistence as data about genocide accrues and, from it, greater comprehension ensues about the Holocaust.

If the above is logically acceptable, then it follows that much of the future agenda of Holocaust studies will, of necessity, emanate from the study of other genocides. Take the case of antisemitism: built on a long thread of uninterrupted hatred that spawned centuries of persecution, this phenomenon of Jew hatred now has a huge literature. In the context of the Holocaust, antisemitism played a central role and, to date, has been examined to a point of exhaustion. Luckily, thanks to other genocides driven by other forms of articulated hatred and institutionalized prejudice, antisemitism needs to be seen and compared to these other antipathies that underlay the genocidal victimizations of Armenians, Gypsies and Tutsis. Each is fueled by its own brand of "anti-ism." How do these animosities differ or resemble each other? Future scholarship of antisemitism will increasingly be dictated less by its past than by its more contemporary counterparts. Much can be learned from anti-Gypsyism and, of course, from any form of racism.

A few studies have already appeared on antisemitism as a form of racism. But they do not yet suffice; too many questions remain. To date, antisemitism as a sub-species of racism has led to an insoluble question, whether the Final Solution was primarily fueled by racism or by antisemitism, a query that, in itself, cannot be answered satisfactorily, if only because the Nazi ideology was simultaneously militantly racist—propounding the supremacy of Aryans—and absolutely antisemitic. Indeed, to be antisemitic in its racist mode the Nazis did not have to be racist supremacists; on their rise to power they had already inherited racist antisemitism which would have sufficed to launch their exterminist, anti-Jewish campaign. It certainly needed no further fortification from any other racist doctrine.

What really needs to be examined is the origins of the exterminationist *mentality*. Neither antisemitism nor racism alone provide a satisfactory explanation. If genocide and, hence, the Holocaust in particular, are to be better understood, then the roots of annihilationism—the origins of ultra-extreme intolerance—need to be explored, identified, and analyzed. One must ask what external factors encourage the ultimate polarization of antagonism to prompt genocidal thought and action. This avenue needs to be followed through to its logical end. The answer certainly does not lie in German or European civilization alone. Given the propensity to eradicate ethnic minorities in all corners of the earth, the answer lies beyond particular civilizations. Perhaps it lies in certain confluences of critical events—economic, political, social—which trigger into action the genocidal mentality. So far, we do not know the answers beyond informal speculation and conjecture, and possible hypothesis, none of which, so far, can be supported by sufficient hard evidence. Psycho-sociological methodologies not yet fully honed will have to be employed to bring about a systematic unraveling of the puzzle. What precisely quickens the genocidal state of mind—not for a brief moment of reflexive rage—but as a sustained commitment to a social goal, namely, the existential excision of a certain segment of a population? Are there some people with a latent propensity for such behaviour or does the potential lie in everyone?

As the number of genocides after Auschwitz grows, this is of *the* highest priority for all scholars. Whereas the Holocaust in itself may not provide the answer, it may come from *outside* itself, from other genocides. If there is to be some progress in human control over the tendency of mass destruction, we must be able to account for the rise to power of the genocidists. This is an imperative, for the scholar, for the politician, and for the general public, which, potentially, can be subjected to a future policy of genocide. Presently, very little has been learned about the structural make-up of the world of genocide. There are, as yet, no models, no all-embracing theories.

Since ethnogenocide is on the rise, more and more in the context of inter-ethnic conflict, a high priority must be given to an understanding of the dynamics of ethnicity and the interplay of inclusiveness and rejection according to ethnic criteria. How much has the struggle for scarce resources got to do with ethnogenocide? When do economic goals set off the mechanism of genocidal thought? Are there any ideological (religious, etc.) preconditions or predispositions for the genocidal mentality? Is everyone a potential genocidist? Or are some persons of a certain cultural make-up more likely to be genocidal if the conditions are right? We still are nowhere near the answers, if only because we lack precision tools.

At this point, scholars simply do not know the answers to these key questions. Nor, indeed, do they yet have dependable methodologies to deal with them professionally. For starters, those accused of genocide need to be thoroughly interviewed and studied in-depth. So far this has not yet ever been the case, if only because the interviewers have lacked the training to travel down the road into the heart of the genocidist's mind and psyche. All one need do to see how woefully unsatisfactory these sessions were is review interrogations of some high Nazi officials and concentration camp guards. Now that they are all dead or mentally too old, the only way to begin research along these lines is to focus on accused and convicted genocidists of other, more recent, instances.

Unfortunately, though understandably, for human and legal reasons, the survivors (as witnesses) have been given the greatest attention. But survivors of genocide cannot introduce us to the mind-sets of those who committed genocide. In fact, what survivors have to say about the genocidists is intellectually tangental, in part because, correctly, they throw up their hands in true despair and claim the impossibility of comprehending the psychological and ideological motivations of their tormentors. Through their eyes the Holocaust, as any other genocide, is "incomprehensible." They cannot identify with their killers for they lack the mentality of the killers. The objects of intense future research must be the architects and foot-soldiers of genocide; the pioneering work of Christopher Browning is a mere beginning.

This is where the study of multi-genocide, *à la* ex-Yugoslavia, or inter-ethnic genocide, *à la* Rwanda/Burundi comes in handy because, in many cases, some survivors were also genocidists and, vice-versa, genocidists were also survivors. Thus, in thousands of cases among the Hutu refugees who fled Rwanda, one can find this combination genocidist/survivor from whom one can elicit what it is that transforms one into a participant in genocide. Much of this information and insight may, perhaps, be applicable to an under-standing of the genocidists who were engaged in the Final Solution.

All too unhappily, the Holocaust—as it recedes into the past—stands out less as an aberration than as prelude. To be historically accurate one should ascribe that "honor" to the Armenian genocide as the one ushering in the 20th century. That would make the Holo-caust a magnification of its predecessor and less a ground-breaker. None of this lessens the criminality of the Final Solution, but it does contextualize it alongside other genocides before and after. Relating it to past and future genocides gives it more meaning in human history than it would otherwise have standing alone in historic and intellectual isolation. As the 21st century approaches and the Holo-caust becomes history, ceasing to be living memory, intellectual enlightenment about it will unavoidably come from an on-going process of comparison with other genocides and near-genocides. Indeed, it would not be wrong to conclude that a brief moratorium be called on Holocaust Studies, allowing its scholars to widen their horizons by familiarizing themselves professionally with other genocides. In so doing, they would unavoidably raise new ques-tions, which they could then transfer over to the Final Solution.

To conclude with an illustration: at present, little more can be said about the Nazi *monde concentrationnaire*, even by studying the Soviet *Gulag* (to which it has often been fallaciously compared.) If new avenues are to be found, it is time also to explore the enormous network of prisons erected since 1949 by the People's Republic of China. Here is a world of merciless human torment and destruction in the millions that raises significant questions useful to those still involved with the genocidal functions of the SS complex of camps that they had strung up across Europe. Designed that only a mini-mum of the inmates survive, these Chinese institutions of slow death may hold the answers to several aspects about the Hitlerian and Stalinist systems of incarcerating those the regime deemed unfit to live. Those administering a German or Chinese or Soviet camp may share similar mentalities; if so, what are they?

The future directions of Holocaust research must be towards the comparative, towards contextualization, towards finding for the Final Solution its rightful niche in human history, both in Europe as well as in the world, both for this generation as well as for the next. These suggestions may displease those insistent on intractable centralization of the Holocaust. But theirs is an intellectual exaggeration and a stance which contains its own danger. Exaggeration is *per se* distortion, and distortion is a form of falsification. Holocaust studies cannot afford this kind of self-promotion. To retain their credibility, scholars of the Holocaust will have to pay more attention to other genocides as well as to genocide in general. One path leads to trivialization, the other to further enlightenment.

NOTES

1. Richard Arens, ed. *Genocide in Paraguay*, Temple University Press, 1976

2. Henry R. Huttenbach, "Locating the Holocaust on the Genocide Spectrum: Towards a Methodology of categorization," *Holocaust and Genocide*, Vol. 3, No. 3 (1988) pp. 287-303

3. Henry R. Huttenbach, "Two Lessons from Rwanda," *The Genocide Forum* I (1994) No. 3, pp. 3-4

4. Henry R. Huttenbach, "Thinking the Unthinkable, Writing the Undescribable," *The Genocide Forum* II (1995) No. 2, pp. 1-2

The Holocaust and Business as Usual: Congressional Source Materials

Daniel Rosenberg

SUMMARY. Fueled by the need to resolve problems in war production and working in the context of New Deal anti-monopoly sentiment, a number of important Senate committees before and during World War II investigated American and other Western corporate ties with German business. Their findings constitute important resources for Holocaust reference. The proceedings and reports of these committees–which include the Subcommittee on War Mobilization of the Committee on Military Affairs and the Special Committee Investigating the National Defense Program–run to many thousands of pages and are located in leading libraries. Careful analysis by researchers may help determine the degree of American and Western responsibility for the Holocaust. *[Article copies available for a fee from The Haworth Document Delivery Service: 1-800-342-9678. E-mail address: getinfo@haworth.com]*

Readers may find it rewarding to examine the reference materials sketched below, which comprise the records of several wartime Senate committees. These contain information on certain aspects of the economic relationship between economic and financial enterprises in the democratic nations and their counterparts in Nazi Germany before and during World War II. What follows is intended to

Daniel Rosenberg is Director of Academic Affairs and Professor of History, University College, Adelphi University.

Address correspondence to: Daniel Rosenberg, Eddy Hall, University College, Adelphi University, Garden City, NY 11530.

[Haworth co-indexing entry note]: "The Holocaust and Business as Usual: Congressional Source Materials." Rosenberg, Daniel. Co-published simultaneously in *The Reference Librarian* (The Haworth Press, Inc.) No. 61/62, 1998, pp. 99-111; and: *The Holocaust: Memories, Research, Reference* (ed: Robert Hauptman, and Susan Hubbs Motin) The Haworth Press, Inc., 1998, pp. 99-111. Single or multiple copies of this article are available for a fee from The Haworth Document Delivery Service [1-800-342-9678, 9:00 a.m. - 5:00 p.m. (EST). E-mail address: getinfo@haworth.com].

highlight the salient findings in these documentary sources, which may be located at leading research libraries. At specific points, the present writer will indicate useful reports, page numbers, and the titles of charts or tables, again to suggest lines of inquiry for researchers wishing to explore the issues further.

The degree to which the liquidation of Jews was a German business and an exercise in science, for which the established and refined competed, is often neglected by researchers. Students of the period may reacquaint themselves with the relevant flavors of the day by remembering the German corporate bids for concentration camp contracts excerpted by William Shirer:

> Following our verbal discussion regarding the delivery of equipment of simple construction for the burning of bodies, we are submitting plans for our perfected cremation ovens which operate with coal and which hitherto have given full satisfaction.
>
> We suggest two crematoria furnaces for the building planned, but we advise you to make further inquiries to make sure that two ovens will be sufficient for your requirements.
>
> We guarantee the effectiveness of the cremation ovens as well as their durability, the use of the best material and our faultless workmanship.
>
> Awaiting your further word, we will be at your service.[1]

BUSINESS TIES

Although German leaders were clearly gearing for war and the "final solution" in the 1930s, and despite the fact that such firms as I.G. Farben were known to be deriving profits from such preparations, a number of American, British, and other enterprises in democratic nations continued long-established partnerships and patent arrangements with German companies involved in production of oil, electrical equipment, chemicals, telescopic and photographic hardware, and other equipment essential to the German war effort and the Holocaust.

A handful of scholars, most notably Christopher Simpson and Charles Higham[2] have studied American-Nazi business ties. Simpson focused on the slave labor employed in Germany by American companies (particularly General Motors) and their subsidiaries, while Higham scrutinized the now quite-notorious Swiss-based Bank for International Settlements, which operated without a hitch under Nazi control and with American and other Western participants throughout the war. And the more general attributes discoloring the American attitude and policy toward the Hitler regime and its anti-Semitism have also been documented: that prominent Americans often saw the Nazi regime as vigorous and effective (in fact a worthy alternative to the New Deal), which perhaps overzealously but successfully instilled pride and industriousness;[3] that its anti-Semitism was likely to be solely rhetorical; that policymakers in key positions refused entry to countless thousands of Jews attempting escape.[4]

But numerous volumes of Senate committee proceedings between 1934 and 1946, detailing cartel and patent agreements permitting free and exclusive German use of technological processes and methods, deserve special mention and attention. In addition to the pressures of anti-Semitism, appeasement, and pro-Hitler sympathies in high places, the relevant data here suggest the importance of studying pecuniary motives as well in understanding America's relationship to Nazism. Indeed, in appraising the relevant American legacy, one might bear in mind a Senate committee's wartime judgement: "These German-American combinations were effective instrumentalities by which the Nazi government was able to supply itself with vital raw materials for its war machine. . . . [5]"

THE MUNITIONS HEARINGS

Consultation of the documents may begin with a series of Senate hearings into the munitions industry between 1934 and 1936. These may be found in reference collections under a rather lengthy description,[6] but are referred to colloquially as the Munitions Hearings. Senators Gerald Nye and Arthur Vandenberg co-chaired the hearings, which straddled the 33rd and 34th Congressional sessions. Testimony and evidence targeted Du Pont de Nemours & Co. Neither Nye nor Vandenberg were anti-Nazi; the former identified with the anti-Semitic priest Father Coughlin and would help found the isolationist America First organization,[7] while the latter was an outspoken rightwinger, close to the fervently anti-Jewish Henry Ford.[8] Insofar as the Du Ponts controlled General Motors, Ford might have welcomed discrediting evidence against them, a possibility which ought to give scholars some pause before investing complete trust in the Nye-Vandenberg Committee.

Nevertheless, the proceedings include testimony by Du Pont spokesmen confirming the firm's sympathy for Hitler's rise and German rearmament. Scholars may find especially interesting the data in Parts 9 and 12. Exhibit 456 indicates that Du Pont possessed stock and voting rights in the German explosives firm Dynamit-Actien Gessellschaft (DAG), invested in the huge chemical conglomerate I.G. Farben and the metals enterprise Deutsche Gold und Silberscheidenanstalt, and participated (along with Imperial Chemicals of Britain) in patent agreements with these enterprises. The participants regularly renewed patent accords right down to the brink of the Holocaust, the formulae worded along the lines of the following sample: "Each party agrees, . . . upon making or obtaining any patented invention or discovering or acquiring any secret invention, to disclose in writing to the other party immediately, or in any event within six months thereafter, full particulars in respect thereof . . . "

Entry of the United States into war against the Axis powers elevated the Senate's scrutiny of American cartel connections, insofar as these affected the war effort and offended public opinion. The Senate hearings also reflected the light of the New Deal and of the just-expired Depression, whose depredations had elicited popular anti-corporate sentiment.[9] Though some may suppose that this bent gave undue attention to financial intrigue, it is more likely that anti-monopoly feeling in the country pushed Congressional investigators to be that much more vigilant and on their toes regarding immoral corporate conduct than they might have been at other moments. It may well have been that this popular sensitivity enhanced the perspicacity of the Senate. Notwithstanding the ebbs and flows of President Roosevelt's policies and the shifting national priorities as war broke out, popular suspicion of the "economic royalists" (to use FDR's term) remained part of the national conscience and undoubtedly helped drive the most important wartime Congressional inquiries during the war.

Of importance was the work of the Senate Committee on Patents which began hearings in 1942, during the 77th Congressional session. Homer T. Bone served as chair (thus, the "Bone Committee"). Patent agreements were integral to cartel relationships with German industry. Suggestive of the derived benefits to the Nazi regime had been the report in the *New York Times* as far back as May 11, 1934, that Boeing had sold equipment to Germany "now being taken apart there and carefully studied with a view to their duplication under a license." The sharing and exchange of technology were at the heart of patent agreements. What may have begun as rather basic licensing arrangements at an earlier period took on different meaning after Hitler came to power. Though many such ties originated in the pre-Hitler decade, evidence discloses that the assumption of power by the Nazis did nothing to bring them to a halt, but rather intensified them (a trend confirmed in data collected by the Kilgore Committee, discussed below). Indeed, it was this latter issue of "license" which characterized the cartel agreements documented by the Bone Committee. In studying the work of the Bone Committee, one cannot dismiss the variety and reiteration of patent agreements it found operating in a battery of fields. Perusal by scholars of its manifold proceedings may yield much information verifying the intricacies of these relationships.[10]

THE TRUMAN COMMITTEE

Though not dealt with in great detail here, the Senate's Special Committee Investigating the National Defense Program, headed by Harry Truman and established in 1941, was especially noteworthy among the committees scrutinizing war production and cartels was.[11] Its hearings often paralleled those of the Subcommittee on War Mobilization, discussed below, likewise producing many thousands of pages of documents and testimony. Though it focused on the Standard Oil of New Jersey-I.G. Farben contacts at first, the Truman Committee examined other industries and companies. A case in point was Dow Chemical, which was found to have given Farben a discount in purchases of magnesium, a vital element in war production.[12] Dating almost from the moment that Hitler assumed office–in fact, Dow had charged German buyers slightly more than others in the pre-Nazi period–and in marked contrast to the higher price charged to British buyers, the markdown remained consistent up through the outbreak of hostilities in September 1939. In such decisive years of Nazi war preparations as 1934 and 1935, the greater part of Dow's foreign magnesium sales were to German purchasers, again at that lower price.[13]

The Truman Committee attributed the oft-reported synthetic rubber (natural sources having been cut off by the war) shortage early in the war to the honoring of cartel agreements by Du Pont, and particularly by Standard Oil of New Jersey.[14] The committee declared that

> The documentary evidence out of Standard's own files requires the conclusion that Standard, as a result of its cartel arrangements with the I.G. Farben, and as a result of its general business philosophy, did hamper the development of synthetic rubber in the United States and did place itself in a position where its officials, although personally honorable men, engaged in activities helpful to the Axis Nations and harmful to the United States.[15]

A Standard memorandum, issued a month after the outbreak of war, was read into the record, suggesting plans to Farben "for a modus vivendi which would operate through the term of the war whether or not the U.S. came in."[16] Committee chairman Truman in fact characterized the activities of Standard of New Jersey as "treason."[17] Assistant Attorney General Thurman Arnold, a key Truman Committee witness, attempted to launch an anti-monopoly suit against Standard, for the limits on synthetic rubber in the United States were considered a threat to the national interest. Business and political pressures were brought to bear, however, resulting in a $50,000 settlement.[18]

THE KILGORE COMMITTEE

Perhaps the most suggestive findings came in 1943-44 before a special group established by the Military Affairs Committee of the

Senate: the Subcommittee on War Mobilization, headed by Senator Harley Kilgore (hence, the "Kilgore Committee"). While the comprehensive title of its final document (Subcommittee of Committee on Military Affairs, Congress 78-1st Session, Senate Resolution 107 and Senate Resolution 102, Scientific and Technological Mobilization, Hearings and Monographs, 1943) tells little, the subjects taken up attest to the range of the investigation.[19] The Kilgore Committee obtained evidence of agreements between American firms and German partners in the chemical, oil, aircraft, pharmaceutical, optical, and metal industries, above all with German companies in the I.G. Farben orbit. American participants were by no means the only enterprises from democratic states to be so engaged: the data show French and British connections as well.

"Schedule A" in Part 4 of the Kilgore committee's inquiry includes a rather exhaustive list of patent agreements among Du Pont, Farben, their subsidiaries, and various affiliates in other countries, covering sharing, transfer, and rules for the limitation or disposal of products in the chemical field. (In pointing out a "gentleman's agreement between Du Pont and I.G. Farben by which each was to give the other the first option on new processes and products," the Senate's Military Affairs Committee recognized the operation of less formal arrangements as well.[20]) These included synthetic resins and plastics, derivatives of polyvinyl, synthetic rubber and nylon, general heavy chemicals, dyes, neoprene products, and organic chemicals. A small number of the agreements date from the years of the Weimar Republic. The great majority were initiated after the Nazis took power, when chemical research took on special meaning.

Noteworthy are the patent and processes accord of March 1934 (amended May 1935) concerning research in cyanides, formaldehyde, and derivatives,[21] the 1933 agreement between Farben, Goodyear, and Du Pont regarding rubber antioxidants,[22] and the September 1938 pact in which Du Pont gave Farben substantial license to manufacture synthetic rubber in Germany, "with certain rights to export from Germany."[23] The variety and number of agreements is quite impressive. Striking indeed is the 1935 project among Britain's Imperial Chemicals, Deutsche Gold und Silberscheidenanstalt, London Fumigation Co., Ltd., and others for "manufacture and sale of [the] fumigation product known as Zyklon."[24] After sufficient experimentation, German chemists would produce Zyklon B, without Zyklon's noxious odor, for mass extermination.[25]

Du Pont was not the only American firm with cartel ties to Nazi-dominated plastics, chemical, and oil firms before, and to an extent, during the war. (Evidence showed that the corporation viewed the war as little more than a temporary stall in the soon-to-be revived rewarding relationships it enjoyed with German holocaust beneficiaries.[26)] Part 6 of the Kilgore investigations indicates that as part of its arrangement with I.G. Farben, Standard Oil of New Jersey delayed production of higher octane gasoline in the United States, though Standard had patented the process. Testimony and evidence brought before the Kilgore committee demonstrated that Standard was in fact instrumental in the transfer of military and Holocaust technology to its German partners, especially in the field of synthetic products. During the 1930s, Farben and Standard operated an American firm in Louisiana, Jasco, producing synthetic acetic acid (acetylene), crucial in making fire-proof materials such as film, paint, and rayon.[27] The cartel agreement between the two giants gave Farben final voice in Jasco's affairs.[28] As the war came and American neutrality weakened, Farben recommended, and Standard of New Jersey agreed, that the plant be dismantled, with inevitable impact on American war production, according to testimony.[29]

RAMIFICATIONS

Not surprisingly, President Roosevelt responded to the various hearings with a declaration in the spirit of America's "half century" of "opposition to private monopolies," that "cartel practices which restrict the free flow of goods in foreign commerce will have to be curbed."[30] Nevertheless, the extent of damage done surely transcends the issue of monopolistic practices, though the latter help explain the former. Cartel connections gave the chemical giants substantial control of basic processes (particularly the "buna" and "butyl" synthetic rubbers) and decisive chunks of the globe in which these might be used, surely lucrative arrangements: especially does this seem true of Du Pont and Standard.[31] As a Farben spokesman acknowledged, their contribution to the Nazi war and extermination effort in the case of at least one basic substance was considerable: "Without tetraethyl lead, the present method of warfare would have been impossible. The fact that since the beginning of the war we could produce tetraethyl lead is entirely due to the circumstances that shortly before, the Americans presented us with the production plans, complete with their know-how."[32] Moreover, Farben credited both Standard and Shell with assistance in producing an assortment of petroleum derivatives.[33]

"Buna," the synthetic rubber first worked on in Du Pont, Farben, and Standard research departments, the rights to which were elaborated, assigned, licensed, and disposed of accordingly by their leading executives, became the name of an Auschwitz extension run by I.G. Farben, where tens of thousands slave laborers worked (though never actually producing any synthetic rubber).[34] The latter, observes a historian, "were worked to exhaustion before meeting their 'final solution' at the nearby ovens of extermination plants. I.G. made the poison gas for this and other death camps."[35] Notwithstanding the failure to manufacture the product as envisioned, prisoners labored until they dropped to build the unit known as I.G. Auschwitz:

> During work we were terribly mistreated. As our working place was situated outside the large chain of sentry posts, it was divided into small sectors of 10×10 meters, each guarded by an SS man. Whoever stepped outside these squares during working hours was immediately shot without warning for having "attempted to escape." Often it happened that out of pure spite an SS man would order a prisoner to fetch some given object outside his square. If he followed the order, he was shot for having left his assigned place. The work was extremely hard and there were no rest periods. The way to and from work had to be covered at a brisk military trot; anyone falling out of line was shot. On my arrival about 3,000 people, of whom 2,000 were Slovak Jews, were working on this emplacement. Very few could bear the strain and although escape

seemed hopeless, attempts were made every day. The result was several hangings a week.[36]

Though the war itself generally led to the suspension of cartel contacts until peacetime, one may suppose that the logic of those arrangements had fed the outbreak of hostilities and helped sustain the machinery of extermination, while proving of material benefit to the partners involved. Apparently the actual outbreak of hostilities did not lead to the total cessation of business relationships among partners whose governments and peoples were at war. A later Kilgore investigation cited evidence that Canadian, American, British, French, and German aluminum companies functioned together throughout the war in the Alliance Aluminum Compagnie, headquartered in Basle, Switzerland. And representatives of German, American, and British chemical concerns reportedly met in Lisbon in May 1944.[37]

In any case, *The New York Times* seemed to put its finger on "one deeply disturbing aspect" of the business ties highlighted above, in its editorial shortly after the Standard revelations:

> The military importance of their products laid upon them a special responsibility. They could not fail to know that in dealing with their German partner they were dealing with an organization compelled to suit its policies and operations to the needs of the developing Nazi plans for world conquest. Yet as late as 1939 they were willing to build aviation gasoline plants for Germany and to convey technical information to Germany. A responsible sense of industrial statesmanship would have told them that this was not just routine business. It should have been clear that this aviation gasoline and these technical developments would ultimately be used against the victims of Germany's military aggression.[38]

The manner in which German firms like Farben put to use the technology apportioned and shared by cartel partners is indeed an intriguing issue when appraising Holocaust responsibility. Though the economic motives would be obvious, it would not be unfounded to suggest that spokesmen of large American (and other Western) enterprises identified with political and social aspects of Nazism as well, as they had so often declared when opposing popular New Deal-era movements and strategies.[39] Nazi leaders and policies left little to the imagination by the middle '30s. Similarly, the German business entities which hitched their hopes to Nazi comets could have had little doubt as to how they would be earning their keep in years to come. The involvement of firms like I.G. Farben in the slave labor and murder apparatus, which was evident before the war, apparently did nothing to dissuade its myriad partners in democratic countries from continued cooperation. Nor does it seem, given the clarity of the Nazi pledge in foreign relations and Jewish affairs, that American cooperators could have harbored illusions that research transfer and patent agreements might have benign purposes after the middle of the '30s. In sum, researchers may find the reference materials discussed above to be of considerable value in determining the extent of complicity.

REFERENCES

1. William L. Shirer, *The Rise and Fall of the Third Reich: A History of Nazi Germany*, New York, 1959, p. 1264.

2. Christopher Simpson, *Splendid Blond Beast: Money, Law, and Genocide in the Twentieth Century*, New York, 1993; Charles Higham, *Trading With the Enemy: An Expose of The Nazi-American Money Plot*, New York, 1983.

3. George Seldes, *1000 Americans*, New York, 1947.

4. Henry L. Feingold, *The Politics of Rescue: The Roosevelt Administration and the Holocaust, 1938-1945*, New Brunswick, 1970; David S. Wyman, *The Abandonment of the Jews: America and the Holocaust, 1941-1945*, New York, 1984.

5. United States Senate. Subcommittee on War Mobilization. *Scientific and Technical Mobilization: Cartels and National Security.* Part II, Analytical and Technical Supplement, 1944, p. 73.

6. United States Senate. Special Committee on Investigation of the Munitions Industry of the United States. Senate Resolution 206. *Hearings and Reports*, 1934-1936.

7. William E. Leuchtenberg, *Franklin D. Roosevelt and the New Deal*, New York, 1963, p. 322; Arthur M. Schlesinger, Jr., *The Politics of Upheaval, 1935-1936*, Boston, 1960, p. 20.

8. George Seldes, *Facts and Fascism*, New York, 1943, p. 77-78.

9. Robert S. McElvaine, *The Great Depression: America, 1929-1941*, New York, 1993.

10. United States Senate. Committee on Patents. Congress 77-2nd Session, *Hearings*.

11. Donald H. Riddle, *The Truman Committee*, New Brunswick, 1964.

12. United States Senate. Special Committee Investigating the National Defense Program. Report No. 10, Part 17: Magnesium, p. 10303-10309.

13. Special Committee Investigating the National Defense Program, Report No. 10, Part 17: Magnesium, exhibit No. 1176, Table 3–*Magnesium ingot and stick foreign sales–Dow (large shipments, accounting department records)*, p. 10719; exhibit No. 1177–*Magnesium ingots*, p. 10720.

14. Richard Sasuly, *IG Farben*, New York, 1947, p. 155-156.

15. Special Committee Investigating the National Defense Program, Report No. 480, Part 7: Rubber, May 26, 1942.

16. Joseph Borkin, *The Crime and Punishment of I.G. Farben*, New York, 1978 p. 92.

17. *New York Times*, March 27, 1942.

18. Alan Brinkley, "The Antimonopoly Ideal and the Liberal State: The Case of Thurman Arnold," *The Journal of American History*, Vol. 80, No. 2 (September 1993), p. 576.

19. Thus, for example: United States Senate. Subcommittee on War Mobilization. *Scientific and Technical Mobilization*. Part 4–Patents, June 4, 1943.

—. Part 5–October 14, 1943.

—. Part 6–Monopoly and Cartel Practices. Vitamin D. October 15, 21, 1943.

—. Part 7–Monopoly and Cartel Practices. Titanium. November 4, 1943.

—. Part 8–Monopoly and Cartel Practices. Universal Oil Products. November 8, 1943.

—. Part 16–Cartel Practices and National Security. August 29, September 7, 8, 12, 13, 1944.

20. United States Senate. Committee on Military Affairs. *Economic and Political Aspects of International Cartels*. Monograph 1, 1944, p. 6. See also Gerald Colby Zilg, *Du Pont: Behind the Nylon Curtain*, Englewood Cliffs, 1974, p. 303.

21. *Scientific and Technical Mobilization*, Part 4–Patents, p. 2315.

22. *Scientific and Technical Mobilization*, Part 4–Patents, p. 2317.

23. *Scientific and Technical Mobilization*, Part 4–Patents, p. 2318.

24. *Scientific and Technical Mobilization*, Part 4–Patents, p. 2320; I.G. Farben owned a third of Deutsche Gold und Silberscheidenanstalt: see Borkin, p. 122.

25. Borkin, p. 123-124.

26. Committee on Military Affairs, Monograph 1, p. 74.

27. *Scientific and Technical Mobilization*, Part 4–Patents, p. 1365.

28. *Scientific and Technical Mobilization*, Part 4–Patents, p. 1367.

29. *Scientific and Technical Mobilization*, Part 4–Patents, p. 1405.

30. *Scientific and Technical Mobilization*, Part 16–Cartel Practices, p. 2038.

31. George Stocking, *Cartels in Action*, New York, 1948, 115-116.

32. Borkin, p. 78.

33. Special Committee Investigating the National Defense Program, *Hearings*, 77th Congress, 1st Session, pp. 4561-4584.

34. Primo Levi, *Survival in Auschwitz*, New York, 1961, p. 21, 66; Borkin, p. 127.

35. Zilg, p. 354.

36. Borkin, p. 113.

37. United States Senate. Committee on Military Affairs, Subcommittee on War Mobilization. *Elimination of German Resources for War.* Hearings, Part 3: pp. 290-292; I. F. Stone, *The Truman Era*, New York, 1953, p. 23.

38. *New York Times*, April 2, 1942.

39. See Simpson, pp. 43-98.

Separating the Qualitative to Quantitative Dimension from the Data versus Analyses Distinction: Another Way to Study Holocaust Survivors

Peter Suedfeld
Erin Soriano

The argument between proponents of qualitative and quantitative research in the social sciences has recently taken on not only re-newed vigor, but also new levels of acrimony. In the hands of some debaters, the choice is not merely between words and numbers, it is between sensitive, contextualized, empathic, postmodern under-standing and cold, scientistic (rather than scientific), decontextual-ized and therefore misleading, "factoids." For others, it is between science, which is rigorous, objective, replicable, generalizable, and disconfirmable (or "falsifiable," to use Popper's ambiguous word),

Peter Suedfeld and Erin Soriano are affiliated with the Department of Psychol-ogy, 2136 West Mall, The University of British Columbia, Vancouver, BC V6T 1Z4, Canada.

The preparation of this paper, and our research on Holocaust survivors, have been made possible by grants to the first author from the Social Sciences and Humanities Research Council of Canada and the Hampton Fund of The Universi-ty of British Columbia, and by the cooperation of Dr. Robert Krell and the Vancouver Holocaust Centre Society for Education and Remembrance.

[Haworth co-indexing entry note]: "Separating the Qualitiative to Quantitative Dimension from the Data versus Analyses Distinction: Another Way to Study Holocaust Survivors." Suedfeld, Peter, and Erin Soriano. Co-published simultaneously in *The Reference Librarian* (The Haworth Press, Inc.) No. 61/62, 1998, pp. 113-129; and: *The Holocaust: Memories, Research, Reference* (ed: Robert Hauptman, and Susan Hubbs Motin) The Haworth Press, Inc., 1998, pp. 113-129. Single or multiple copies of this article are available for a fee from The Haworth Document Delivery Service [1-800-342-9678, 9:00 a.m. - 5:00 p.m. (EST). E-mail address: getinfo@haworth.com].

113

and interpretation, which is essentially private, fuzzy, intuitive, selective, and therefore susceptible to many kinds of biases. Even
though the basic alternatives, and their predecessors such as nomothetic vs. idiographic approaches (Allport, 1942; Gergen, 1982;
Harré & Secord, 1972), have been with us for a long time, the
barrage of moral disapproval that each side now focuses on the
other makes this much more than a routine epistemological disagreement among colleagues (see, e.g., Denzin & Lincoln, 1994;
Gross, Levitt, & Lewis, 1996).

Research on Holocaust survivors is an interesting arena for this
contest, for several reasons. All contenders feel that reporting
"mere" statistics about survivors is not enough. A rhetorical question asked in a recent symposium put it well: "Can't the survivors
themselves say more on the topic than can a p-value?" (Isaacowitz,
1996)—and even the most dedicated number-cruncher wants to put it
on record that he or she does in fact realize the (qualitative) anguish
and horror of the Holocaust. More importantly, perhaps, in this
particular area the two approaches have led to very different conclusions. Thus, the debate has real consequences for the content of the
scientific literature, which is not necessarily the case generally, and
may even have real-world implications—e.g., for policies regarding
therapy and restitution, and for expectations as to the aftermath of
analogous tragedies such as those of Cambodia, Tibet, Bosnia,
Rwanda, etc.

Much of the literature about the Holocaust and Holocaust survivors is qualitative, originating in personal narratives and clinical
interviews, frequently interpreted in psychoanalytic terms. On the
basis of these descriptions, survivors of the Holocaust have long
been assumed to be universally, uniformly, and irreversibly suffering from "survivor syndrome," "concentration camp syndrome,"
and/or "post-traumatic stress disorder (PTSD)," all denoting a mix-
ture of chronic anxiety, pervasive guilt, depression, sleep distur-
bances, social withdrawal and isolation, psychosomatic symptoms,
inability to cope with new stressors, and impaired intellectual and
emotional functioning (Bettelheim, 1943; Eitinger, 1961; Friedman,
1949; Niederland, 1964). Survivors who did not present such syndromes were assumed to be suffering from "alexithymia" or "psy-
chic numbing" (Steinberg, 1989). A recent review (Lomranz, 1995)

of 108 publications, the majority of which are reports of clinical and case studies, classified over 70 as focusing specifically on pathology and/or its treatment, with another 10 or so dealing with processes related to PTSD (intrusive memories, nightmares, and the like). Most of the others discuss such issues as family and parenting, religious and political attitudes, etc. Not one is categorized as reporting successful coping and adaptation.

On the other hand, broader-based empirical studies using psychometric—i.e., quantitative—instruments, even those (such as the MMPI) that are based on clinical concepts, have generally led to the conclusion that there is nothing much wrong with most survivors. They feel happy, satisfied, successful, sociable, and well-adjusted, sometimes more so than members of the general population. Although they may experience an occasional subdromal sign of PTSD (e.g., an intrusive memory or a nightmare), this is not sufficient to disturb their high level of well-being (Kahana et al., 1988; Leon et al., 1981; Lomranz, 1995). Some survivors express the thought that in some ways the events of the Holocaust had what Antonovsky (1979, 1987) called salutogenic effects—those that enhance health, including psychological health—rather than, or as well as, pathogenic consequences, which lead to illness or dysfunction. Some attribute their drive, achievement motivation, and occupational success to their experiences; others feel that it made them stronger and more self-sufficient, increased their sensitivity to other people's suffering, or led them to a greater appreciation of what is truly important in life (Lomranz, 1995). The possibility of salutogenic effects is seldom considered by clinical investigators. The same blind spot has been identified in studies of the Second Generation—i.e., the children of survivors (Hass, 1990).

What underlies the different findings and conclusions of these two alternative research methods? There are several possibilities, not mutually exclusive, each of which derives from the different strengths and weaknesses of each approach.

QUALITATIVE RESEARCH

Much of the case study literature is based on survivors who were accessible to the researcher because they sought therapy and/or restitution. This sample, which may comprise as many as 3/4 of all research participants to date (Helmreich, 1992), cannot be assumed to be representative of the survivor population in general. In fact, a questionnaire study with 211 survivors of the Holocaust (Helmreich, 1992) found that only 18% had ever sought psychological help from a professional—a much smaller percentage, incidentally, than among a control group of 295 American Jews, of whom 31% had at some time consulted a psychiatrist, psychologist, or social worker. If Helmreich's figures are correct, 75% of Holocaust survivors who have participated in research are drawn from the 18% who felt that they needed therapy or counseling. One cannot justify generalizing the results of these clinical participants to all Holocaust survivors (Eitinger & Major, 1982).

Another problem with qualitative research when trying to assess the impact of the Holocaust is the greater susceptibility of such methods to researcher biases and expectations. For example, therapist-interviewers may be searching for symptoms and syndromes. This is well illustrated in a study by Robinson, Rapaport-Bar-Sever, and Rapaport (1994). The researchers, two senior psychiatrists and one psychiatric resident, interviewed 103 survivors, and found that most of them were still suffering from symptoms of "survivor syndrome." These results are not surprising considering that psychiatrists are trained to search for pathology, and generally assume that the impact of traumatic events (especially of such magnitude as the Holocaust) is necessarily deleterious and long-lasting.

Researcher biases in qualitative research may also affect the interpretation of results. Because the "data analysis" and interpretation are selective, researchers may overlook, discount, or de-emphasize evidence contrary to their expectations. They may also put an interpretive slant on data that are in themselves neutral. For example, two eminent scholars have written the following: "Fifty years after the Holocaust, the memory of those traumatic years continues to haunt the lives of the survivors. Even though one marvels at the remarkable adaptation of child survivors of the Holocaust, the anguish of the past remains a part of their conscious and unconscious life" (Kestenberg & Fogelman, 1994, pp. 204). The pathogenic orientation of these authors is revealed not only in their marveling at the subsequent adaptation of child survivors, but also in how they report what is essentially the finding that survivors remember the Holocaust (not a very surprising datum). But in this report, they don't merely remember it: they are "haunted by" the memory. The fact that the remembered anguish is "part of their . . . life" is again nothing more than saying that they remember it—the emotional implications added by the researchers go far beyond the bare fact.

It is not only the interviewer who can influence the results of qualitative research; difficulties may also arise in the interview setting if the survivor has certain expectations. For example, if the interviewer is a therapist, the survivor may be more inclined to emphasize problems of adjustment, assuming that this is what a healer should hear about. After all, we don't go to the doctor to talk about what *doesn't* hurt. Survivors' motives for participation in the interview can also lead to specific emphases. For example, if the context of the interview is evaluation for 'restitution, the survivor may be more inclined to emphasize losses and negative consequences (Suedfeld, 1996).

This is not to imply that the accretion of negative affect and psychological dysfunction that characterizes qualitative studies is completely wrong or inaccurate. The point is that there is no way of telling to what extent the reports describe all survivors, most survivors, the average survivor, the exceptional survivor, or for that matter, the perceptions of the author.

All of the problems associated with qualitative, idiographic research violate fundamental principles that are pertinent to credible, reliable, and sound behavioral research (Suedfeld, 1996a; Suedfeld & Bluck, 1996). Despite these limitations, the importance of qualitative data should not be overlooked: such data do contribute valuable information. They offer richly textured insights into the survivor's perceptions and memories, with high degrees of individuation and contextualization. "To ignore such criteria is to risk trivializing the survivor's experiences as well as to present only a superficial picture" (Suedfeld, 1996, p. 169a). Narrative data put flesh on the skeleton of the "p-value," illustrating the personal meaning of both the general trends discovered by quantitative methods and exceptions to those trends. Another important role played by such descriptions is that they can be sources of testable hypotheses and theories, to be further explored by more rigorous methods (Barabasz & Barabasz, 1992).

QUANTITATIVE RESEARCH

Quantitative research on Holocaust survivors is hardly faultless. Lomranz (1995) has accumulated a list of its shortcomings. Some of these are endemic. Most studies use relatively small samples (although larger than is feasible in case studies), drawn from selected subpopulations of survivors (here, usually not clinical patients but, perhaps, people attending a survivors' conference, belonging to a survivor group, or participating in Holocaust education or documentation). This makes it difficult to disaggregate the sample by, e.g., demographic variables, Holocaust experiences, prewar and postwar adjustment, postwar country of settlement, and other interesting and important characteristics. Studies suffer from a lack of control or comparison groups. It is admittedly difficult to decide who would comprise appropriate groups for this purpose, because of the wide diversity among survivors as to national and religious backgrounds, Holocaust experiences, postwar emigration and resocialization, language skills, etc. Last, various artifacts are not well controlled.

Other flaws are not as widespread, but many studies have drawn conclusions on the basis of measures derived from instruments that may not be validated for such respondents or may not measure the most relevant variables. Quantitative research may take place in an environment or context that discourages full disclosure, and frequently uses formats that constrain the participant's responses to categories predetermined by the researcher. Purely numerical data do not allow for descriptions nor qualification of responses: for example, the fact that 18% of survivors in Helmreich's study (1992) had sought treatment tells us nothing about the severity or nature of their problems, nor even about the extent to which these problems were actually related to the Holocaust.

Among the advantages of quantitative approaches is that researchers are able to work with larger samples, thus allowing for broader representation of the survivor population. With a combination of wide sampling, a larger sample size, and inferential statistics, results become much more representative of survivors, enabling scholars to make more accurate, reliable, and valid generalizations. In this type of research, the questions asked are still susceptible to researcher expectancy effects, but the data are less so: it is more difficult to ignore, omit, or selectively interpret numbers than parts of narratives.

TOWARD RESOLUTION

How can one interpret a handful of personal interviews and generalize one's conclusions to the large group of survivors? Or, how can one expect to communicate the experience of a survivor from answers to a paper and pencil questionnaire? It is important that the two research methods not be viewed as mutually exclusive. In fact, the use of both offers unusual scope for novel procedures. Instead of debating the issue of the appropriateness of qualitative versus quantitative research, investigators should benefit from the strengths of each.

In our research on Holocaust survivors, we have used both quantitative and qualitative methods to collect as well as to analyze data; but while we sometimes analyze qualitative data qualitatively, and quantitative data quantitatively, we also break tradition by analyzing qualitative data quantitatively. Table 1 shows the orthogonal relationship between quantitative and qualitative types of data and analyses; although we will not discuss them all here, our program of research on Holocaust survivors has components in four of these quadrants.

GENERAL METHODOLOGY

Our research on the Holocaust uses two data-collection approaches, a battery of Child Survivor Questionnaires, and narratives

TABLE 1. Types of Data and Types of Analyses

Analysis	Qualitative	Quantitative
Qualitative	Clinical case studies	Interpretation of numerical patterns
Quantitative	Thematic content analysis	Psychometric measures

from the Vancouver Holocaust Documentation Project. The questionnaires are designed to assess survivors experiences of the Holocaust and their judgments about its possible long-term consequences. In particular, we have been interested in whether, and how, the Holocaust may have influenced various aspects of a survivor's life, such as life satisfaction, achievement motivation, attributional style, child-rearing practices, religious beliefs, and world assumptions. Quantitative scales in the battery of questionnaires, some of them well-established and widely used and others devised specifically for our study, assess these and other factors.

The Vancouver Holocaust Documentation Project has collected over 120 eyewitness testimonies of Holocaust survivors. The Project is a cooperative effort of the Vancouver Holocaust Centre for Education and Remembrance and the Departments of Psychology and Psychiatry at the University of British Columbia, and is directed by Dr. Robert Krell, a child psychiatrist who during the Holocaust was a hidden child in the Netherlands. The interviews, lasting 2-3 hours each, are videotaped and are used for educational purposes. They deal with how people lived before, during, and after the Holocaust, and how the experience of the Holocaust may have affected later life course, relations with others, and outlook on life. Our studies on the Holocaust use both data bases, sometimes in tandem.

QUANTITATIVE DATA ANALYSES OF INTERVIEW PROTOCOLS

Our research group analyzes the videotaped narratives through the use of a number of techniques sometimes referred to as "measurement at a distance" or, more technically, thematic content analysis (Smith, 1992). Such techniques can be applied to a variety of verbal data sources: writings, interviews, speeches, and conversations, live or recorded, in any language familiar to the researcher. They do not eliminate the initial decision underlying the selection of research questions and scoring methods (e.g., the investigator may choose to score for successful or unsuccessful coping methods); they do, however, ensure that the rest of the research process is not slanted by that initial decision.

These techniques share the characteristics of other quantitative research methods in psychology. Materials are selected randomly from the total database, the interjudge and test-retest reliabilities of the scoring system are reported, and the data can be disaggregated along any desired variables or compared to equivalent data from other groups. Thus, one could compare the responses of Holocaust survivors with survivors of other extreme stressors–natural disasters, other mass atrocities, or individual tragedies–or with control groups, such as Jews who during the war resided in neutral or safe countries. The procedures are replicable by anyone trained in the scoring technique, and the hypotheses are disconfirmable. The data are not subject to the interpretation of the researcher: any scoring unit either does or does not fit the criteria of the specific system being applied. Thematic content analysis allows these advantages of quantitative research to apply to qualitative materials such as interviews.

The scoring procedure will vary depending on what psychological variable is being studied. Each of the systems mentioned below has extensive materials and explicit procedures for how scorers must be trained; in each case, there is also a criterion (usually a correlation of at least 0.85 with expert scorers on a set of test passages) for defining when the individual is qualified to score independently.

SAMPLE VARIABLES

Thematic content analysis does not lend itself well to global questions such as, "How well do survivors adapt in their new country?" or "How was the later personality development of hidden children affected by their experience?" The questions must be more focused: "How high a level of achievement motivation do survivors show?" or "Are former hidden children likely to seek help from others when they have a problem?"

There exist reliable and tested systems for a wide range of specific psychological and behavioral functions, some of which are presented in Table 2a. New scoring systems can be developed for an even wider range that a particular researcher may want to investigate. A short list of possibilities is given in Table 2b.

Our research group has applied the scoring systems for integra-

TABLE 2(a). Currently Scorable Variables

Cognitive Functioning

Integrative Complexity–Scope and effectiveness of information search and processing, consideration of alternative decisions, points of view, motives, etc.

Explanatory Style–Beliefs about why things happen (or do not happen) in one's life: optimism and pessimism, feelings of being in control.

Motivational Factors

Achievement–The desire to perform tasks well, to excel, to meet challenges.

Affiliation–Concern with establishing, maintaining, or restoring positive emotional ties with another person or persons.

Intimacy–Preference for warm, close, and communicative relations with other people, sharing one's thoughts and feelings.

Power–Concern with influencing, dominating, or controlling another person or persons while avoiding such influencing on oneself.

Psychosocial Orientation

Psychological Nonimmediacy–A subtle and nonobvious measure of how psychological distance, hostility or coldness versus warmth and positive emotions.

Responsibility–Concern with standards of conduct and the critical evaluation of one's own behavior.

Coping Strategies–Uses of different behavioral styles (emotion- or problem-oriented, self-reliant or help-seeking, etc.) to solve problems.

tive complexity, coping strategies, achievement motivation, and a number of other variables to the videotaped interviews. We have found that the techniques fulfilled our expectations for random sampling of materials and interscorer and test-retest reliability, as well as for amenability to quantitative analysis and therefore for generating testable hypotheses.

QUALITATIVE ELABORATIONS OF STATISTICAL ANALYSES

In one study (Suedfeld, Krell, Wiebe, & Steel, 1997), the videotaped narratives were scored for the appearance of various coping strategies. The coding categories were developed from two sources. Eight were adopted from the "Ways of Coping" scales described by

TABLE 2(b). Potentially Scorable Variables

Trust-Mistrust	Anxiety
Quality of Life	Moral Reasoning
Uncertainty Orientation	Aggression

Folkman et al. (1986). This schema is clearer and less cumbersome than other coping scale categories, has been widely used to measure coping in a wide variety of situations, and has demonstrated reliability and validity. In a pilot study with four videotapes, we determined that the categories could indeed be used with the material; however, we also identified five additional categories that are not in the Folkman et al. taxonomy but appeared in our tapes and are also referred to frequently in Holocaust autobiographies (see Table 3).

Next, each autobiographical narrative was divided into four time periods: "Pre-Holocaust" (before the person's country of origin was involved in World War II or came under German influence), "Early Holocaust" (when official and systematic anti-Jewish persecution had begun, but while the interviewee and his or her family remained in their normal home), "Late Holocaust" (after the individual had been forced to leave his home by flight, hiding, or deportation), and "Post-Holocaust" (after liberation).

Each narrative was next divided into "meaning segments," defined as the memory of one problematic event or experience and the interviewee's response to it. Each segment was then coded within one or more of the 13 response categories. Test-retest reliability for the main coder was a satisfactory $r = 0.88$, and interjudge reliabilities between the main coder and other members of the research group (on one-third of the tapes) were $r = 0.85$ or higher.

We found a large number of differences in coping strategies as a function of Holocaust phase, and some as a function of the survivor's age at the time. We will not summarize these here; but, to illustrate the qualitative elaboration of the statistical results, let us look at two coping categories: Supernatural Protection (which we further divided into superstition and religion) and Self-Control. There were both age- and phase-related differences on religion. Statistical analysis showed three significant effects. Such references peaked in memories of the Late Holocaust period [$F(3, 15) = 3.51$,

TABLE 3. Coping Categories and Definitions[a]

1. Confrontation	Effort to resolve situation through assertive or aggressive interaction with another person
2. Distancing	Effort to detach oneself emotionally from the situation
3. Self-Control	Effort to regulate one's own feelings or actions
4. Accept Responsibility	Acknowledging that one has a role in the problem
5. Escape/Avoidance	Efforts to escape or avoid the problem physically
6. Planful Problem-Solving	Deliberate (rational, cognitively-oriented) effort to change or escape the situation
7. Positive Reappraisal	Effort to see a positive meaning in the situation
8. Seeking Social Support	Effort to obtain sympathy, help, information, or emotional support from another person or persons
9. Endurance/Obedience/ Effort	Effort to persevere, survive, submit, comply with demands
10. Compartmentalization	Effort to encapsulate the problem psychologically so as to isolate it from other aspects of life
11. Denial	Ignoring the problem, not believing in its reality
12. Supernatural Protection	Attribution of survival to religious or superstitious practices; efforts to gain such protection (e.g., prayer)
13. Luck	Attribution of survival to good fortune

[a]From Suedfeld et al., 1997. Categories 1-8 were adapted from Folkman et al., 1986.

$p < .05$], were consistently highest among adolescents and very low (actually zero, except in the Late Holocaust period) among child survivors [$F(2, 17) = 4.34$, $p < .05$]. There was a steady decrease from Pre- through Post-Holocaust memories among adolescents and, although less consistently, among adults. No pattern emerged among children [interaction $F(6, 30) = 2.46$, $p < .05$].

Looking at the data qualitatively tells us more about the personal meaning of these differences. Adolescent survivors, speaking of the pre-Holocaust period, tended to provide descriptions of their religious education. In contrast, references during the Holocaust phase (especially the Late Holocaust, with comments about faith made by all three age groups) were more likely to cite faith as a source of strength to survive—that is, as a true coping strategy, e.g., through prayer. Interestingly, child survivors made no references to faith except in reference to the Late Holocaust period. This may follow from the fact that for these survivors, Jewish religious education and worship were interrupted very early in life. Child survivors were also more likely than either adults or adolescents to comment that the events of the Holocaust destroyed their religious faith. References to religion were particularly frequent among adolescent survivors, perhaps because of the proximity of such major events as the male survivors' Bar Mitzvah and the beginning of full participation in religious life by both male and female adolescents.

For Self-Control, there were also main effects for Time ($F = 8.85$, $p = .001$) and Age Group ($F = 6.50$, $p < .01$), and a significant interaction ($F = 3.86$, $p < .01$). This strategy was mentioned most during the Late Holocaust period, with children being particularly highly elevated. Qualitative analysis showed that children in hiding, many of them separated from their parents, had to exert exceptional degrees of self-control in order to survive. On some occasions, the need for concealment required them to stay quiet, in small and uncomfortable places, for long periods. At other times, they had to ingratiate themselves with the adults who were sheltering them. They learned not to cry, not to complain, not to admit feeling ill, and so on. Many also had to remember at all times such things as a false identity and personal history or newly learned Christian religious rituals.

To sum up, the numerical patterns and differences across age groups and temporal phases can be used as markers for important aspects of survival-related behavior, the details and personal meanings of which can then be elucidated through examination of the narrative. One important point is that with such a combined use of the two approaches, the researcher is less tempted to build elaborate interpretations of phenomena that in fact may not be typical or reliable.

CONVERGENT USE OF QUALITATIVE AND QUANTITATIVE DATA

We are currently analyzing data that address the same topic, achievement motivation. It has been thought that Holocaust survivors not only manifest high levels of this motive (Helmreich, 1992), but that perhaps high achievement orientation may be one of the more common salutogenic consequences of discrimination and persecution, including those connected with the Holocaust. It may also, however, be a more general consequence of immigration and assimilation in a new country where the merit principle is considered a basic societal axiom, and may also be fostered by Jewish family life and values.

To study these issues, we are using independently obtained qualitative and quantitative information. The qualitative material is derived from the survivor videotapes used in our other research. The methodology for scoring Need for Achievement (nAch) from many kinds of discourse is well established (e.g., Winter, 1987). The motive is considered to be present when a narrative refers to success in competition with a standard of excellence, or a unique accomplishment, or long-term pursuit of an occupational, educational, or other goal. Explicit references to a desire to achieve such a goal are also scored for nAch. In addition, there are coding categories for successful, doubtful, and unsuccessful instrumental activity in pursuit of achievement, anticipatory goal states, obstacles to achievement, and affective state.

The quantitative data are scores on the Ray Achievement Motivation Scale (Ray, 1979), a closed-ended psychometric instrument using 14 items balanced for acquiescent response set. The measure has been validated on British, Australian, and South African samples, and includes questions such as, "Have you always worked hard in order to be among the best in your own line (school, organization, profession)?" and "Do you get restless and annoyed when you feel you are wasting your time?"

The scale was administered to volunteer participants attending any of several child survivor conferences in 1994-95, as part of the packet of questionnaires referred to earlier. At this point, no results are available for either the thematic content analysis or the self-report scale; however, we intend to use the convergent validation between the two to assess the reliability and pervasiveness of achievement orientation among survivors, especially child survivors. The available norms for the Ray scale, and its administration to a comparison group of Jews who lived in North America during the war, will be used to investigate whether levels of achievement motivation among the survivors are in fact different from those found among non-Holocaust survivor, non-Jewish and Jewish groups.

CONCLUSIONS

In our opinion, strict adherence to the qualitative-quantitative distinction is counterproductive. Both approaches have unique advantages (as well as drawbacks), and data collected in either approach can be analyzed on the basis of the other. Given the problems of sample size arid representativeness, the difficulty of finding appropriate, reliable, and valid measurement instruments, the dangers of researcher and participant expectancy artifacts, the impossibility of finding a truly satisfactory comparison population, and so on–none of them restricted to, but perhaps all exacerbated in, Holocaust survivor research–it seems to us foolhardy to reject any potentially useful source or kind of data.

The ongoing and not very useful debates in this field, and in others that are characterized by similar battles between pathology-oriented and adaptation-oriented researchers (such as the psychology of aging; Lomranz, 1997, in press) could be avoided with a more eclectic, integrative epistemology. Perhaps the result would be an understanding of the survivors that would at the same time be more reliable and more complete than one or the other school would produce–a change that could benefit both scientific progress in the area and the people who are its focus of interest. "For if the survivors could somehow deal with their problems, they may serve as a model for all individuals who have gone through crises, be it a life-crippling disease, a debilitating accident, financial ruin, social ostracism, or the loss of loved ones. The mere fact that so many survivors live and function indicates that there are important lessons to be learned from them" (Helmreich, 1992, p. 218). But we have to be sure we know what the lessons are before we learn them.

REFERENCES

Allport, G.W. (1942). *The use of personal documents in psychological science.* New York: Social Science Research Council.

Antonovsky, A. (1979). *Health, stress, and coping.* San Francisco: Jossey-Bass.

Antonovsky, A. (1987). *Unraveling the mystery of health: How people manage stress and stay well.* San Francisco, CA: Jossey-Bass.

Barabasz, A. F., & Barabasz, M. (1992). Research designs and considerations. In E. Fromm & M. Nash (Eds.), *Contemporary research* (pp. 173-201). New York: Guilford.

Bettelheim, B. (1943). Individual and mass behavior in extreme situations. *Journal of Abnormal and Social Psychology, 38*, 417-452.

Denzin, N.K., & Lincoln, Y.S. (Eds.) (1994). *Handbook of qualitative research.* Thousand Oaks, CA: Sage.

Des Pres, T. (1976). *The survivor: An anatomy of life in the death camps.* New York: Oxford Univ. Press.

Eitinger, L. (1961). Pathology of the concentration camp syndrome. *Archives of General Psychiatry, 5*, 375-379.

Eitinger, L., & Major, E.F. (1982). Stress of the Holocaust. In L. Goldberger & S. Breznitz (Eds.). *Handbook of stress* (pp. 617-640). New York: Free Press.

Folkman, S., Lazarus, R.S., Dunkel-Schetter, C., DeLongis, A., & Gruen, R. (1986). Dynamics of a stressful encounter: Cognitive appraisal, coping, and encounter outcomes. *Journal of Personality and Social Psychology, 50*, 992-1003.

Friedman, P. (1949) Some aspects of concentration camp psychology. *American Journal of Psychiatry, 105*, 601-605.

Gergen, K.J. (1982). *Toward transformation in social knowledge.* New York: Springer-Verlag.

Gross, P.R., Levitt, N., & Lewis, M.W. (Eds.) (1995). *The flight from science and reason.* New York: New York Academy of Sciences.

Harré, R., & Secord, P.F. (1972). *The explanation of social behavior.* Totowa, NJ: Rowman & Littlefield.

Hass, A. (1990). *In the shadow of the Holocaust: The second generation.* Ithaca, NY: Cornell Univ. Press.

Helmreich, W.B. (1992). *Against all odds: Holocaust survivors and the successful lives they made in America.* New York: Simon & Schuster.

Higgins, G. O'C. (1994). *Resilient adults: Overcoming a cruel past.* San Francisco: Jossey-Bass.

Isaacowitz, D. (1996, Nov.). *Opening comments.* Symposium on "Aging among Holocaust survivors: The status of behavioral science research" (D. Isaacowitz, Ch.). Annual Scientific Meeting of the Gerontological Society of America, Washington, DC.

Kahana, E., Kahana, B., Harel, Z., & Rosner, T. (1988). Coping with extreme stress. In J. Wilson, Z. Harel, & B. Kahana (Eds.), *Human adaptation to extreme stress: From the Holocaust to Vietnam* (pp. 55-78). New York: Plenum.

Kestenberg, J.S., & Fogelman, E. (Eds.) (1994). *Children during the Nazi reign: Psychological perspective on the interview process.* Westport, CT: Praeger.

Krell, R. (1993). Child survivors of the Holocaust–strategies of adaptation. *Canadian Journal of Psychiatry, 38*, 384-389.

Leon, G., Butcher, J., Kleinman, M., Goldenberg, A., & Almagor, M. (1981). Survivors of the Holocaust and their children: Current status and adjustment. *Journal of Personality and Social Psychology, 41*, 503-506.

Lomranz, J. (1995). Endurance and living: Long-term effects of the Holocaust. In

S.E. Hobfoll & M.W. de Vries (Eds.), *Extreme stress and communities: Impact and intervention* (pp. 325-352). Amsterdam: Kluwer.

Lomranz, J. (1997, in press). An image of aging and the concept of integration: Coping and mental health implications. In J. Lomranz (Ed.), *Handbook of aging and mental health: Towards an integrative approach.* New York: Plenum.

Niederland, W.G. (1964). Psychiatric disorders among persecution victims: A contribution to the understanding of concentration camp pathology and its aftereffects. *Journal of Nervous and Mental Diseases, 139,* 458-474.

Ray, J.J. (1979). A quick measure of achievement motivation–validated in Australia and reliable in Britain and South Africa. *Australian Psychologist, 14,* 337-344.

Robinson, S., Rapaport-Bar-Sever, M., Rapaport, S. (1994). The present state of people who survived the Holocaust as children. *Acta Psychiatrica Scandinavica, 242-245.*

Smith, C.P. (Ed.) (1992). *Motivation and personality: Handbook of thematic content analysis.* Cambridge: Cambridge Univ. Press.

Steinberg, A. (1989). Holocaust survivors and their children: A review of the clinical literature. In P. Marcus & A. Rosenberg (Eds.), *Healing their wounds: Psychotherapy with Holocaust survivors and their families* (pp. 23-48). New York: Praeger.

Suedfeld, P. (1996a). Thematic content analyses: Nomothetic methods for using Holocaust survivor narratives in psychological research. *Holocaust and Genocide Studies, 10,* 168-180.

Suedfeld, P. (1996b). The social psychology of "Invictus": Conceptual and methodological approaches to indomitability. In C. McGarty, & S.A. Haslam (Eds.), *The message of social psychology* (pp. 328-341). Oxford: Basil Blackwell.

Suedfeld, P., & Bluck, S. (1996). Cognitive concomitants of life events–Finding a balance between generalizability and contextualization: Reply to Pennell (1996). *Journal of Personality and Social Psychology, 71,* 781-784.

Suedfeld, P., Krell, R., Wiebe, R., & Steel, G.D. (1997). Coping strategies in the narratives of Holocaust survivors. *Anxiety, Stress, and Coping, 10,* 153-179

Winter, D.G. (1987). Leader appeal, leader performance, and motive profiles of leaders and followers: A study of American presidents and elections. *Journal of Personality and Social Psychology, 52,* 196-202.

The Nazi Origins of Eduard Pernkopf's
Topographische Anatomie des Menschen:
The Biomedical Ethical Issues

Howard A. Israel

SUMMARY. The atrocities produced by Nazi doctors during the Holocaust have left a lasting imprint on contemporary society and, in particular, the health professions. The discovery of the Nazi origins of a classic anatomy atlas is just one of many examples of scientific information obtained by doctors who violated the Hippocratic Oath and abused their power in the name of science. The focus of this paper is on how the origins of the Pernkopf anatomy atlas became known over 50 years after its creation. The ethical dilemmas that doctors and medical centers face as a result of this and other potentially tainted data is reviewed. *[Article copies available for a fee from The Haworth Document Delivery Service: 1-800-342-9678. E-mail address: getinfo@haworth.com]*

Howard A. Israel is Associate Professor, School of Dental and Oral Surgery, Division of Oral & Maxillofacial Surgery, Columbia University, New York, NY 10032.

The author wishes to acknowledge the contributions of the following individuals who assisted in many aspects with the material presented in this paper: Professor William Seidelman, University of Toronto, Toronto, Canada; Hope Zimmerman, Columbia University, New York, New York; Dr. Steven Syrop, Columbia University, New York, New York; Monica Oswald, Columbia-Presbyterian Medical Center, New York, New York; and Mindy Packer Israel, Great Neck, New York.

[Haworth co-indexing entry note]: "The Nazi Origins of Eduard Pernkopf's *Topographische Anatomie des Menschen:* The Biomedical Ethical Issues." Israel, Howard A. Co-published simultaneously in *The Reference Librarian* (The Haworth Press, Inc.) No. 61/62, 1998, pp. 131-146; and: *The Holocaust: Memories, Research, Reference* (ed: Robert Hauptman, and Susan Hubbs Motin) The Haworth Press, Inc., 1998, pp. 131-146. Single or multiple copies of this article are available for a fee from The Haworth Document Delivery Service [1-800-342-9678, 9:00 a.m. - 5:00 p.m. (EST). E-mail address: getinfo@haworth.com].

INTRODUCTION

The destructive impact of the Holocaust continues to exert its influence on contemporary society in numerous ways. The atrocities produced by the unethical abuse of power by doctors and scientists from academic institutions have been documented. However, the impact of the issues raised by Nazi medicine on the health professions and medical centers today has not received adequate attention. Important decisions must be made by individual health professionals and medical centers concerning the use of data and information derived from Nazi doctors. The bioethical questions which relate directly to the use of such data are numerous and profound. Should the medical information derived from such unethical sources be used, and if so, under which conditions? Is it unethical not to disclose the source of such data? Should such data be totally censored, as some have suggested, or should the truth about the data be revealed to allow each individual to make their own decision? How should medical center libraries deal with such data? What obligations do we have to the victims and the families of the victims and how should they be approached? If free use of such data is permitted is history more likely to repeat itself? Does the use of data obtained from Nazi medical experiments honor those who lost their lives, or, will medical researchers be more likely to use the name of science to rationalize the abuse of humans for medical experimentation?

The anatomy atlas entitled *Pernkopf Anatomy*, which can be found in medical center libraries throughout the world, represents just one example of a book which contains potentially tainted material derived from the unethical abuse of power by doctors and scientists. The focus of this essay will be on how the controversy surrounding this anatomy book has recently been brought to the attention of the public, and how the health professions and information sciences have responded to the bioethical issues raised.

DISCOVERY AND BETRAYAL

As an oral and maxillofacial surgeon at Columbia-Presbyterian Medical Center, I had been using Pernkopf's *Atlas of Topographical and Human Anatomy of the Head and Neck* for over 20 years.

The highly detailed paintings of dissections of human cadavers brought precise anatomic relationships into focus unlike any other anatomy atlas I had seen. Extremely complex anatomic structures, such as those of the head and neck, are illustrated in superb and clear detail, bringing the anatomy laboratory to the pages of a book. My very worn, but well preserved edition had been used regularly, during my days as a student and resident, and for over a decade as a surgeon and member of the faculty of Columbia University. Pernkopf's atlas was the most valued book I had in preparing myself and my residents for surgical procedures.

Prior to April, 1994, I had no awareness or knowledge concerning the origins of the Pernkopf atlas. I had never thought about how this work had been created nor did I have any idea who Pernkopf was. The beginning of my discovery about the origins of this work began one day in April, 1994 as I was sitting at my desk preparing for an operation that I was to perform the next day. My edition of Pernkopf's atlas was open to an anatomic drawing of a male cadaver which showed the various layers of fascia and muscle of the neck, face and jaws. A colleague stopped by my office to chat for a few moments. He saw what I had been doing and after a few minutes he told me that he had been aware of the atlas as a student and he recalled that there was evidence that the illustrations in the atlas were of cadavers of murdered Nazi victims. I stared at the page that I had been looking at. I studied the picture which I had looked at thousands of times, but this time in a different way. Had I been using an anatomy book that had Nazi origins? Had I unknowingly benefited all these years by looking at pictures of Nazi murder victims? Who were these people in this book? What kind of lives did they live? What were their names? How did they die? Did they suffer? Who was Pernkopf?

THE LIBRARY STACKS AND NAZI SIGNATURES

The artist who had created the illustration of the male cadaver that I had been studying signed his work, Lepier. Later that day in April, 1994, I went to the stacks of the Health Sciences Library at Columbia University. I searched and found other copies of the Pernkopf books written in German. They were very old and appeared to be in poor condition, sitting on the shelves. I found copies of the Pernkopf books published in 1937, 1943 and 1952 (2,3,4). I opened the 1943 volume of *Topographische Anatomie des Menschen, Lehrbuch und Atlas der regionar-stratigraphischen Praparation*, von Eduard Pernkopf. The publisher was Urban & Schwarzenberg, located in Berlin and Wien. On page 586 of the 1943 edition was a drawing of a pregnant woman. The abdomen was dissected open exposing the intestines and the enlarged uterus. The artist was Lepier and his signature included a swastika. Also in this edition opposite page 604 was another drawing of a dissection showing the developing fetus within the uterus. Again, Lepier signed his name with a swastika. In this same edition the illustration opposite page 672 revealed an anatomic dissection of the thigh of a male cadaver with an apparently circumcised penis. The artist, Endtresser, signed his name with the Nazi icon "SS".

Appalled and astonished by my discovery, I shared my initial findings with a few very select people who I thought would have greater knowledge of the history of these books. One of these individuals, a prominent professor, responded to my questions about the origins of this book with the following question: "If what you are suggesting is true, so what?" This is a troubling question and represents the very essence of the dilemma faced by health professionals and the information sciences. If it is true that these books contained drawings of Nazi murder victims, how should one proceed? Should they continue to be used? Should I continue to use them if it helps me and my patients? Should I have been informed of the Nazi origins of the book 20 years ago?

I was very fortunate to meet Dr. Robert Jay Lifton, the author of "Nazi Doctors: Medical Killing and the Psychology of Genocide."[1] Dr. Lifton was a guest speaker at the Columbia University Health Sciences Center Campus on April 7, 1994 at a program to commemorate the Holocaust. Dr. Lifton was able to put me in touch with several individuals who are on the forefront of issues such as this today. The more I spoke to people who were knowledgeable on the continuing effects of the Holocaust on medicine today, the more disturbed I became.

Dr. William Seidelman, from The Wellesley Hospital, University of Toronto, Canada, has been involved in considerable research on patho-anatomical specimens from the Nazi era. Dr. Seidelman informed me about a scandal in West Germany that erupted in 1989 when it was discovered that anatomical and pathological collections in institutions in the former West Germany contained remains of Nazi victims.[2,3,4,5] Amongst these included brain specimens from the Nazi euthanasia program in the collections of the Max Planck Institute for Brain Research in Frankfurt[2,6] and the Vogt Collection from the University of Dusseldorf.[2,7,8] Since 1994, Dr. Seidelman and I have jointly researched the origins of the Pernkopf atlas and its creator and much disturbing information has been uncovered.

THE NAZI ORIGINS OF PERNKOPF'S ATLAS OF TOPOGRAPHIC AND APPLIED HUMAN ANATOMY: WHAT IS KNOWN?

Eduard Pernkopf's *Topographische Anatomie des Menschen (Topographical Anatomy of Man)* is generally considered by anatomists and surgeons to be a classic among anatomy atlases that is unique and will probably never be duplicated. This seven book anatomy masterpiece was originally produced at the University of Vienna under the direction of Professor Eduard Pernkopf of the Institute of Anatomy from 1933-1955. The combined efforts of Eduard Pernkopf, his highly skilled anatomic artists and the publisher, led to the development of a four color separation printing technique, which resulted in the reproduction of over 800 paintings of highly detailed anatomic dissections.[9] The first volume (2 books) was published in 1937, the second in 1943 (2 books), and the third (1 book) in 1952. The fourth and final volume (2 books) was completed after Pernkopf's death in 1955 and published between 1956 and 1960.

English language editions of the book have been published in 1963, 1980 and 1989 and have received widespread acclaim in the American medical literature. A review of Pernkopf's *Atlas of Topographic and Applied Human Anatomy* appeared several years ago in the *New England Journal of Medicine*,[10] in which the reviewer indicated that "this outstanding book should be of great value to anatomists and surgeons" and "is in a class of its own and will continue to be valued as a reference work even if its prohibitive cost and great detail make it unsuitable for purchase by medical students." Another review from the *Journal of the American Medical Association*[11] indicated that this atlas is a "classic among atlases of anatomy" that "will be most useful to otolaryngologists, plastic surgeons, head and neck surgeons, ophthalmologists, oral surgeons, and orthopedists."

Volumes of Pernkopf's *Atlas of Topographic and Applied Human Anatomy* can be found in leading medical centers throughout the United States and the world. Undoubtedly, this classic anatomy atlas has helped train and assist numerous anatomists, surgeons and other physicians throughout the years. The significant contribution of this classic anatomy atlas to the health professions over the years remains unquestioned. However, an exploration of the background of Eduard Pernkopf and his artists and, in particular, how this work was produced, raises significant questions of biomedical ethics which are extremely relevant to the health professional community today.

In March, 1938, after the Nazi takeover of Austria, Eduard Pernkopf, director of the Anatomy Institute of the University of Vienna, was appointed Dean of the Faculty of Medicine. As a devout Nazi, Pernkopf led the purge against the Jewish faculty. Pernkopf also became the editor of the prestigious *Viennese Medical Weekly* (*Wiener Klinische Wochenschrift*) in which he espoused his racist views. In a 1938 address to the Faculty of Medicine of the University of Vienna, Pernkopf summarized the role of medicine in the new state:[12,13]

To assume the medical care–with all your professional skill of the Body of the People (Volkskorper) which has been entrusted to you, not only in the positive sense of furthering the propagation of the fit, but also in the negative sense of eliminating the unfit and defective. The methods by which racial hygiene proceeds are well known to you: control of marriage; propagation of the genetically fit whose genetic, biologic constitution promises healthy descendants; discouragement of breeding by individuals who do not belong together properly, whose races clash; finally, the exclusion (Ausschaltung) of the genetically inferior from future generations by sterilization and other means.

The talented artists who painted the illustrations for Pernkopf's *Atlas of Topographic and Applied Human Anatomy* were also active members of the National Socialist Party. Erich Lepier, Franze Batke and Karl Endtresser frequently demonstrated their allegiance to the Nazi cause by signing their anatomic paintings with Nazi icons. Erich Lepier often signed his name with a swastika and an example of this can be readily demonstrated in his illustration of an anatomic dissection of a pregnant woman, which is in Pernkopf's *Topographische Anatomie des Menschen*, Edition 1943, Volume 2, opposite page 604, Figure 172, Tafel 94.[14] Karl Endtresser signed his name with an "SS" symbol in his painting of an anatomic dissection of the thigh of an apparently circumcised male, which is in Pernkopf's *Topographische Anatomie des Menschen*, Edition 1943, Volume 2, opposite page 672, Figure 188, Tafel 102.[14] Franz Batke's signature is followed with an "SS" symbol for the year '44, in his painting of an anatomic dissection of the neck, which is in Pernkopf's *Topographische Anatomie des Menschen*, Edition 1952, Volume 3, opposite page 48, Figure 14, Tafel 9.[15] These are just a few of the examples in which Nazi icons appear in the German language editions of the book.

More recent editions of the book[16,17] contain the same illustrations, only this time, with most* of the Nazi icons eliminated, or with the signatures altered. The student or surgeon using the more current versions of Pernkopf's *Atlas of Topographic and Applied Human Anatomy* would have no knowledge of the Nazi sympathies of Eduard Pernkopf and his artists. Some of the illustrations from Pernkopf's *Atlas of Topographic and Applied Human Anatomy* can also be seen in other current anatomy atlases, such as *Clemente's Anatomy: A Regional Atlas of the Human Body*. In the 1987 edition of this popular anatomy atlas, Figure 399 is the same anatomic illustration by Lepier, of the pregnant woman from the 1943 Edition of Pernkopf, only this time, the signature with the swastika has been eliminated.[18]

---

*Some of the more recent editions still contain the "SS" symbol in the signatures of the artists.[16,17]

THE PRECISE ORIGINS OF THE INDIVIDUALS PORTRAYED IN PERNKOPF'S ATLAS OF TOPOGRAPHIC AND APPLIED HUMAN ANATOMY: THE HEART OF THE CONTROVERSY

The precise origins of the subjects portrayed in the Pernkopf atlas remain a subject of debate. Evidence concerning the possible origins of these individuals is circumstantial and suggestive. As of the date of this writing, the names of the individuals portrayed in Pernkopf's *Atlas of Topographic and Applied Human Anatomy*, where they were from, when they died and the cause of death remain unknown.

It is known that many of the cadavers that were used by the Anatomy Institute of the University of Vienna, during the war, were from people who were executed in the Wiener Landesgericht, the Vienna district court.[9,19] This court executed individuals who were declared enemies of the state and included non-Jewish Austrian patriots, communists and other enemies of the Nazis. Ernst[19] has indicated that "Pernkopf worked on the publication of an anatomic atlas which contained material from children killed in a Viennese hospital. His institute of anatomy also used the corpses of executed persons for teaching purposes; part of this material is believed to be still in use at the university."[19] Williams[9] has indicated that many of the dissections from the anatomy institute while under the direction of Pernkopf "have survived and may be seen in the University of Innsbruck's Anatomy Institute, Innsbruck, Austria."

According to Lehner,[20] in a 1990 dissertation from the University of Vienna, Pernkopf was very concerned about a shortage of cadavers in the anatomy institute in 1938 and 1939. Pernkopf requested from the authorities in Berlin the use of cadavers of persons executed in German occupied Poland; however, this request was denied. Pernkopf allegedly put pressure on the City of Vienna's administration to order all city hospitals to refrain from dissecting corpses and to hand them over to the anatomy institute. Apparently, due to a wave of executions in Vienna, sufficient numbers of corpses were available in the anatomy institute by 1940. In the last year of the war, corpses were supplied from execution chambers in Linz, Munich and Prague.

After the war, Pernkopf was imprisoned for three years in Gla-senbach, an Allied prison camp near Salzburg.[9] Why he was held for three years is not known as he was never charged with any specific crimes. However, in 1948, Pernkopf was released and he returned to the University of Vienna where he continued to work on the anatomy atlas until his death in 1955.[9]

The illustrations that appear in Pernkopf's atlas do not provide any direct evidence concerning the origins of the subjects por-trayed. However, some of the illustrations raise questions which provide further fuel for the controversy surrounding the origins of the individuals portrayed. An illustration by Lepier of a dissection of the head and neck of a cachectic, younger appearing male[15] can be seen in the 1952 edition (Volume 3, Figure 50, Tafel 43, oppo-site page 97). The subject's crudely shaven hair is demonstrated in considerable detail. The man's relative youth, cachectic appear-ance and the haircut, raise the question that the subject may have been a prisoner from wartime. In the same 1952 edition (Volume 3, Figure 9, Tafels 3 & 4, opposite page 44) are head and neck illustrations by Batke, which reveal the cadaver to have hair of approximately one inch in length.[15] Again, these illustrations raise the question as to why the hair was not completely shaven, as is generally performed for hygienic purposes prior to anatomic dis-sections. Other questions are raised concerning Endtresser's paint-ings of a dissection of the femoral region of an apparently circum-cised male subject, published in the 1943 edition.[14] Illustrations from the 1943 edition by Lepier of the male genitalia showing an apparently circumcised penis of an adult (Volume 2, Figure 5, page 38) and the uncircumcised penis of an infant with the umbilical cord still attached (Volume 2, Figure 6, page 39) also raise further questions concerning the origins and cause of death of the subjects in Pernkopf's atlas.[14]

The illustrations seem to raise more questions than answers. Although there is no conclusive evidence demonstrating the true origins of the cadavers in Pernkopf's atlas, enough questions have been raised to support a thorough investigation to determine the precise origins and cause of death of these individuals.

DISCUSSION:
RELEVANCE OF THE "PERNKOPF ISSUE" TODAY

The question may be raised as to whether it is really that important to determine the origin of the subjects used in Pernkopf's atlas. The quality of the anatomic illustrations and the value of Pernkopf's *Atlas of Topographic and Applied Human Anatomy* in the education of anatomists, medical students and surgeons remain unquestioned. The issue is one of biomedical ethics. If a thorough investigation reveals that the Pernkopf atlas contains victims of Nazi execution, is it appropriate to use this information? In order to thoroughly understand this issue, it is important to realize that the "Pernkopf issue" is potentially just one of numerous examples in which there have been horrific violations of medical ethics by Nazi doctors, which continue to influence medicine today. To understand the importance of the "Pernkopf issue" requires a retrospective look at the devastating consequences of the abuse of power by doctors who violate the Hippocratic Oath.

The tremendous abuse of power by Nazi doctors is well documented. How today's medical profession handles the scientific data which has resulted from those medical atrocities will impact greatly on biomedical ethical issues of today and in the future. Dr. Sigmund Rascher's notorious Dachau hypothermic experiments were not the work of a deranged madman working in the isolation of the concentration camp. Rascher's experiments, which involved the immersion of concentration camp prisoners into freezing water, were performed for the Luftwaffe. The results of Rascher's hypothermia experiments continue to be cited in the medical literature.[21]

German medical science also seized on the murders of the Hitler period as an opportunity to exploit the remains of the dead. There were regular transports from the execution chambers of Gestapo prisons to university institutes of anatomy.[22] During the war the Institute of Anatomy at the University of Tubingen received the cadavers of 429 victims of Nazi terror. Some were Russian and Polish prisoners of war exploited as slave laborers and executed for socializing with German women.[23] It is not known exactly how many medical school institutes of anatomy received the cadavers of political victims. Tubingen is the only university to have made a credible and serious attempt to determine the truth.[24]

Although the transport of bodies from concentration camps is believed to be rare, this did happen in the case of August Hirt in Strasbourg.[25] Hirt requested Jewish prisoners from concentration camps who were murdered then sent to the Anatomy Department. The purpose of Hirt's "research" was to develop a collection of Jewish skulls. After the war, some of Hirt's specimens are believed to have unknowingly been used by French medical students as cadavers for anatomy dissections.

So how should health care professionals handle scientific data derived from Nazi atrocities? Some would argue that no matter how horrible the Nazi crimes were, these acts were in the past. If some benefit could be derived from it today, to save a life or enable a surgeon to perform more skillfully, it honors those who suffered and sacrificed their lives. Others may argue that the real purpose of science is to serve humankind by relieving suffering and improving the quality of life. They will indicate that science and ethics are inseparable and that it is impossible to justify the use of scientific data that has emanated from evil and caused incomprehensible human suffering. Furthermore, they will argue that using scientific data that emanated from Nazi crimes creates the environment for a repeat of such breaches of biomedical ethics, in which there is further potential justification and rationalization for unethical medical experimentation in the name of furthering scientific research.

CONCLUSIONS

How the community of health care professionals handles scientific data from Nazi medical crimes is very important to the future practice of health care. A more detailed exploration of the Nazi origins of Pernkopf's *Atlas of Topographic and Applied Human Anatomy* is relevant today because English, German, Japanese and Italian language editions of this book continue to be used in medical centers throughout the world. However, there is no indication to the unsuspecting user of Pernkopf's *Atlas of Topographic and Applied Human Anatomy* that there is any link to Nazi medicine or of the controversy which exists concerning the origins of the subjects portrayed in the dissections. It is an established fact that Eduard

Pernkopf and his artists were Nazis who actively embraced the policy of racial hygiene. It is known that Pernkopf's *Atlas of Topographic and Applied Human Anatomy* contains Nazi icons throughout the earlier editions of the book. However, more current editions since 1963 have included the same anatomic illustrations as the earlier editions, but with these Nazi icons eliminated. There is strong evidence to suggest that many of the cadavers used in the Institute of Anatomy under Pernkopf during the war years came from individuals executed by Nazis in a Viennese prison and from a local Viennese hospital. The exact names and cause of death of the subjects portrayed in Pernkopf's *Atlas of Topographic and Applied Human Anatomy* remain unknown.

The obliteration of the Nazi icons together with suppression of the truth has resulted in medicine's ignorance of the Pernkopf history. However, recent publications[19,26,27,28,29,30] have created awareness of the disturbing history of the Pernkopf era in Vienna and stimulated interest in the origins of the Pernkopf atlas. Although some have proposed that the Pernkopf atlas be removed from circulation, in my view suppression of the work is inappropriate. Furthermore, censorship of this work is reminiscent of the book burnings that took place in Nazi Germany. The position put forward by The Israel Holocaust Martyrs' and Heroes Remembrance Authority, Yad Vashem, to the Universities of Vienna and Innsbruck and the publisher,[31,32] is the most appropriate course of action:

1. *Investigation:* There should be a proper investigation by outside experts to determine who the subjects portrayed in the Pernkopf atlas were and where and how they died. An official report of the investigation should be published in the public domain.
2. *Commemoration:* If it is established that some of the subjects had in fact, or could possibly have been, victims of the Nazis, there should be a public commemoration of the victims by the institutions and organizations concerned and every future edition of Pernkopf's atlas should include a commemoration to them.

3. *Acknowledgment:* The book should continue to be published with an appropriate acknowledgment in every future edition of the book documenting the history of Pernkopf, the University of Vienna Faculty and the Institute of Anatomy.

On February 12, 1997 the University of Vienna announced at a press conference[33] that it will conduct a broad investigation into the precise origins of the specimens used for the detailed drawings in Pernkopf's atlas. At that conference, it was revealed that during the era of National Socialism, the bodies of individuals executed for political reasons were routinely given to the Institute of Anatomy. The recktor of the university, Alfred Ebenauer, indicated "I agree with the contemporary efforts of American physicians to add an explanation to the Pernkopf Atlas." These represent important first steps in arriving at the truth and confronting the past. However, the question still remains for clinicians today as to how we should handle the information contained in Pernkopf's atlas, as well as other potentially tainted scientific data.

Controversial scientific information also poses a significant problem for the information sciences. Medical center libraries have not reacted uniformly to the Pernkopf atlas controversy, demonstrating a wide range of responses to the biomedical ethical issues raised. Upon discovering the background of the Pernkopf atlas, one physician had his medical center library "expunge it from its collection and retain it in a symbolic manner, so that we might remember those events in those times and their lessons."[30] The medical library at the National Institutes of Health has placed the Pernkopf atlas on reserve with a note in the book referring readers to a binder of materials which contains a collection of articles and papers describing the Pernkopf controversy.[34,35] Other medical center librarians have raised the issue of how to label certain materials as being controversial, but not others. Until the publisher agrees to include an acknowledgment in the book, indicating its Nazi background, medical center library and ethics committees will have to make a determination as to how to best handle this controversial material in their respective institutions.

As we wait for the scientific community, academic centers, and the publisher to respond to the issues raised by Pernkopf's atlas, the individual must make their own personal decision as to how to deal with information and data obtained from Nazi medicine. The implications on how we proceed with these issues today are quite profound. Health professionals care for patients based on the information they receive through continual education and training that takes place throughout their professional lives. We all want to be cared for by physicians who believe that all people are life worthy of the highest quality of life.

REFERENCES

1. Lifton, Robert J. The Nazi Doctors: Medical Killing and the Psychology of Genocide. Basic Books, New York, 1986.

2. Dickman, Steven. Scandal over Nazi victims' corpses rocks universities. Nature 337:195, 1989.

3. Seidelman, William. In Memoriam: Medicine's Confrontation with Evil. Hastings Center Report, November/December, 1989, pp. 5-6.

4. Seidelman, William. "Medspeak" for Murder: The Nazi Experience and the Culture of Medicine, in "When Medicine Went Mad: Bioethics and the Holocaust." Caplan, Arthur L (ed), Humana Press, Totowa, New Jersey, 1992, pp. 271-279.

5. Kater, Michael. Unresolved questions of German medicine and medical history in the past and present. Central European History, 25(4):407, 1993.

6. Dickman, Steven. Brain sections to be buried? Nature 339:498, 1988.

7. Bogerts, Bernhard. The Brains of the Vogt collection. Arch Gen Psychiatry 45:774, 1988 (letter to editor).

8. Gershon, E.S. and Hoehe, M.R. Comment: On the deaths of Ernst and Klaus H. Arch Gen Psychiatry 45:774, 1988 (letter to editor).

9. Williams, D. The history of Eduard Pernkopf's "Topographische Anatomie des Menschen." Journal of Biocommunication 15:2, 1988.

10. Snell, R.S. Pernkopf Anatomy: Atlas of Topographic and Applied Human Anatomy, vol. 2, Thorax, Abdomen and Extremities, 3rd ed., Platzer, W. (ed), Monsen, H. (Transl). The New England Journal of Medicine 323(3):205, 1990.

11. Hast, M.H. Pernkopf Anatomy: Atlas of Topographic and Applied Human Anatomy, vol. 1, Head and Neck, 3rd ed., Platzer, W (ed). Journal of the American Medical Association 263(15):2115, 1990.

12. Weissmann, G. Springtime for Pernkopf, in "They All Laughed at Christopher Columbus: Tales of Medicine and the Art of Discovery." Times Books, New York, pp 48-69, 1982.

13. Pernkopf, E. Originalabhandlungen Nationalsozialismus und Wissenschaft. Wiener Klinische Wochenscrift 51:545, 1938.

14. Pernkopf, E. Topographische Anatomie des Menschen, II. Band: Bauch, Becken und Beckengliedmasse. Urban & Schwarzenberg, Berlin und Wien, 1943.

15. Pernkopf, E. Topographische Anatomie des Menschen, III. Band: Der Hals. Urban & Schwarzenberg, Berlin und Wien, 1952.

16. Pernkopf Anatomy: Atlas of Topographical and Applied Human Anatomy, Volume I, Head and Neck. Platzer, W. (Ed), Third edition, Urban & Schwarzenberg, Baltimore and Munich, 1989.

17. Pernkopf Anatomy: Atlas of Topographical and Applied Human Anatomy, Volume II, Thorax, Abdomen and Extremities, Platzer, W. (Ed), Third edition, Urban & Schwarzenberg, Baltimore and Munich, 1989.

18. Anatomy: A Regional Atlas of the Human Body, Clemente, C.D. (ed), Third edition, Lea & Febiger, Philadelphia and London, Urban & Schwarzenberg, Baltimore and Munich, 1987.

19. Ernst, E. A leading medical school seriously damaged: Vienna 1938. Annals of Internal Medicine 122(10):789, 1995.

20. Lehner, M. Medizinische Fakultat der Universitat in den Jahren 1938-1945 (Dissertation). University of Vienna, 1990.

21. When Medicine Went Mad: Bioethics and the Holocaust. Caplan, Arthur L. (ed), Humana Press, Totowa, New Jersey, 1992.

22. Seidelman, W. Complicity, complacency and conspiracy: the enduring legacy of medicine in the Third Reich. From Conference "Hippocrates Betrayed: Medicine in the Third Reich, " The United States Holocaust Memorial Museum, Washington, DC, January 24, 1996.

23. Pfeiffer, J. Neuropathology in the Third Reich: memorial to those victims of National Socialist atrocities in Germany who were used by medical science. Brain Pathology 1:125-131, 1991.

24. Berichte Berichte: der Kommission zur Uberprufung der Praparaesammlungen in den medizinschen Einrichtungen der Universitat Tubingen im Hinblick auf Opfer des Nationalsozialismus. Herausgegeben vom Prasidenten der Eberhard-Karls-Universitat Tubingen Abdruck–auch auszugweise–nur mit Genehmigung des Herausgebers. 1990.

25. Kasten, F.H. Unethical Nazi medicine in annexed Alsace-Lorraine: the strange case of Nazi anatomist Professor Dr. August Hirt, in "Historians and Archivists: Essays in Modern German History and Archival Polic." Kent, G. (ed), University Press, Fairfax, Virginia, pp 173-208, 1991.

26. Israel, H., Seidelman, W. Nazi origins of an anatomy text: The Pernkopf atlas. JAMA, 276(20):1633, 1996 (letter).

27. Broder, J. The corpses that won't die. Jerusalem Report, pp 24-25, February 22, 1996.

28. Wade, N. Doctors question use of Nazi's medical atlas. The New York Times, pp C1, November 26, 1996.

29. Wade, N. The Nazi's medical atlas. Linacres, pp 32-36, Spring, 1997.

30. Panush, R.S. Upon finding a Nazi anatomy atlas: the lessons of Nazi medicine. Pharos, pp 18-22, Fall, 1996.

31. Letter from Amb. R. Dafni, Vice-Chairman of Yad Vashem to Univ. Prof. Dr. Alfred Abenauer: Rector, University of Vienna. March 23, 1995.

32. Letter from Amb. R. Dafni, Vice-Chairman of Yad Vashem to Univ. Prof. Dr. Hans Moser: Rector, University of Innsbruck. March 23, 1995.

33. Press Conference of the University Vienna, "Examination of Anatomical Studies Conducted at the University of Vienna, 1938-1945." February 12, 1997.

34. Gejman, P., Nussenblatt, R. Personal correspondence, December, 1996.

35. Letter from Grefsheim, S., NIH Library, April 17, 1997.

"Getting It Right":
Some Thoughts on the Role
of the Holocaust Historian

Michael R. Marrus

To consider the place of the Holocaust in our society is immediately to pose questions. Is there too much or too little? Is the emphasis right? How do we deal with it? Is it unique? Is it misused? What to do next? There are numerous opinions, and an abundance of authorities. Survivors have special preoccupations, although these are less easily collapsed into a single viewpoint than is customarily assumed. Jewish community leaders may speak with one voice, but there are plenty of dissenters, and not all of them agree. Some use the rhetoric of the Holocaust for fundraising purposes; others are revolted by the prospect. Some stimulate Holocaust consciousness as a way of energizing Jewish identity, but others warn that it is unhealthy to define oneself as a perpetual victim, particularly when this defies current reality. Non-Jews are all over the map as well. Some have had enough. Some want to dig deeper. Some ethnic communities have special preoccupations, and are concerned with how the presentation of the Holocaust might reflect upon themselves. There are different connotations on the left and on the right.

Michael R. Marrus is affiliated with the Department of History, University of Toronto, 100 St. George Street, Toronto, Ontario, Canada M5S 3G3.

An earlier verson of this article appeared in *Beyond Imagination: Canadians Write about the Holocaust*, edited by Jerry S. Grafstein (Toronto: McClelland and Stewart, 1995). The author has permission to reprint.

[Haworth co-indexing entry note]: " 'Getting It Right': Some Thoughts on the Role of the Holocaust Historian.' " Marrus, Michael R. Co-published simultaneously in *The Reference Librarian* (The Haworth Press, Inc.) No. 61/62, 1998, pp. 147-156; and: *The Holocaust: Memories, Research, Reference* (ed: Robert Hauptman, and Susan Hubbs Motin) The Haworth Press, Inc., 1998, pp. 147-156.

Educators voice interest, but their students sometimes do not. Media offerings vary considerably, from the thoughtful and carefully executed to the shamelessly exploitive.

I come to these debates as a historian, and what I want to say here reflects how I bring professional preoccupations to issues that can easily be looked at from other standpoints as well. And since my starting point is often misunderstood, I begin with a word of explanation. Each of us has a variety of roles we perform in society, flowing from aspects of our personal identities: I am, at once, a Canadian, a Jew, a father, a husband, a professor, and so on. Each of these roles involves obligations and aspirations, feelings and ways of looking at the world. To some degree, the Holocaust may be caught up in every one of these roles. At one time or another, the Canadian, the Jew, and so on, responds to the wartime massacre of European Jewry in particular ways or defines him or her self in a manner that draws upon that catastrophe.

But when it comes to the Holocaust the historian in me is different. As a historian I have publicly declared responsibilities quite different from those prescribed by my other identities. I remember, in the mid-sixties, debating with fellow graduate students at the University of California, in Berkeley, about the historian's craft. What was the historian's vocation? Opinions varied, but in my circle, in that heady Vietnam and civil rights era, most of us saw our task as social and political change. Politics lurked just beneath the surface of everything, we believed. (I even wrote a book entitled *The Politics of Assimilation*.) We were to hold a mirror to society, to show the seamy underside, and help set things right.

The challenge to that view, however, which I remember to this day, and which I now believe to have been the wiser course, came from one of our teachers, universally respected as a master at his craft—even if not admired by us for his politics at the time. "The historian's job," he insisted—and I can remember his intonation still, after some thirty years—"is *to get it right!*" "Getting it right" was a sober injunction to youthful idealists, because it suggested the diversion (as we saw it) of extraordinary energy into detail, and tests of accuracy. It meant the greatest care in research, wide-ranging reading, seeing documents in their original form, learning foreign languages, and studying the idioms of particular contexts.

More often than not, it meant visits to dreary, ill-appointed archives, sifting through seemingly worthless paper for hours on end. It required plenty of *Sitzfleisch*. This was a program sure to bring high-flying generalizations down to earth, or discourage some from even getting off the ground. But it was the best advice we ever had.

"Getting it right" is what I try to do as a historian of the Holocaust. Jews and non-Jews, parents and spouses, teachers and politicians, clerics and artists, and everyone else will make of the Holocaust what they will, according to their conscience, inclinations, and fundamental beliefs. I do not in the least disparage such approaches–far from it; at various moments, in other roles I perform, I may well think of the wartime murder of European Jews in precisely the same manner. Some, however, have to make sure that the Holocaust upon which people act and ruminate is faithful to the events themselves, or at least as faithful as we can possibly make it. Some have to be counted on for historical accuracy, for generalizations that match the evidence, and for a balanced view. Those are the historian's tasks, making him or her the custodian, in a sense, of the public memory of the event itself.

Just putting it this way, I know, makes some people uneasy, and quite often when I elaborate, they feel even worse. No one takes kindly to assertions of external authority in matters close to the heart, and when memory has become sacred, as in the case with the murder of European Jewry, it can clash sharply with history as historians understand it. That is why academic lectures to the Jewish community on Holocaust themes sometimes finish in a stormy question-and-answer period, with the lecturer rushing for the door at the end of the evening. "Young man," I have been addressed often enough (I am fifty-four), "when were you born? Let me tell you, it was not quite the way you have told us."

"Getting it right" sometimes involves questioning the recollections of Holocaust survivors (although almost invariably there are other survivors who remember things differently), disputing received wisdom, pitting book learning against cherished or traumatic memories. To younger colleagues contemplating this challenge, I can only say *bon courage*!

For obvious reasons, we defer to those who have suffered and survived–and so we should in listening to people recount their own traumatic experiences. For the historian, trouble comes when the anguish and suffering of the victim becomes a warrant for historical analysis and wide-ranging generalization. For while experts in their own pain, survivors have to struggle like the rest of us to understand the bigger picture. To achieve a balanced, objective view, they frequently must lift aside a mountain of emotion; and it is hardly surprising that many do not care or dare to do so. I would be the last to say that they should try. My point, however, is that testimony is no substitute for historical inquiry.

Historians are necessary, therefore, and for at least two reasons we are sure to have more, rather than less, recourse to them in the future. First, historians become increasingly important as the ranks of survivors grow thinner. In a few decades, it is often pointed out, those who have firsthand recollections of these events will be no more, and historians will become the principal custodians of public memory of the Holocaust. Second, memory itself grows faint, at least in some cases, and needs constant verification. Primo Levi, the cultivated Italian Jew who endured a year in Auschwitz, was very preoccupied with this issue both for himself and others. "Human memory is a marvelous but fallacious instrument," he wrote in his last book, *The Drowned and the Saved*. "The memories that lie within us art not carved in stone; not only do they tend to become erased as the years go by, but often they change, or even grow, by incorporating extraneous features." Levi worried about how memory, when "evoked too often, and expressed in the form of a story, tends to become fixed in a stereotype, in a form tested by experience, crystallized, perfected, adorned, installing itself in the place of the raw memory and growing at its expense." Memory, he felt, had constantly to be tested, analysed, probed–something he did with his own memories, doubtless at great personal cost.

So there is much work for Holocaust historians to do. Yet many people feel that we already know more or less all that there is to know about the Holocaust, and that to insist on the kind of painstaking verification I am advocating here is to duck moral responsibility. To them, the real problem is not this or that detail, but rather Holocaust denial or the societal questions alluded to at the beginning of this essay. Like Virginia Woolf they might well prefer accounts of the Holocaust that are "more truth than fact." Some people have even been surprised when I explained I teach a university course on the Holocaust. "A whole *course*? Don't you get bogged down? Isn't this really just a morbid curiosity?"

The truth is, however, not only that there is much we don't know, but that the history of the Holocaust poses historical problems at least as challenging, and generally more challenging, than any other field one can find. "Getting it right" is far more difficult and exhilarating than people assume. Leave aside the deepest questions: How could people do it? How could others allow them to do it? These questions ultimately fall outside the historian's province, I believe, for the answers–if there are answers–are tied up with notions of humanity itself and its capacities for good and evil. But there are also garden-variety questions, asked all the time by historians, but which for the Holocaust are of extraordinary import, because we are, after all, talking about the murder of millions of people: Who decided? How were decisions reached? Who acted? When? And how? What did people know? How did one place differ from another? What alternatives presented themselves?

"Getting it right" involves posing such questions and addressing them with the best tools the historical culture of our society provides. It also requires some measure of objectivity, which brings us to perhaps the most important methodological challenge for the historian of the Holocaust. Among the least appreciated attributes of the historian these days, objectivity is nevertheless what we insist upon in many other aspects of life. There are many appropriate ways to respond to murder, but if we are speaking about an investigating officer, a coroner, or a judge, for example, we feel that their task requires them to keep an open mind about the evidence they assess and a capacity to weigh evidence fairly and dispassionately. When it comes to a serious illness of someone close to us, we can respond appropriately as friend, parent, spouse, or whatever, but we have quite different expectations when it comes to the surgeon conducting an operation. Indeed, with surgery, as with the practise of law or many other professional activities, we usually feel that too intimate a relationship would interfere with sound discharge of professional responsibilities. Simply put, we feel that practitioners such as these carry out their responsibilities best when they act as professionals.

No one expects, or wants, historians to perform like machines. But there is a world of difference between history taken up as a sacred duty, keeping faith with those who were murdered–intimately involved with mourning, commemoration, denunciation, or a warning for future generations–and the quite different task of historical analysis, trying to make sense of it all in terms understood by the historical culture of our day. This last is the objective I am talking about here, an effort to integrate the history of the Holocaust into the general stream of historical consciousness, to apply to it the modes of analysis, the scholarly discourse and the kinds of analyses used for other historical issues.

The need to achieve such an integration has been obvious to many historians of my generation, those of us who received our historical training in the mid-sixties or just before. For us, at that time, the Holocaust was simply absent. A quarter of a century after the destruction of so much of European Jewry, mass industrial murder in the heart of Western Civilization had scarcely appeared in the historical record. No one would have thought to mention it in a lecture. Textbooks on the modern era skirted the issue. Discussions of the Second World War avoided it scrupulously. In 1953 a distinguished historian at the University of Toronto wrote a modern history of Germany without referring to it at all. And when a colleague revised his book some years later, he included nothing on Jews or the Holocaust. And in this, I hasten to add, historians reflected the wider absence in the culture of the day.

Non-Jews, but also Jews, did not speak about the Holocaust. Western countries, it has been said, in explanation of their reticence, suffered from a "guilt complex" in the postwar years. But I have found no evidence of this, or indeed of any other strong feeling about the issue. People just weren't interested in discussing it. Jews, too, whether from shame or fears of renewed anti-Semitism, or relief that it was over, remained silent. Survivors found that their stories made listeners uncomfortable. In the immediate postwar period, there was not even a word to designate what had happened. The term "Holocaust" hardly appeared before the end of the fifties, and even then it was largely restricted to Jews–and specialists in the subject at that. Raul Hilberg's landmark book *The Destruction of the European Jews* appeared only in 1961, and this was among the very first works on the subject intended for a wide, general audience. It was only towards the end of the sixties that writings began to accumulate and that a few of these caught the eye of the general public. In 1968 the Library of Congress, for the first time, created a major entry card: Holocaust–Jewish, 1939-1945.

The great change occurred in the seventies, a decade or more after the trial of Adolf Eichmann in Jerusalem, an event intended by its organizers to stimulate public consciousness of the murder of European Jews. Major landmarks included the publication of Lucy Dawidowicz's widely successful *War Against the Jews*, (1975), the convocation of several international historical conferences, a lively dispute over a book by David Irving claiming Hitler's ignorance, until 1943, of the Final Solution, and Gerald Green's extraordinarily popular NBC docudrama "Holocaust" (1978). Historians and others began to publish well-researched monographs on the subject, intended for the wider audience of interested readers. Since then, historical inquiry has proceeded apace, to the point that it may be impossible, now, for a single person to master all of the literature.

More than anything else, "getting it right" involves digesting this literature and asserting the place of the Holocaust in the wider history of our time. No one contemplating what has happened to mankind in the twentieth century can skirt the Nazis' assault on European Jewry. Historians of the Third Reich now must all come to terms with it. Those who study the Second World War must do the same. Jewish issues are closely intertwined with the history of occupation regimes, the Barbarossa campaign, the functioning of the Nazi state, and the roles of Hitler, the SS, soldiers, bureaucrats, and popular opinion. And just as no one can understand the war without understanding what happened to the Jews, so the latter must be understood in terms of what was happening on the wider historical stage.

Most important, the effort to eliminate an entire people, set as a major objective by a highly developed industrial society and carried out on a European-wide scale, eventually using the most up-to-date technology, is now widely seen to be unprecedented, not only for Western Civilization but for humanity itself. Germans, with helpers, not only intended this, but for three or four years actually set about doing it. In the past, peoples have constantly been cruel to one another, have tormented others in various ways, and have fantasized horribly about what might happen to their enemies. But there were always limits, imposed by technology, humane sensibilities, religious scruples, geography, or military capacity. During the Second World War mankind crossed a new threshold. Nazi Germany operated without historic limits, until crushed by military defeat.

As a result, we have a different sense of human capacities than we did before. Some, particularly Jews who suffered at the hands of the Nazis but who miraculously survived, draw the bleakest conclusions of all. "Every day anew I lose my trust in the world," wrote Jean Améry not long before his suicide. Others think that a warning is all one can deduce. Primo Levi's message was: "It can happen, and it can happen everywhere." Levi, too, ended his life, but while he lived he argued that reflecting on the Holocaust might help prevent another catastrophe. Whatever one's view, the Holocaust has become a major reference point for our time, constantly kept in view for one's judgement about the state of the world, as might the French Revolution, say, or the First World War.

In addition to studying perpetrators, "getting it right" involves looking at victims, and refusing to see them as endowed by their victimhood with a special aura of heroism, righteousness, or other admirable qualities. When the Israeli research and commemorative institute Yad Vashem was founded in 1953, it was called in English "The Martyrs' and Heroes' Remembrance Authority." At the centre of attention, according to the law establishing the institution, was a distinctly Israeli appreciation of the victims' experience–"the sublime, persistent struggle of the masses of the House of Israel, on the threshold of destruction, for their human dignity and Jewish culture." The accent was on combativeness, rebellion, and unwillingness to submit. The most important outcome was national regeneration through resistance and armed struggle. No sooner had Yad Vashem been established, however, than a different Israeli voice was heard. In 1954 the Hebrew poet Natan Alterman, who has been called "the uncrowned poet laureate" of his generation, and who lived in Palestine during the war, wrote a famous poem celebrating Jewish *opponents* of the insurgents–those who claimed that "resistance will destroy us all." A dissident voice at the time, Alterman took care to appreciate as the real heroes those Jews who were caught in the middle: heads of the Jewish Councils or *Judenräte*, confused and harassed community leaders, those responsible elders who "negotiated and complied" rather than the relatively small number of young people who managed to take up arms. Following Alterman's intervention, an intense debate began, which has continually renewed itself ever since with new discoveries and new historical writing. The result, I believe, has been a more mature historical understanding, enriched by research and the confrontation of different points of view.

Finally, "getting it right" involves finding the right language, expressing oneself in the right idiom—speaking with a voice, in short, appropriate both for the most terrible events, but also for the present generation, including young people. Holocaust history is like all history in this respect; it must constantly be rewritten if it is not to vanish from public perceptions or lose the significance we want ascribed to it. Here again, Holocaust history poses special challenges. In his *Reflections on Nazism*, Saul Friedländer dwells upon the difficulties historians and others have in finding the right words to discuss the massacre of European Jewry. Friedländer is disturbed by the continuing fascination with Nazism, evident particularly in films and literature. This is part of the problem of how we communicate things that are deeply disturbing to us, but also strange and difficult to grasp emotionally. Historians neutralize horror, he seem to say; and he is concerned with expression that "normalizes, smooths and neutralizes our vision of the past." Does scholarly discourse anaesthetize in this way? Friedländer knows there is no easy answer. "There should be no misunderstanding about what I am trying to say: The historian cannot work in any other way, and historical studies have to be pursued along the accepted lines. The events described are what is unusual, not the historians' work. We have reached the limit of our means of expression."

There is no alternative, I conclude, but to keep at it. Historians of the Holocaust are called upon to provide one kind of explanation, and their preoccupation is not only the intractable material with which they work, but also a public that is constantly renewing itself, coming forward with new layers of experience, new interests, and new unfamiliarity. Diaries and memoirs of survivors reflect a widely shared obsession of those who went through the Holocaust: "How will what happened to us be understood?" "Could a postwar world possibly grasp what we went through?" Imagine how those victim might understand the generation that now looks back on their agonies. The gap grows wider, and with it the challenge to the historians and everyone else.

To all of those concerned to see knowledge about the Holocaust extended, I think I can provide some reassurance. The Holocaust has become history, has entered into the historical canon, with all of its strengths and weaknesses. This means debate and disagreement, but also research, new questions, and new ways of looking at old problems. It means historians of many backgrounds are applying themselves to the task, many of whom share concerns I articulate here that they "get it right." This is the way, in our culture, that historical understanding is preserved and advanced. It seems plain now that after the shock of the postwar era the Holocaust has become history. And that is the best guarantee we have that it will be remembered.

PART III:
REFERENCE

Holocaust Autobiography

Martin Goldberg

SUMMARY. Students have a need to go beyond their assigned texts when studying the events of the Holocaust. Autobiographies are often the most moving, personal accounts of these horrific times. Reference librarians can offer much assistance for research on specific autobiographies, working in concert with faculty. This article reviews the state of Holocaust education in general, an academic reference department's role in student projects, and an overview of the wide variety of autobiographies that exist. *[Article copies available for a fee from The Haworth Document Delivery Service: 1-800-342-9678. E-mail address: getinfo@haworth.com]*

In Germany they came first for the Communists and I didn't speak up because I wasn't a Communist. Then they came for the Jews, and I didn't speak up because I wasn't a Jew. Then they came for the trade unionists, and I didn't speak up be-

Martin Goldberg is Head Librarian, Penn State University, Beaver Campus, Monaca, PA 15061.

[Haworth co-indexing entry note]: "Holocaust Autobiography." Goldberg, Martin. Co-published simultaneously in *The Reference Librarian* (The Haworth Press, Inc.) No. 61/62, 1998, pp. 157-163; and: *The Holocaust: Memories, Research, Reference* (ed: Robert Hauptman, and Susan Hubbs Motin) The Haworth Press, Inc., 1998, pp. 157-163. Single or multiple copies of this article are available for a fee from The Haworth Document Delivery Service [1-800-342-9678, 9:00 a.m. - 5:00 p.m. (EST). E-mail address: getinfo@haworth.com].

cause I wasn't a trade unionist. They came for the Catholics and I didn't speak up because I was a Protestant. Then they came for me, and by that time no one was left to speak up.

Martin Nummular (1892-1984)

INTRODUCTION

Perhaps the most popular and unforgettable first-person account of the devastation of the Jews was Anne Frank's moving day to day memoir; it has sold well over 16 million copies, read by countless more library borrowers and been translated into at least 50 different languages. The power of television and motion pictures seems to perpetuate interest in study of the Holocaust. *Schindler's List*, technically a work of fiction, found sales skyrocketing once the movie was released. The popularity of this moving film resulted in more autobiographical accounts of the Holocaust being written by survivors; publishers tell me of the rising number of submissions as survivors finally feel the need to tell their stories. As a result, if ever there was a *Golden Age of Holocaust Autobiographies*, it is now.

Despite the fact that this gruesome, unexplainable period of history has been studied, researched and documented more than any other, deniers seem to be multiplying. More than once I have heard in the library a student saying that the Holocaust was exaggerated. As librarians, we are not supposed to comment on a patron's questions/statements, but it is often difficult not to: recently, a student I was helping find some material on a particular concentration camp said "You know, Hitler wasn't so bad. He really was a very bright man."

Clearly, more, not less, needs to be taught about the Holocaust. We cannot rely on our textbooks which faculty depend upon (public schools more than college) to inform the students. One study of over 40 American history textbooks from major publishers found that none adequately covered the Holocaust. Five of those books did not even contain a single sentence on this topic (Dong, 1979). Not even the Anne Frank Diary (thought by many to be the "least threatening" and thereby most acceptable in schools) made it into some reading lists in many high school texts since no Holocaust supplementary reading lists were included. Of 17 major history titles for grades seven through twelve, only five contained more than 31 lines about the Holocaust and 85 lines was the more generous. None described the concentration camps and ignored any aspect of the survivors (Braham, 1987). College history anthologies did little better than the high school texts. In describing the results of the National Assessment of Educational Progress evaluation of students' history and literature proficiencies, it was noted that "narratives, journals and biographies ought to be used in each history course to enliven events and to illuminate concepts" (Finn and Ravitch, 1988).

In our library, we have developed a number of resource files relating to the Holocaust autobiographies. These resources come in handy when students often need more precise information about particular autobiographies, such as questions about how events occurred in certain geographical areas, and persecution of different groups (by religion, gender, nationality, and politics). A number of students request photos, maps, newspaper clippings, texts of speeches, Nazi propaganda, etc., to utilize for class presentations and papers. Recently, one student group requested portions of the Nuremberg trials transcripts in order to demonstrate how some of the victims who did not survive might have testified. Another group needed Nazi propaganda used in Germany and compared it with some material distributed to some of the conquered nations, as well as anti-Nazi propaganda used by the Allies. A fairly common technique is for students to read *The New York Times* accounts on specific days noted in some diaries and try to understand what forces were at play in particular areas. The faculty that use autobiographies as part of class assignments have also invited reference librarians to present basic research tools and techniques to their students. This has resulted in students getting a good understanding of basic historical research in order to obtain a well informed overview of the outside forces working upon the autobiography's author.

AUTOBIOGRAPHY

Daniel Stern in a book review of Livia Jackson's *Elli, Coming of Age in the Holocaust* (Times Books, NY, 1980) wrote: "What do we do with the survivors and their awful claim on mankind's attention. There is one thing we must do—we must listen" (Stern, 1981). The autobiographies, first-person accounts and diaries include those written when events occurred, often secretly recorded with the writer knowing the future at best to be doubtful. Others were written years later in order to reflect on one's past and accept responsibility for what one did "using their current values to weigh behavior that their memories progressively return to consciousness" (Magee, 1988). In short, the bond between the writer of a good autobiography and the reader becomes a one-to-one experience that cannot be replicated elsewhere. Robin Berson in an article about biography notes "the examination of individual lives can offer us direct examples of other human beings like ourselves who faced similar challenges and struggled, with varying degrees of success, to find meaningful responses to those challenges" (Berson, 1994).

"Biographical dictionaries are among the most frequently used books in the academic library (or in any library). Questions about notable people and about people in the news—their lives, interests, education, background, affiliations, position and even their addresses—come from faculty and students alike" (Gates, 1974). In surveys of public library patrons' preferences for "something to read," after ranking fiction as first, biographies and autobiographies were next in demand. "If the reader's main requirement from biography is for "something to read," then the public librarian's first job is to identify the classic works in the genre which, as with classic works of fiction, should be ever-present, in attractive editions, on the shelves of the smallest library service point" (Spiller, 1988).

Then what do we offer our patrons? There is a wide variety of titles from the victims themselves, from the oppressors and even some from bystanders. These autobiographies cross all geographic boundaries, include all religions and languages, from all age groups, from the living to the dead, providing a wide diversity of experiences and writings. On May 20, 1941, Mary Berg, a 16 year old whose father was an American, experienced most of the horrors of the Warsaw Ghetto wrote this description of despair before she fortunately made her way to the United States: "On the other side of the barbed wire spring holds full sway. From my window I can see young girls with bouquets of lilac walking on the Aryan part of the street. I can even smell the tender fragrance of the opened buds. But there is no sign of spring in the ghetto. Here are rays of the sun are swallowed up by heavy gray pavement. On a few window sills, long, scrawny onion stalks, more yellow than green, are sprouting. Where are my lovely spring days of former years, the gay walks in the park, the narcissus, lilac and magnolia that used to fill my room?" (Berg, 1945).

A young Polish woman and her sister were on the first Jewish transport to Auschwitz and writes of a song from the camps: "There used to be tangos, fox trots, and fanfares sung by dancing pairs. There were tangos of dreams and lovers, but now we're at war. Nobody writes songs. It's a waste of our young years. So sing this new song, our head held up high. Sing, sister, behind the German iron bars this tango of tears, suffering and desperation–what the war means to us today. Our hearts are crying hot tears. Are we ever going to see the sun? Are we going to see the beautiful world again? From the distance through the iron bars freedom is laughing at us and about freedom we are constantly dreaming" (Gelissen, 1995).

Perhaps one of the most misunderstood groups, the Jewish ghetto police, are heard in a 100-day diary written by a 25 year old in Warsaw, who experienced harsh conditions and seeing his wife and young daughter taken away on a train to Treblinka. His diary survived his death in 1944: "Today we indeed have proof of how good it is to find oneself under the power of divine protection. And a time will come when the democratic world will win and fanfares will announce the freedom of peoples. Jews will then be able to live freely, go back to Palestine–although from the 3 million will remain perhaps twenty thousand, a tiny number. But the most important fact is that justice will prevail again . . . No! Jews, if you believe this, you are mistaken! We have lost the war. If maybe there is a God in the world, the worst for Him–evidently it is a God of the strong and mighty, not of the weak and persecuted. And is there is no God at all, well then there is nothing to argue about" (Perechodnik, 1996).

Equally haunting, Gabriele Silten's *Between Two Worlds* describes how at the age of ten, she and her family were sent to Terezin, where they remained for 16 months until liberation. She explains how she had four companions: hunger, fear, cold and death. "I do not want to go with her; I do not go looking for her, but she comes to me without my asking. I do welcome her care though; no one else has much time to care for me. Her name is Death, and she is my loyal friend" (Silten, 1995). She also wrote an autobiographical collection of poems describing her childhood (Silten, 1991).

Nechama Tec provides an excellent first-person account as her family is forced to live apart as Christians. "Once, in town, a Polish friend and I saw a small group of Jewish workers from a factory walking along the middle of the road, surrounded by German soldiers with machine guns. They wore tattered clothes of an indefinite tired, colorless gray that, in a strange way, seemed to blend with their bodies. They look exhausted, depressed, depleted or energy almost of life itself. Moving listlessly, their eyes mostly stayed fixed on the ground; when they glanced up their eyes had a vacant, empty look, which saw nothing and cared about nothing. They were pathetically shrunken into themselves, totally apart from their surroundings. Occasionally, roughly and contemptuously, a soldier would push one of them with his machine gun, but they continued to move automatically. If dead people could walk, I would expect them to walk that way" (Tec, 1984).

These and other autobiographies demonstrate the excellent, vivid descriptions that one can only get from personal accounts. The bond between writer and reader is often personal and always strong. We learn that truth and values are universal and timeless. "The truths told in autobiography . . . are not necessarily verifiable in objective, external reality or expressible as simple facts and ideas. Rather, the cultural value of autobiography is often subjective and internal. Its value is a matter of the heart and spirit as well as of the mind" (Goodwin, 1993).

REFERENCES

Berg, Mary. (1945). *Warsaw Ghetto*. New York: L.B. Fischer, 59.

Berson, Robin. (1994). A Passion for Biography. *Wilson Library Bulletin*, 69 (2): 65.

Braham, Randolph L. (ed.) (1987). *The Treatment of the Holocaust in Textbooks: the Federal Republic of Germany, Israel, the United States of America*. New York: Columbia University Press, 240-3.

Dong, S. (1979). Study Criticizes Coverage of the Holocaust by 43 Current History Textbooks. *Publishers Weekly*, 216 (9): 296.

Finn, Chester E. and Diane Ravitch. (1988). No Trivial Pursuit. *Phi Delta Kappan*, 69 (81): 561.

Gates, Jean Key. *(1974). Guide to the Use of Books and Libraries (3rd ed.).* New York: McGraw-Hill, 116.

Gelissen, Rena Kornriech. (1995). *Rena's Promise*. Boston: Beacon, 220.

Goodwin, James. (1993). *Autobiography: The Self-Made Text*. New York: Twayne, 23.

Magee, James J. (1988). *A Professional's Guide to Older Adults' Life Review: Releasing the Peace Within*. Lexington, Mass.: Lexington Books, 4.

Perechodnik, Calel. (1996). *Am I A Murderer? Testament of a Jewish Ghetto Policeman*. Boulder, Colorado: Westview, 172-3.

Silten, R. Gabriele. (1995). *Between Two Worlds: Autobiography of a Child Survivor of the Holocaust*. Santa Barbara, California: Fithian Press, 128.

Silten, R. Gabriele. (1991). *High Tower Crumbling: Poems*. Santa Barbara, California: Fithian Press.

Spiller, David. (1988). A Strategy for Biography Provision in Public Libraries. *Library Review*, 37: 40-41.

Stern, Daniel. (1981). A Survivor's Memoir. *Midstream*, (April): 58.

Tec, Nachama. (1984). *Dry Tears, The Story of a Lost Childhood*. New York: Oxford, 142-3.

Examining the Holocaust
Through the Lives and Literary Works
of Victims and Survivors:
An Ideal Unit of Study
for the English Classroom

Samuel Totten

INTRODUCTION

Teaching about the adverse impact of prejudice and discrimination and the horror of human rights violations is *vitally significant*;
and no matter how difficult it is to accomplish, there is a moral
imperative–or so it seems to this author–to address such issues in
the classroom. This becomes particularly evident when one ponders
the words of Thomas Hammarberg (1983), former Secretary General of Amnesty International, when he argues that " . . . the oppressors [of people across the globe] are relying on ignorance and
indifference . . . among the citizens in their countries and public
opinion abroad. . . . " (p. 5). That was certainly true during the
perpetration of the Holocaust; and unfortunately, it is also true
vis-à-vis a multitude of human rights violations, including genocide, today.

Samuel Totten is affiliated with the University of Arkansas, College of Education, 107A Peabody Hall, Fayetteville, AR 71701.

[Haworth co-indexing entry note]: "Examining the Holocaust Through the Lives and Literary
Works of Victims and Survivors: An Ideal Unit of Study for the English Classroom." Totten, Samuel.
Co-published simultaneously in *The Reference Librarian* (The Haworth Press, Inc.) No. 61/62, 1998,
pp. 165-188; and: *The Holocaust: Memories, Research, Reference* (ed: Robert Hauptman, and Susan
Hubbs Motin) The Haworth Press, Inc., 1998, pp. 165-188. Single or multiple copies of this article are
available for a fee from The Haworth Document Delivery Service [1-800-342-9678, 9:00 a.m. - 5:00 p.m.
(EST). E-mail address: getinfo@haworth.com].

While education alone will not lead to the end of discrimination and/or genocide in our world, education can contribute to raising the consciousness of people in regard to what it means to be a caring and just human being in a world rife with indifference, injustice, and brutality. Concomitantly, genocide, in general, and the Holocaust, in particular, as well as those actions that often set the stage for genocide (e.g., prejudice, discrimination, racism, anti-Semitism, ethnic cleansing) are not only within the purview of social studies and history teachers, but also those who teach English. How so? An examination of the aforementioned issues legitimately involves the study of language and its usage. For example, it could involve the study of stereotyping by examining racial slurs and slang and/or the calumny, propaganda and diatribes often targeted at a particular group of people in order to ostracize and isolate them. It might involve an examination of the use of euphemism to hide evil intentions and/or acts (e.g., as in the case of the Nazis' use of "Final Solution" for the total annihilation of the Jewish people). And, of course, the study of powerful literature is a must. The latter combines the cognitive (i.e., thinking and knowing) and affective (i.e., likes/dislikes, feelings, beliefs) domains, which is capable of producing a thought-provoking and unforgettable learning experience.

Too often, we (educators, parents, politicians and others) fail miserably in educating the young to truly care about the world beyond the boundaries of their homes, schools or local community. Ideally, educators and others should strive to create a world in which all citizens truly are their brothers' and sisters' keepers. Ultimately, that would mean that when one *hears about, reads about* or *observes* an injustice being committed, one would not turn away out of apathy or indifference as so many bystanders did during the Holocaust years and have continued to do in the post-World War II years as one genocide after another has been committed in such places as Bangladesh, Burundi, Bosnia, Cambodia, East Timor, and Rwanda.

Fortunately, an ever-greater number of educators across the United States are becoming increasingly interested in *and* engaged in pedagogical activities that focus on issues of prejudice, racism, anti-Semitism, discrimination and genocide. This is evidenced in many different ways. For example, as of May 1997 fourteen states (California, Connecticut, Florida, Illinois, New Jersey, New York, Nevada, North Carolina, Ohio, Pennsylvania, South Carolina, Tennessee, Virginia and Washington) have established various sorts of state recommendations or mandates in regard to teaching about human rights violations, the Holocaust and/or other genocidal acts. Additionally, some states have developed of teacher guides and/or curricula on such issues. On a different but related note, an ever-increasing number of sessions at various annual educational association conventions (including but not limited to the National Council of Teachers of English, the National Council for the Social Studies, the National Middle School Association, and the Association for Supervision and Curriculum Development) are being conducted on such concerns. And, with the establishment of the U.S. Holocaust Memorial Museum and its teacher and administrators' workshops, large numbers of teachers are beginning to develop their own lessons on various facets of the Holocaust.

Not surprisingly, social studies and English teachers are at the forefront of much of this activity. That is possibly due to the fact that these are the two disciplines in which teachers often address key social issues. At the same time, though, as an ever-increasing number of English teachers have become interested in teaching about the Holocaust, many are asking, "How can we do justice to this complex and significant topic and still teach the set curriculum dictated by state and district standards?" It is a significant question that needs to be addressed. It is also a question that I have been wrestling with over the past decade and a half. In wrestling with it, my goal has been to develop various methods and units that provide students with an in-depth—versus a perfunctory or superficial—study of the Holocaust while also focusing on the "stuff" of the English classroom. I began tackling this concern as a beginning English teacher in a combination junior high/high school in Victoria, Australia, and continued my work on it as a high school teacher in rural northern California. Having established some rudimentary ideas, I began to hone them as I proceeded to teach English to 8th, 9th, and 10th grade students at the American School in Israel and eleventh graders at the U.S. House of Representatives Page School in Washington, D.C.

It is worth noting that a study of the kind to be described herein (e.g., an in-depth examination of how an author's life–in this case, an author who lived through the Holocaust–influenced his/her style, content, and themes as a writer) begins to get at what schools often do not avail to students. Most significantly, it provides students with an opportunity to pursue a topic in-depth. As Fred M. Newmann (1988), a professor of education at the University of Wisconsin at Madison, has written:

> We are addicted to coverage. This addiction seems endemic in high schools[,] but it affects all levels of the curriculum, from kindergarten through college. We expose students to broad surveys of the disciplines and to endless sets of skills and competencies. The academic agenda includes a wide variety of topics; to cover them all, we give students time to develop only the most superficial understandings. The press for broad coverage causes many teachers to feel inadequate about leaving out so much content and apologetically mindful of the fact that much of what they teach is not fully understood by their students.
>
> . . . The alternative to coverage, though difficult to achieve, is depth: the sustained study of a given topic that leads students beyond superficial exposure to rich, complex understanding. . . . To gain rich understanding of a topic, students must use a great deal of information, use that information to answer a variety of questions about the topic, and generate new questions that lead to further inquiry. In demonstrating their knowledge of the topic, they should go beyond simple declarative statements to differentiation, elaboration, qualification, and integration. (p. 346)

It also provides students with an opportunity to conduct an unique examination of one of the major events in the history of humanity, the Holocaust. Too often in the past, and even today, many students have not been introduced to this watershed event during their secondary schooling years. As Elliot Eisner (1979), a professor of education at Stanford, has perspicaciously argued:

> . . . what schools do not teach may be as important as what they do teach. I argue this position because ignorance is not simply a void, it has important effects on the kinds of option[s] one is able to consider; the alternatives one can examine, and the perspectives on can view a situation or problem. (p. 83)

Among the other reasons–some of which are related to the above points–why I find the assignment so powerful are: (1) It provides students with an opportunity to become a "classroom expert" on a single author and his/her works; (2) It provides a student with an opportunity to glean unique and powerful insights into how an author's life often influences his/her artistic literary efforts, and this is something that many students, including those in college, never glean; (3) It provides the students with an opportunity to plumb the depths of a person's experiences who has lived through such a watershed event; (4) It provides the students with an opportunity to examine how prejudice, anti-Semitism, racism and hatred of the other can, if allowed to go unchecked, culminate in genocide; and (5) The entire study raises a host of important issues in regard to those who were perpetrators, collaborators, bystanders, and victims, and addresses the fact that everyone in society "plays" one (or more) of those roles when an injustice or atrocity is committed.

THE BIOGRAPHIES OF HOLOCAUST LITTÉRATEURS

The project was purposely designed to be carried out as an independent project, and thus much of the work is done outside of class time. In light of that, the project, for the most part, should not subtract from the time needed for the study of the "mandated" or set curriculum. Put another way, while it is true that certain days may be given over to providing instruction in regard to footnoting, the development of proper bibliographic forms, and/or the sharing of findings by students, *the regular course of study as required by the district or state is still, for the most part, taught each and every day.* This procedure is followed for two key reasons: one, many teachers feel that they cannot take large chunks of time out of their schedules for major projects such as the one about to be described; and two, a project of this nature requires ample time for students to conduct their research and fashion their findings into a cogently written essay.

In light of the sophistication of analysis as well as the "research" involved in a study of this nature, this project is best suited for advanced and/or the most motivated students at the tenth, eleventh and twelfth grade levels. That said, I have used variations of this assignment (where the focus was not on the Holocaust but writers' lives in general) with tenth and eleventh grade students in "regular" (as opposed to advanced) English classes.

In order to cogently delineate the process of the project, I will list each component in chronological order and then briefly discuss it.

1. Prior to having the students undertake this project, I make a concerted effort to provide them with the "tools" to critique a work of literature (e.g., how to ascertain and gain an understanding of literary pieces vis-à-vis their key character development, symbolic structure, allusions, metaphors, motifs, etc.). I *always* interweave this more traditional approach with "reader response theory" in which students respond via their own lives, experiences and perspectives (O'Neill, 1994; Rosenblatt, 1968; Rosenblatt, 1978; Sheridan, 1991). As O'Neill (1994) has noted:

> Basically, reader response theory differs most radically from previous theories about teaching literature in the degree of emphasis placed on the reader's response to an interpretation of the text . . . In reader response theory, the text's meaning is considered to reside in the 'transaction' between the reader and the text, not from the text alone.
>
> . . . In practice, reader response theory considers very carefully how students respond intellectually and emotionally to the text . . . By validating students' responses, teachers can spark a lively discussion from which a careful literary analysis will flow. . . . Rather than beginning with a discussion of symbolism or metaphor, for example, teachers should allow an exploration of these aspects to develop from students' own observations about the work.
>
> . . . the emphasis on getting students to respond to the literature doesn't mean that any response is as good as another. Students are continuously urged to return to the text to find validation for their views. (pp. 7, 8)

Personally and philosophically, I think it is extremely important that students have ample opportunity to respond to a work from their own perspective, but also think it is important to teach the students that there are systematic and engaging ways to begin to gain a deeper appreciation of a work through an understanding of an author's use of allusions, metaphors, motifs, symbols, etc.

In regard to the latter concern, I have found that a particularly engaging and effective manner for doing this is to initially have the students create their own characters and place them in a setting in which they include other characters (including antagonists) with whom they interact. Gradually, as I teach various literary conventions (e.g., characterization, setting, conflict, dialogue, personification, analogy, smile, metaphor, allusion, symbol, irony, etc.) and provide powerful and clear examples of such literary conventions found in highly engaging pieces of literature, I require the students to add the components, in the most artistic way possible, to their own stories. Through both creating and sharing (e.g., reading, listening and commenting on their own as well as other student developed stories), the students gain a clearer understanding and greater appreciation of the use and value of such conventions in a work of literature.

2. Following the initial exercise I always have the students read a literary work (usually a novel such as *A Separate Peace* by John Knowles) that is engaging, easy to understand, and packed with literary conventions that are fairly readily accessible for those students who have been prepped to detect and analyze them. (Note: A teacher, of course, could have the students read a novel about the Holocaust but if he/she does so, the key–again–is to use a work that is readily accessible to students and packed with powerful symbols, allusions, images, and motifs so that students can gain practice in analyzing a work along the lines suggested above.) During the course of the in-depth study of the literary work, which generally spans a four to six week period of time, the students engage in both reader response [theory] activities as well as a more conventional "literary" analysis of the work. Such a process serves two main purposes: one, to provide the students with opportunities to respond to a novel in two unique and powerful ways; and two, to specifically prepare them for the forthcoming assignment in which they will

be required to develop a major paper where they analyze how an author's life possibly influenced his/her plots, characterization, themes, images, settings, symbols, allusions, motifs, etc.

3. Upon completion of the above two steps, I provide the students with the focus of the assignment: Each student will select an author (a poet, novelist, short story writer, or playwright) who experienced, in some major way, the Holocaust. The student will then conduct an in-depth analysis as to how the author's life possibly influenced his/her plots, themes, character development and use of key images, allusions, symbols, motifs. The final paper may be written in any format (e.g., formal paper; interview or question and answer format; and/or creative use of rhetorical stance methodology where the components of voice, audience, purpose and form are used in a unique fashion but also complement one another–that is, a unique voice is speaking to a specific and unique audience for a specific purpose in a specific and unique mode or format). In all cases, I inform them that they must heed and use sound rules of scholarship by properly citing works they use in their research.

In writing the paper (which generally is about 15-20 pages in length), the students are required to read at least three major works (plays or novels) by the author. If a student selects a poet or short story writer then the student and teacher will need to work out specific requirements. A student is also required to read at least one major biography (that is, one by a noted critic or noted biographer and/or an acclaimed critical biography, e.g., *Paul Celan* by John Felstiner), and three critical essays that have been written by respected scholars. Students are encouraged to rely on both the biographer's and critics' insights as well as their own critical faculties to assess how the author's life possibly influenced the writing of his/her works. If autobiographical works such as Elie Wiesel's *All Rivers Run to the Sea: Memoirs* are available then students should be encouraged to use those as well.

It is the teacher's duty to make sure that there is an ample number of literary works available by each author before encouraging a student to conduct a study of a particular author. That will require the ready availability of an adequate number of novels, short stories, plays or poems, critical essays, and at least one major biography (or, short of that, a solid number of in-depth biographical essays; or at the very least, an ample number of short interviews, biographical statements, and articles and/or autobiography). This is imperative for if there is a dearth of such literature and information then the student is being "set up" for frustration, disappointment and, ultimately, failure.

Students need to be encouraged *and* shown how to be "literary sleuths" for this project. That is, if a complete biography or autobiography does not exist on a particular author then students need to be taught where and how to cull out various types of information about an author's life. For example, students might be encouraged to (1) examine scholarly criticism about an author's work in order to cull out key biographical information; (2) locate interviews with and/or about an author; (3) locate pertinent information from short essays and popular pieces about an author, and/or from introductions to an author's work; (4) make use of such resources as the *Contemporary Authors Series*, Volume 1-47 (Detroit, MI: Gale Research Inc.), *World Authors 1950-1970: A Companion Volume to Twentieth Century Authors* (New York: The H.W. Wilson Company, 1975), and *Who's Who in Twentieth Century Literature* by Martin Seymour-Smith (New York: Holt, Rinehart and Winston, 1976); and (5) possibly write to an author or a scholar who has written extensively about an author in order to solicit key information. In order to enable students to successfully use some of the aforementioned resources (e.g., *Contemporary Authors Series*) as well as others (e.g., *Reader's Guide to Periodical Literature* and pertinent databases), teachers will have to avail their students of their existence as well as teach them how to use them.

The aforementioned volumes are invaluable as students search for key biographical information on an author. For example, the *Contemporary Authors Series* includes information on "approximately 100,000 authors, both living and deceased, a large portion of whom cannot be found in other reference works" (n.p., introductory material to the volume). *World Authors* contains autobiographical and biographical information on 959 authors. It basically follows the same format as its two predecessors: *Twentieth Century Authors*, which was edited by Stanley J. Kunitz and Howard Haycraft in 1942, and included information on 1,800 authors, and *The First Supplement* (which was published in 1955 and in addition to updating the original entries found in *Twentieth Century Authors*, included an additional 700 more).

4. In light of the complexity of the assignment, I make a point of providing my students with at least one example of the type of sophisticated and analytical paper that I expect them to write. In order not to tempt them to model their paper on the example, I make sure that the "example" is on a totally different subject.

Thus, instead of providing a sample paper on the Holocaust, I give them a paper in which a student has studied the life and works of, say, Willa Cather, F. Scott Fitzgerald, Richard Wright, J.D. Salinger, James Baldwin, Sylvia Plath, Truman Capote, Gabriel Garcia Marquez, Aleksandr Solzhenitsyn, George Orwell, or Nadine Gordimer. Providing such an example generally takes the mystery out of the project, and makes them more at ease with what lies ahead.

5. Immediately after providing the students with the focus of the assignment, deliver a short commentary on *at least* twenty authors who have written highly engaging literary works (e.g., poetry, drama, short stories, novels) on some aspect of the Holocaust. Among the authors I generally highlight during this part of the assignment are: Aharon Appelfeld, Tadeusz Borowski, Paul Celan, Charlotte Delbo, Ida Fink, Chaim Grade, Uri Zvi Greenberg, Pierre Julitte, Yitzhak Katzenelson, Ivan Klima, Gertrud Kolmar, Abba Kovner, Jerzy Kosinski, Primo Levi, Jakov Lind, Arnost Lustig, Don Pagis, Miklos Radnoti, Piotr Rawicz, Tadeusz Rozewicz, Nelly Sachs, Andre Schwarz-Bart, Jorge Semprun, Abraham Sutzkever, Wladyslaw Szlengel, and Elie Wiesel. (NOTE: If teachers and/or their students have difficulty locating key information on a good number of these authors, then it is fine to have more than one student conduct a study on a particular author. The key, though, is to make sure that each student does his/her own work. Certainly the use of notecards (e.g., making sure that the students are gleaning different types of information, or at least not all of it being the same or uniform) is one way for teachers to ascertain whether students are, in fact, conducting their own research. If a student decides to study an author not mentioned by the instructor then he/she has to seek the instructor's permission.)

At this point I highlight some of the most fascinating aspects of the aforementioned authors' life experiences and literary efforts.

The key is to whet the students' appetite to discover more about a particular author's life and works and how, if at all, the author's life experiences during the Holocaust influenced his/her plots, themes, and style. In other words, it is the teacher's job to try to "sell" *all* the authors and their works to the students. In light of that, the tone, tenor and type of information relayed should be engaging and informative.

If the teacher is well prepared, each author and his/her works can be covered in a span of two to three minutes. Prior to providing the students with this information, though, they should be told that as they listen to the summaries about the authors they need to write down the names of at least three of the authors they find most intriguing. The key to having them write down at least three is that once students begin to gather information on "their" author, some will invariably find that the lives or works of their first or second choices (e.g., authors) are not as interesting as they initially thought they would be. This method provides them with back-ups.

Alternatively, instead of taking a period to present this information orally (though I think it is worth doing it orally because the teacher can emphasize and add material as he/she presents the information, and by presenting it in an exciting manner one is more likely to engage a student's interest) a teacher could provide some of the more basic information on a handout. Or, the teacher could provide a brief handout with key elements (this way the students will be sure to have something to refer back to as they attempt to select an author to study) and still present the information orally— though not necessarily all the information on the sheet.

In introducing such writers to the students, my comments would be something along the following line: "*Elie Wiesel*, who was born in the town of Sighet in Transylvania in 1928 and grew up in a highly religious Jewish family, was deported at the age of about thirteen along with his family to Auschwitz where his mother and youngest sister were immediately murdered in a gas chamber. Following a series of harrowing experiences, including a death march to Buchenwald, after which his father perished, Elie was liberated from the camps and eventually reunited with an older sister in Paris. For many years, and primarily due to the trauma he experienced under the Nazis, he refused to speak. Later, he began to write of his experiences and eventually became a well known novelist and humanitarian. He now resides in New York City and teaches at Boston University. In 1986 he was the recipient of the Nobel Prize for Peace for his work on the behalf of those across the globe who have been deprived of their human rights. Among his most well known and powerful works is *Night*, a vivid depiction of what he experienced in Auschwitz. His description of his deportation and eventual arrival at Auschwitz is unforgettable: "The Hungarian police made us get in–eighty people in each [box] car . . . The cars were sealed . . . Lying down was out of the question, and we were only able to sit by deciding to take turns. . . . After two days of traveling we began to be tormented by thirst. Then the heat became unbearable. . . . On the first day of the journey [Madame Schachter, who had gone out of her mind] began to moan and to keep asking why she had been separated from her family. As time went on, her cries grew hysterical . . . The heat, the thirst, the pestilential stench, the suffocating lack of air–these were as nothing compared with these screams which tore us to shreds. A few days more and we should all have started to scream too. . . . As the train stopped, we saw this time flames were gushing out of a tall chimney into the black sky. We looked at the flames in the darkness. There was an abominable odor floating in the air" (Wiesel, 1982, pp. 32, 33, 34, 36, 38).

"*Tadeusz Borowski*, who was born to Polish parents in the Russian Ukraine in 1922, published poetry both prior to and following World War II. Following the war, he also published short stories. When Borowski was four years old, his father was exiled to a labor camp near the Arctic Circle, and just four years later his mother was deported to Siberia. This resulted in Borowski being raised by an aunt. By 1934 both of his parents had been set free and he was reunited with them in Warsaw, Poland.

"Due to his association with an underground group of writers who were critical of the Nazis, he was arrested by the Gestapo and for the next three years (1942-1945) he was incarcerated in the notorious death camp named Auschwitz as well as the infamous concentration camp named Dachau. While incarcerated, he served as a kapo or low level functionary for the Nazis. His most famous work, *This Way for the Gas, Ladies and Gentlemen*, is comprised of harrowing short stories about life and death in the camps. For a variety of reasons, including the impact of what he had witnessed during his incarceration in Auschwitz and Dachau, he committed suicide in 1951. He was not yet thirty years old."

"*Abba Kovner* was born into a Jewish family in the Ukraine in 1918. During the Nazi reign of terror against the Jews, he was involved in armed resistance in the Vilna Ghetto. He escaped from the ghetto and led Jewish partisan units against the Nazis in the outlying forests. (In the Rudninkai Forest, Kovner commanded a Jewish unit made up of Vilna ghetto fighters, as well as the Jewish Camps "Revenge" battalion.) He eventually emigrated to Israel where he became a well known poet who wrote extensively about the Holocaust."

"*Aharon Appelfeld*, a Jew who was born in the Bukovina region of Romania in 1932, was torn from his family when he was eight years old after the Germans killed his mother and sent his father to a labor camp. Appelfeld was also eventually incarcerated in the camp but escaped and spent the next three years hiding in the woods. When he was eleven he was discovered by Russian troops and became a kitchen helper in the Soviet army. In 1945, upon the conclusion of World War II and at the age of thirteen, Appelfeld was sent to a displaced persons camp in Italy. A year later, at the age of fourteen, he emigrated to Palestine, which is now known as Israel. Under the assumption that his father perished in the labor camp, he began to make a new life for himself. It was not until 1960, at the age of 28, that he discovered that his father was still alive and also a resident of Israel. Appelfeld has written numerous short stories and novels about various aspects of the Holocaust."

In certain cases I have read the students a poem and/or an excerpt from a short story or a novel, again, to whet the students' appetites. For example, among the many pieces I have read to the students are an excerpt from Tadeusz Borowski's *This Way for the Gas, Ladies and Gentlemen.*

> A cheerful little station, very much like any other provincial railway stop: a small square framed by tall chestnuts and paved with yellow gravel. Not far off, beside the road, squats a tiny wooden shed, uglier and more flimsy than the ugliest and flimsiest railway shack; farther along lie stacks of old rails,

heaps of wooden beams, barracks parts, bricks, paving stones. This is where they load freight for Birkenau: supplies for the construction of the camp, and people for the gas chambers. Trucks drive around, load up lumber, cement, people–a regular daily routine.

"The transport is coming," somebody says. We spring to our feet, all eyes turn in one direction. Around the end, one after another, the cattle cars begin rolling in . . . The train backs into the station, a conductor leans out, waves his hand, blows a whistle. The locomotive whistles back with a shrieking noise, puffs, the train rolls slowly alongside the ramp. In the tiny barred windows appear pale, wilted, exhausted human faces, terror-stricken women with tangled hair, unshaven men. They gaze at the station in silence. And then suddenly, there is a stir inside the cars and a pounding against the wooden boards.

Water! Air!–weary, desperate cries. (From "This Way for the Gas, Ladies and Gentlemen" by Tadeusz Borowski, p. 33-34, 36 in *This Way for the Gas, Ladies and Gentlemen* by Tadeusz Borowski (New York: Penguin Books. 1976))

At the conclusion of this session, the students peruse the literary works or biographies (or other biographical information) of those authors they are considering for the focus of their study. A quick examination, I explain, may facilitate and expedite their selection of an author. (Note: Ideally, a teacher should bring both literary works and biographies of the various authors to class for this activity. Alternatively, of course, a teacher could take the students to the library during class.)

At this juncture it is important for the teacher to inform the students that while he/she (the teacher) has selected those authors whose lives are fascinating and/or whose works are extremely engaging, they have the right and opportunity to select another author for the study as long as his/her life has been informed in some major way by the Holocaust.

6. At the outset of the students' study (and ideally, throughout the course of the study), *it is imperative* to provide the students with an overview of some of the major issues of the Holocaust. This will assist the students to contextualize what they're reading and study-

ing. Among the facts and issues teachers might consider for such an overview are: the definition of genocide, a definition of the Holocaust, what the Holocaust was, who the Nazis were and why and how they came to power, the steps the Nazis took to isolate and deprive Jews and others of their rights, the various reasons as to why the Nazis wanted to kill large numbers of innocent people, the ways in which the Nazis carried out their policy of genocide, and why and how the Holocaust is unique vis-à-vis the issue of genocide. Certainly there are many other facts, issues and concerns that a teacher could address, and ideally these should be addressed in class as they bubble up out of the students' research.

Excellent resources (which are highly readable and accessible to young people) for discussions of the history are: *The World Must Know: The History of the Holocaust as Told in the United States Holocaust Memorial Museum* by Michael Berenbaum (Boston: Little, Brown and Company, 1993); *Tell Them We Remember: The Story of the Holocaust* by Susan D. Bachrach (Boston: Little Brown, 1994); *The Destruction of the European Jews* by Raul Hilberg (New York: Holmes and Meier, 1985); an essay entitled "Holocaust: The Genocide of the Jews" by Donald L. Niewyk (in Samuel Totten, William S. Parsons and Israel W. Charny (Eds.) *Genocide in the Twentieth Century: Critical Essays and Eyewitness Accounts* (New York: Garland Publishers, 1995)); the series of articles in the October 1995 special issue ("Teaching About the Holocaust") of *Social Education*, *59*(6) edited by Samuel Totten, Stephen Feinberg and Milton Kleg. Included in the latter are two particularly helpful pieces of information developed by the U.S. Holocaust Memorial Museum and The President's Commission on the Holocaust: "Frequently Asked Questions About the Holocaust" and "The Uniqueness of the Holocaust"; and a pedagogical essay entitled "The Start is as Important as the Finish: Establishing a Foundation for a Study of the Holocaust" by Samuel Totten (forthcoming, *Social Education*).

An informative and interesting film to show at the outset of the study in order to begin to establish a foundation for understanding what the Holocaust was is "Genocide" from "The World at War Series" (available from Arts and Entertainment, 800-423-1212 or write to A&E Video, P.O. Box 2284, South Burlington, Vermont 05407).

7. As we proceed with the project, certain days are taken to present and teach certain components critical to the project. Thus, for example, early on in the process, we spend at least two days on the "whys, whens, and hows" of citation (including the proper method for footnoting as well as the issues of paraphrasing and plagiarism). Again, I provide key examples on how to footnote different types of sources (e.g., information from critical essays, biographies, novels, journals, popular magazines, etc.). I also provide examples of correct and incorrect methods of paraphrasing as well as the proper way to cite the sources. Finally, we also go over that which constitutes both subtle and blatant examples of plagiarism.

8. Next, I teach the students procedures for setting up their note cards, which is a key requirement of this project. I provide them with models of well developed note cards and also actually model how to select information and create a series of cards on different topics (e.g., key experiences during youth; major influences, which may be broken down into those involving family members or friends, other authors, teachers, books, experiences such being deported to a ghetto or concentration camp or the murder of a loved one; key symbols or allusions found in a particular work; and soon). Additionally, I teach them how to assign the cards specific code numbers vis-à-vis key topics. In addition to showing them how to develop cards that contain succinct but key information, we also discuss how cards that include scant information may prove to be useless when one goes to write his/her research paper. In illustrating the latter concern, I give the students handouts of positive and negative exemplars, and then we discuss the value and/or weaknesses of each.

At the same time, I go over the most effective way to properly cite a work or another person's words/ideas (e.g., author's name, title of the source, date of publication, page number(s)). I note that complete information along these lines must be included on the cards; and in doing so, explain the rationale for the requirement (e.g., it facilitates the writing of the paper, prevents the need at a later time to seek out pertinent bibliographical information, and provides a check on inadvertent plagiarism).

Next, due dates are established as to when the first, second and third set of cards are due (each set must include a minimum of twenty cards). I explain that after each set of cards is turned in, I will carefully scrutinize each and every card in regard to the amount, type and usefulness of detail included on them as well as the breadth of information included within the set. When critiquing the cards, I make a point of raising questions in regard to anything that is not clear, not detailed enough, marginal or useless information, and/or if the card is bereft of key bibliographical information (e.g., full title of citation, author's name, page number, date of publication, etc.). The cards are returned to the students with a grade and notes as to what, if anything, they need to do to improve their next set of notecards. The reason I require three sets of cards is because it prods students to do ample research. Also, the staggered check of the cards generally cuts down on student procrastination in which they try to research and write a paper at the last minute.

9. I have found that it is always a good idea to periodically provide the students with in-class time to work on their projects. This is a legitimate use of classroom time, and it will avail the teacher of an opportunity to act as a trouble shooter for those students who have questions, concerns, and/or have run into "snags." Equally important, such time will likely help to ease some of the stress and strain students may experience due to the nature of such a project.

10. About once every two and a half to three weeks it's a good idea to devote a class period to a discussion of the students' most interesting and telling findings and/or any problems they have encountered in their research. Initially, students are somewhat reluctant to do this but once the ice is broken and some begin to share their findings, many others become eager to share their own.

It is not unusual for such sessions to naturally lead into discussions of such issues of prejudice, the Nazis' virulent anti-Semitism and racism, the horrors perpetrated by the Nazis as well as a myriad of questions concerning the perpetration of the Holocaust (e.g., whys, hows, whens, etc.). These sessions prove to be the opportune time and place for the teacher to purposely incorporate additional information about the Holocaust. The aim of such sessions should be to assist the students to gain a more thorough understanding of that event and period.

NOTE: For those who wish to have their students examine issues of prejudice, discrimination, racism, and anti-Semitism in a more systematic fashion, he/she could personally conduct special sessions in which the students share their research findings about such issues. For example, on a given day (spaced every couple of weeks throughout the study), students could be required to bring in examples from both an author's life and works that speak to the incipient prejudice and ongoing and more blatant discrimination and brutality that they and their characters faced/face during the Nazi onslaught. At this time, the students could address pertinent questions posited either by the teacher and/or themselves, thus lending a certain coherence to the discussion. Among such questions might be: What were the first signs of people acting upon their prejudices? Did the government issue edicts, pass legislation, etc., in an attempt to ostracize a certain group of people? How did various groups react to the ever-increasing discriminatory acts?

To establish an even more systematic procedure, the teacher could require students to prepare short talks and handouts delineating their major findings along the aforementioned lines. These "discussion starters" could serve as the basis for gaining a deeper understanding of such issues.

All of the above approaches enable students to explore the subtle and not so subtle effects of discriminatory actions, and how they can, if left unchecked or purposely fanned, manifest themselves in ever-increasing and more overt actions that over time can become, sometimes through "legal" means, a way to isolate and create scapegoats of innocent people. It also provides a unique lens on how, in certain extreme cases, those who are cast as outsiders can become, when a society acts out its hate in a barbaric fashion, victims of mass murder.

CONCLUSION

Teachers often avoid projects of this nature because of their complexity and/or time-consuming nature. However, if set up in a systematic manner neither situation should prove overwhelming. Indeed, I have found that students love to be challenged, especially when they have ongoing guidance and support. When approached by both the instructor and the students in a systematic manner, the project becomes much less daunting. Also, by assigning this project as an outside project, teachers and students are less overwhelmed by the time factor. That said, since a great deal of the research that *is completed outside of class*, teachers need to provide their students with an ample period of time to work on this project. That basically translates into a minimum of three to four months. And, as long as teachers set up a check and balance system to prevent the students from procrastinating, the lengthy period of time poses no problem.

When all is said and done, the results of this project are extremely exciting. The thought, work, and creativity that goes into them is often quite remarkable. The learning that results from the project is equally astounding. Not surprisingly, at the outset of the project many complain vociferously about the heavy workload, but by the end many are proud of their final accomplishment.

The project constitutes a study that immerses students in a "world" (the world of Nazi-occupied Europe, the ghettos, and the concentration and death camps) that is not only new to them but one which engages them in wrestling with such key issues as prejudice, discrimination, anti-Semitism, racism, stereotyping, and the roles of perpetrators, collaborators, and bystanders. Indeed, it is one which makes them ponder what it means to live in a world where such horrors could be perpetrated. At one and the same time, through the study of the literature and the author's lives, it also engages them in a study of how victims and survivors have taken their experiences and forged literature and new lives out of horrific sorrow and pain.

As educational philosopher Maxine Greene (1988) has perspicaciously noted:

> It is through and by means of education . . . that individuals can be provoked to reach beyond themselves. . . . It is through and by means of education that they may become empowered to think about what they are doing, to become mindful, to share meaning, to conceptualize, to make varied sense of their lived worlds. It is through education that preferences

may be released, languages learned, intelligences developed, perspectives opened, possibilities discovered. (p. 12)

Over the years, it has been my ardent hope and goal that the project described in this essay has, at least for a good number of students, resulted in the sentiments expressed by Maxine Greene.

REFERENCES

Eisner, Elliot (1979). *The Educational Imagination: On the Design and Evaluation of School Programs*. New York: Macmillan.

Friedlander, Henry (1979). "Toward a Methodology of Teaching About the Holocaust." *Teachers College Record*, *80*:519-542.

Greene, Maxine (1988). *The Dialectic of Freedom*. New York: Teachers College Press.

Knowles, John (1988). *A Separate Peace*. New York: Bantam Books.

Newmann, Fred (January 1988). "Can Depth Replace Coverage in the High School Curriculum?" *Phi Delta Kappan*, *69*(5):345-348.

Niewyk, Donald (1995). "Holocaust: The Genocide of the Jews," pp. 167-207. In Samuel Totten, William S. Parsons, and Israel W. Charny (Eds.) *Genocide in the Twentieth Century: Critical Essays and Eyewitness Accounts*. New York: Garland Publishers.

O'Neill, John (1994). "Rewriting the Book on Literature: Changes Sought in How Literature is Taught, What Students Read . . ." *ASCD Curriculum Update*, 1-4, 6-8.

Rosenblatt, Louise M. (1968). *Literature as Exploration*. New York: Noble and Noble.

Rosenblatt, Louise M. (1978). *The Reader, the Text, and the Poem: The Transactional Theory of the Literary Work*. Carbondale, IL: Southern Illinois University Press.

Sheridan, Daniel (November 1991). "Changing Business as Usual: Reader Response in the Classroom." *College English*, *53*(7):804-814.

SELECT BIBLIOGRAPHY

Autobiographies, Memoirs, and Interviews

Appelfeld, Aharon, and Roth, Philip (1994). *Beyond Despair Three Lectures and a Conversation with Philip Roth*. New York: Fromm International.

Cargas, Harry James (1976). *In Conversation with Elie Wiesel*. New York: Paulist Press.

Delbo, Charlotte (1990). *Days and Memory*. Marlboro, VT: Marlboro Press.

Delbo, Charlotte (1968). *None of Us Will Survive*. Boston: Beacon Press.

Grade, Chaim (1986). *My Mother's Sabbath Days*. New York: Knopf.

Katzenelson, Yitzhak (n.d.). *Vittel Diary*. Tel Aviv: Ghetto Fighters' House.

Levi, Primo (1985). *Moments of Reprieve: A Memoir of Auschwitz*. New York: Summit Books.

Levi, Primo (1985). *Survival in Auschwitz* and *The Reawakening: Two Memoirs*. New York: Summit Books.

Lind, Jakov (1969). *Counting My Steps: An Autobiography*. New York: Macmillan.

Radnoti, Miklos (1985). *Under Gemini: A Prose Memoir and Selected Poetry*. Athens, OH: Ohio University Press.

Wiesel, Elie (1995). *All Rivers Run to the Sea: Memoirs*. New York: Alfred A. Knopf. [First of two volumes.]

Wiesel, Elie (1982). *Night*. New York: Bantam.

Wiesel, Elie (1978). "Why I Write." In Alvin H. Rosenfeld and Irving Greenberg (Eds) (1978). *Confronting the Holocaust: The Impact of Elie Wiesel*. Bloomington: Indiana University Press.

Biographies and Biographical Selections

Bloch, Sam E. (January 1992). "Abba Kovner–His Life & Poetry." *Midstream*, pp. 36-38.

Chalfen, Israel (1993). *Paul Celan: A Biography of His Truth*. New York: Persea Books.

Colin, Amy (1991). *Paul Celan: Holograms of Darkness*. Bloomington: Indiana University Press.

Felstiner, John (1995). *Paul Celan: Poet, Survivor, Jew*. New Haven: Yale University Press.

Friedlander, Albert H. (1993). *Riders Towards the Dawn: From Holocaust to Hope*. New York: Continuum. [Note: This volume contains numerous short but informative biographical statements on such authors as Aharon Appelfeld, Paul Celan, Uri Zvi Greenberg, Abba Kovner, Primo Levi, Don Pagis, and Nelly Sachs.]

Harshav, Benjamin (1991) "Sutzkever: Life and Poetry," pp. 1-23. In Barbara and Benjamin Harshav (Eds. and Translators) *A. Sutzkever: Selected Poetry and Prose*. Berkeley: University of California Press.

Kott, Jan (1980). "Introduction" [A biographical statement about Tadeusz Borowski], pp. 11-26. In Tadeusz Borowski's *This Way for the Gas, Ladies and Gentlemen*. New York: Penguin.

Rosenbloom, Noah H. (1980). "The Threnodist and the Threnody of the Holocaust," pp. 91-133. In Noah H. Rosenbloom's (Ed.) *Yitzhak Katzenelson's The Song of the Murdered Jewish People*. Beit Lohamei Haghetaot, Israel: Hakibbuttz Hameuchad Publishing House, 1980. [A short but informative biographical essay on Yitzhak Katzenelson.]

Wirth, Andrej (Summer 1967). "A Discovery of Tragedy: The Incomplete Account of Tadeusz Borowski." *Polish Review*, *12*(3):45-46.

Literary Criticism (while much of this criticism should be accessible to secondary level students, some of it is rather abstruse. That said, many of these works, including the most accessible, include key biographical information about certain authors)

Aaron, Frieda W. (1990). *Bearing the Unbearable: Yiddish and Polish Poetry in the Ghettos and Concentration Camps: Yiddish and Polish Poetry in the Ghettos and Concentration Camps*. Albany, NY: State University of New York Press.

Aaron, Frieda W. (1983). "Poetry in the Holocaust Dominion," pp. 119-131. In Randolph L. Braham (Ed.) *Perspectives on the Holocaust*. Boston: Kluwer Nijhoff Publishing. [Includes a critique of some of the poetry by Katzenelson, Sutzkever, and Szlengel.]

Alexander, Edward (1979). "Holocaust and Rebirth: Moshe Flinker, Nelly Sachs, and Abba Kovner," pp. 31-71. In Edwards' *The Resonance of Dust: Essays on Holocaust Literature and Jewish Fate*. Columbus, OH: Ohio State University Press.

Alexander, Edward (1979). *The Resonance of Dust: Essays on Holocaust Literature and Jewish Fate*. Columbus, OH: Ohio State University Press.

Bahr, Ehrhard (1980). *Nelly Sachs*. Munchen, Germany: Beck.

Cargas, Harry James (Ed.) (1978). *Responses to Elie Wiesel*. New York: Persea Books.

Ezrahi, Sidra DeKoven (1994). "Conversation in the Cemetery: Dan Pagis and the Prosaics of Memory," in pp. 121-133. In Geoffrey H. Hartman (Ed.) *Holocaust Remembrance: The Shapes of Memory*. Cambridge, MA: Blackwell Publishers.

Ezrahi, Sidra Dekoven (1982). *By Worlds Alone: The Holocaust in Literature*. Chicago: The University of Chicago Press.

Fine, Ellen (1983). *The Legacy of Night: The Literary Universe of Elie Wiesel*. Albany, NY: State University of New York Press.

Glenn, Jerry (1973). *Paul Celan*. New York: Twayne Publishers.

Lamont, Rosette C. (1983). "Holocaust Imagery in Contemporary French Literature, pp. 133-147. In Randolph L. Braham (Ed.) *Perspectives on the Holocaust*. Boston: Kluwer Nijhoff Publishing. [Includes a critique of Charlotte Delbo's work and provides some key biographical information about her.]

Langer, Lawrence L. (1995). *Admitting the Holocaust: Collected Essays*. New York: Oxford University Press.

Langer, Lawrence L. (1995). *Art from the Ashes: A Holocaust Anthology*. New York: Oxford University Press.

Langer, Lawrence L. (1995). "Aharon Appelfeld and the Language of Sinister Silence," pp. 125-137. In Lawrence L. Langer's *Admitting the Holocaust. Collected Essays*. New York: Oxford University Press.

Langer, Lawrence L. (1978). "Charlotte Delbo and a Heart of Ashes," pp. 201-244. In Langer's *The Age of Atrocity: Death in Modern Literature*. Boston: Beacon Press.

Langer, Lawrence L. (1982). "Elie Wiesel: Divided Voice in a Divided Universe," pp. 131-189. In Langer's *Versions of Survival: The Holocaust and the Human Spirit*. Albany, New York: State University of New York Press.

Langer, Lawrence L. (1982). "Gertrud Kolmar and Nelly Sachs: Bright Visions and Songs of Lamentation," pp. 191-250. In Langer's *Versions of Survival: The Holocaust and the Human Spirit*. Albany, New York: State University of New York Press.

Langer, Lawrence L. (1975). *The Holocaust and the Literary Imagination*. New Haven, CT: Yale University Press.

Lavers, Norman (1982). *Jerzy Kosinski*. Boston: Twayne.

Leftwich, Joseph (1971). *Abraham Sutzkever: Partisan Poet*. New York: Thomas Yoseloff.

Ramras-Rauch, Gila (1994). *Aharon Appelfeld: The Holocaust and Beyond*. Bloomington, IN: Indiana University Press.

Rosenfeld, Alvin H. (1980). *A Double Dying: Reflections on Holocaust Literature*. Bloomington: Indiana University Press.

Rosenfeld, Alvin H. (February 1974). "Jakov Lind and the Trial of Jewishness." *Midstream 20*:71-75.

Rosenfeld, Alvin H. (November 1971). "Paul Celan" in *Midstream 17*:5-80.

Rosenfeld, Alvin H. (1978). "The Problematics of Holocaust Literature, pp. 1-30. In Alvin H. Rosenfeld and Irving Greenberg (Eds) *Confronting the Holocaust: The Impact of Elie Wiesel*. Bloomington: Indiana University Press.

Rosenfeld, Alvin H., and Greenberg, Irving (Eds) (1978). *Confronting the Holocaust: The Impact of Elie Wiesel*. Bloomington: Indiana University Press.

Syrkin, Marie (May 1966). "The Literature of the Holocaust." *Midstream 12*:3-20.

Syrkin, Marie (March 1967). "Nelly Sachs–Poet of the Holocaust." *Midstream*, pp. 13-23.

Wisse, Ruth (1979). "The Ghetto Poems of Abraham Sutzkever." In *Jewish Book Annual*, NY: Jewish Book Council.

Adjunct Materials

Darsa, Jan (1991). "Educating About the Holocaust," pp. 175-193. In Israel W. Charny (Ed.) *Genocide: A Critical Bibliographic Review. Vol. 2*. London and New York: Mansell Publishers and Facts on File, respectively.

Friedlander, Henry (1979). "Toward a Methodology of Teaching About the Holocaust." *Teachers College Record*, *80*:519-542.

Fuchs, Elinor (Ed.) (1991). *Plays of the Holocaust: An International Anthology*. New York: Theater Communications Groups.

National Council for the Social Studies (October 1995). Special Issue ("Teaching About the Holocaust") of *Social Education* co-edited by Samuel Totten, Stephen Feinberg and Milton Kleg, *59*(6).

Niewyk, Donald (1995). "Holocaust: The Genocide of the Jews," pp. 167-207. In Samuel Totten, William S. Parsons, and Israel W. Charny (Eds.) *Genocide in the Twentieth Century: Critical Essays and Eyewitness Accounts*. New York: Garland Publishers.

Parsons, William S., and Totten, Samuel (1994). *Guidelines for Teaching About the Holocaust*. Washington, D.C.: United States Holocaust Memorial Museum.

Skloot, Robert (1988). *The Darkness We Carry: The Drama of the Holocaust*. Madison: University of Wisconsin.

Totten, Samuel (forthcoming). "Incorporating Poetry into a Study of the Holocaust via Reader Response Theory." *The Social Studies*.

Totten, Samuel; Feinberg, Stephen; and Fernekes, William (forthcoming). *Teaching About the Holocaust: Critical Essays*. Needham Heights, MA: Allyn and Bacon Publishers.

United States Holocaust Memorial Museum (1993). *Annotated Bibliography* [on the Holocaust]. Washington, D.C.: Author.

Selected Issues
in Holocaust Denial Literature
and Reference Work

Suzanne M. Stauffer

SUMMARY. The author presents some of the personal issues related to providing access to Holocaust denial materials, and explores the subjective reasons which make this topic a unique problem. It is suggested that librarians afford themselves of various opportunities to educate the public about this material, while providing access to it in accordance with Constitutional rights and professional practice. *[Article copies available for a fee from The Haworth Document Delivery Service: 1-800-342-9678. E-mail address: getinfo@haworth.com]*

One day, while serving on the reference desk in a public library in the New York City area, I was approached by a very blonde young man, who, in a heavy German accent, asked if we had "The Protocols of the Elders of Zion." My immediate, internal reaction was "Nazi!", but, knowing my duty, I checked the on-line catalog. We did not own it. I told him that we did not own it, but I did not mention that we might be able to acquire it through inter-library loan, or conduct any kind of a reference interview, which was my standard practice. I have felt ashamed and ambivalent about my reaction ever since.

Suzanne M. Stauffer is a doctoral student in the Department of Library and Information Sciences, University of California, Los Angeles, Los Angeles, CA 90095-1521.

[Haworth co-indexing entry note]: "Selected Issues in Holocaust Denial Literature and Reference Work." Stauffer, Suzanne M. Co-published simultaneously in *The Reference Librarian* (The Haworth Press, Inc.) No. 61/62, 1998, pp. 189-193; and: *The Holocaust: Memories, Research, Reference* (ed: Robert Hauptman, and Susan Hubbs Motin) The Haworth Press, Inc., 1998, pp. 189-193. Single or multiple copies of this article are available for a fee from The Haworth Document Delivery Service [1-800-342-9678, 9:00 a.m. - 5:00 p.m. (EST). E-mail address: getinfo@haworth.com].

189

I relate this incident because I believe that it reflects the feelings of many of us when it comes to Holocaust denial literature. We provide access to information on every other topic without restriction or reservation. We meet challenges to other controversial literature as professionals and as individuals, relying on both our professional and our personal ethics to respond to those who would control access to information. For instance, most libraries bought "The Bell Curve," even though, or precisely because, its racist pronouncements about intelligence were contradicted by nearly every reputable expert in the field, responding not only to demand for the work, but also believing that open discourse is the most effective means for educating the public about any issue.

And what about the patron who is truly confused, having heard only bits and pieces from each side? Or the patron doing legitimate research, or reading this material in order to be able to refute it? Do we require a justification or rationale from patrons doing research in any other area?

So, why is this issue different from all these other issues? First, for the obvious reason that the Holocaust is a documented, historical fact. While the causes and meaning of the Holocaust are still being uncovered, discussed, and interpreted, the occurrence itself is not a matter of conjecture, debate, or belief. That six million Jews were exterminated is not a matter of ideology, philosophy, or theology, it is an historical fact. So, it is understandable that many librarians may feel that providing Holocaust denial information is, essentially, providing misinformation, fabrication, and outright lies.

More importantly, I believe that, as much as anything else, it is because we find ourselves having to meet challenges not only from our patrons, but from ourselves. Our professional ethics require one stance and our personal ethics demand another. The question is as much "How do I convince myself that access to this information is a 'right'?", as it is, "How do I respond to public challenges to this material?" In fact, answering the challenges of the public may be easier than answering the challenges from ourselves. For that reason, I am not going to quote the "Library Bill of Rights" or the First Amendment, because we all know what they say, we accept them, and we abide by them, when we do not champion them, but in this case, they may not be enough to allow us to do our jobs and to feel good about ourselves. For the same reason, I have elected not to present statistics about normative practice, historical precedence, or other objective measures, because this is a subjective, emotional issue to which such arguments are irrelevant.

We are, justifiably, repulsed, repelled, and disgusted by the claims of these authors, we feel that their works are an affront and an outrage to the suffering and death of millions of innocents, and we fear, perhaps also justifiably so, that such fallacies may ultimately lead to like persecution and oppression of minorities once again. However, we also know that one of the first steps taken by a tyrannical, oppressive, totalitarian state is the control of the presses and the censoring of information.

A new facet to this problem is the presence of such materials on the Internet, some of it sponsored by "hate groups," others by otherwise reputable professionals, such as Professor Butz at Northwestern University. We may have been able to avoid buying this material by resorting to collection development policies, lack of community interest, and the availability of inter-library loan for those few who requested the material, but how will we justify filtering those sites or refusing to aid in searching for them, when they are available to individuals for no additional charge and require no storage space?

I raise these issues without knowing exactly how to respond to them, except to suggest that in this case, as in so many others, education is the only acceptable response. This may mean that we will have to re-evaluate our duties and responsibilities as reference librarians, if we believe that we only provide access to information without advice on what it is and how to use it. That is an issue for another series of papers, and may never be finally resolved, but I would like to suggest that, although it may not have been recognized, advice, guidance, and education about information has always been a function of reference work, and the most effective librarians are those who can do more than point the patron to the right source. Most of us routinely advise patrons about the sources of information, the reliability of those sources, and the availability of other sources of information on the same topic; if a patron asks for "Consumer Reports," don't we generally suggest that she also might want to consult "Consumer's Digest"?

In addition to direct referrals to supplementary sources, this guidance may take other forms, some subtle, some more obvious. For instance, I was one of those librarians who responded to the Library of Congress when it polled Judaica librarians on their feelings about the classification of this material. The result is that we now have a separate LC classification, so that these items are no longer shelved cover-to-cover with Holocaust studies, but are grouped together in a different area. This is a subtle method of signaling that these items do not hold the same intellectual status as the recognized, accepted works. Public librarians can request the same treatment from their cataloging agencies, or create a new classification at the local level, if necessary.

This same poll also resulted in a new subject heading, "Holocaust, Jewish (1939-1945)–Errors, inventions, etc.", which sends quite a different message from "Controversial literature," particularly since, for most of us, there is no "controversy" about these works. These are small changes, but they have their own impact and can be opportunities for the librarian to explain the difference between the two classifications or subject headings, and perhaps suggest additional materials that give the "other side" of the issue.

Book displays and library activities commemorating Yom ha'Shoah and other appropriate observances are also opportunities for addressing these materials. Some patrons may complain that works such as these should not be dignified with a response, but they can be reminded that it was precisely such silence and ignorance that allowed the anti-Semitic acts of the Nazis to evolve into the Holocaust; that we must protest this material in public forums so that it cannot have an unseen influence on our society.

A more difficult issue is that of balanced presentations; if a speaker is invited to speak against this material, must one be invited to speak for it? In most libraries, this will be less of an issue, since, thankfully, such proponents will not be locally available. Where they are, then they must be invited, and they must be treated with the same respect as their refuters. What about security for the speakers and the public? And what about possible protesters from both sides? These are all problems that the library administration in each community must deal with, and which may create insoluble barriers to this type of activity. Again, I am raising an issue without a recommendation, but in the hopes of engendering discussion, at the very least.

Access to information on the Internet must follow the same policies as access to information from any other source, and reference librarians must provide assistance to all patrons equally. If it is the practice of the library to bookmark sites, then these sites must be bookmarked. If it is the policy of the library to create links, then links must be created. On the other hand, the Internet offers as many opportunities for educating users about this material as it does for providing access to it. A Web page could be created that would present links to sites such as the Simon Wiesenthal Center as well as to Professor Butz's home page, for instance; searches for all subjects could routinely list a variety of sites, providing a balanced coverage of all topics. In fact, such practices would result in improved reference work in general.

As I said, I am as interested in raising these issues as in responding to them. Education provides the only acceptable answer to both professional and personal concerns; we satisfy our professional ethics by providing access and our personal ethics by protesting those materials, at one and the same time. In fact, since our response to this issue is to provide even more information, our professional ethics are satisfied on more than one level, and we can feel personally gratified in that we have been able to fulfill our professional responsibilities and our private obligations.

Research Strategies
and Reference Sources
About the Holocaust:
A Case Study

Linda K. Menton

SUMMARY. This article uses the Hawaii Holocaust Project as a case study to describe the research strategies and reference sources used in conducting videotaped oral history interviews to document the World War II experiences of three groups of Hawaii residents. It includes a description of the project itself and the research undertaken before interviews were conducted, followed by a discussion a research issue unexpectedly encountered in the course of the project and efforts made to address it. It continues with a brief account of the transcript review process, followed by a description of the reference sources used in adding explanatory notes to the transcripts. *[Article copies available for a fee from The Haworth Document Delivery Service: 1-800-342-9678. E-mail address: getinfo@haworth.com]*

"Do you know what a Seder plate is?" an elderly Jewish woman asked me, as we watched a group of technicians set up lights, cameras and microphones at the Jewish Federation office in Honolulu. "Have you ever heard of *Kristallnacht*?" I was glad, for her

---

Linda K. Menton is Associate Professor of Education, Curriculum Research & Development Group, University of Hawaii, 1776 University Avenue, Honolulu, HI 96822.

[Haworth co-indexing entry note]: "Research Strategies and Reference Sources About the Holocaust: A Case Study." Menton, Linda K. Co-published simultaneously in *The Reference Librarian* (The Haworth Press, Inc.) No. 61/62, 1998, pp. 195-211; and: *The Holocaust: Memories, Research, Reference* (ed: Robert Hauptman, and Susan Hubbs Motin) The Haworth Press, Inc., 1998, pp. 195-211. Single or multiple copies of this article are available for a fee from The Haworth Document Delivery Service [1-800-342-9678, 9:00 a.m. - 5:00 p.m. (EST). E-mail address: getinfo@haworth.com].

sake and my own, that I could answer "yes" to both questions, although I am not Jewish and was born several years after the November 1938 "Night of Broken Glass," when the Nazis destroyed Jewish homes, businesses, and synagogues in Germany and Austria, and then began to round up Jews in large numbers and send them to concentration camps.

The woman's questions were a test of sorts. She was asking, as a prospective interviewee, how much, if anything, I and others involved in the Hawaii Holocaust Project, knew about Judaism and about the historical events that had indelibly marked her life and that of her family. Where would she have to start as she tried to explain why and how she had fled Germany with her two young children in the late 1930s? How much historical context would she have to supply to us and to other "young" people who wanted to interview her? Could she entrust her life story to us?

This woman's questions, asked and unasked, have important implications that transcend her legitimate personal concern. They indicate how important it is that those involved in Holocaust-related projects, including reference librarians who are usually called upon for assistance in the course of such projects, have the research and reference skills necessary for such endeavors.

THE HAWAII HOLOCAUST PROJECT

The Hawaii Holocaust Project was founded in 1986 to preserve the little-known World War II story of the Nisei (second-generation Japanese American) veterans of the 522nd Field Artillery Battalion, a part of the famous all-Nisei 100th Battalion/442nd Regimental Combat Team. Like their comrades in the 100th and the 442nd, after basic training the artillerymen of the 522nd were sent to fight in Italy and France. However, in the final months of the war, the 522nd was detached from the 100th/442nd and temporarily attached to the Seventh Army and sent to fight in Germany. There, in the last days of the war, the 522nd provided supporting fire for seven different Army divisions. Events moved so quickly at that time that the Nisei artillery men sometimes found themselves ahead of the infantry as they pushed further and further into Germany. There in the spring of 1945, these young Japanese American men, some of whom had families interned in relocation camps in the United States, came upon the striped-clothed survivors of Dachau and its many subsidiary camps.[1]

The Hawaii Holocaust Project was subsequently expanded to include the life experiences of two additional groups: Holocaust survivors who now live in Hawaii, and other members of Hawaii's Jewish community who fled Europe before or during the war. Today the project has hundreds of hours of videotaped oral history interviews with thirty-two respondents, seventeen Nisei veterans and one of their Caucasian officers, and fourteen Jews. These interviews were transcribed by the Center for Oral History at the University of Hawaii and were published and distributed in 1991 in a two-volume set entitled *Days of Remembrance: Hawaii Witnesses to the Holocaust.*[2]

PRE-INTERVIEW RESEARCH STRATEGIES

Oral history is a method of "doing" history that often focuses on the life experiences of ordinary people. It can give voice, literally and figuratively, to those whose life stories rarely figure in conventional historical accounts. However, oral history demands more than simply sitting down with an interviewee and turning on a tape recorder or a video camera. Rather, it requires the interviewer to know enough of the time period under discussion, and about the interviewee, to guide the interview and to ask the right question at the right time, without interfering with the interviewee's ability to tell his or her own story.

Preparing to Interview Nisei Interviewees

In preparing to interview the Japanese American respondents for the Hawaii Holocaust Project, we initially sought assistance from other institutions that have conducted similar projects. Both the Witness to the Holocaust Project at Emory University in Atlanta and the Center for Holocaust Studies in Brooklyn, New York sent us the interview questions they had developed for their projects on the liberation of concentration camps.

Although these questionnaires proved helpful, we found that it was necessary for us to devise our own interview questions. Doing so required research in three main subject areas. First, we needed a broad knowledge of Hawaii's history, especially the history of the Japanese immigrants who arrived in the islands in large numbers from the mid-1880s until 1924 to work on Hawaii's numerous sugar plantations. General historical sources such as *A Pictorial History of the Japanese in Hawaii, 1885-1924* by Franklin Odo and Kazuko Sinoto (Honolulu, 1985); *Kodomo No Tame Ni (For the Sake of the Children)* by Dennis Ogawa (Honolulu, 1978); and *Pau Hana: Plantation Life and Labor in Hawaii: 1835-1920* by Ronald Takaki (Honolulu; 1983) were particularly useful.

Second, it was important for us to be conversant with information about the attack on Pearl Harbor and especially how it affected people of Japanese descent in Hawaii and the mainland United States. *Personal Justice Denied*, published by the Commission on Wartime Relocation and the Internment of Civilians (Washington, DC, 1982), was a good place to begin reviewing the extensive literature on this subject. J. Garner Anthony's *Hawaii Under Army Rule* (Honolulu, 1975 reprint) provided valuable information on the subject of martial law in Hawaii.

Finally, we needed to learn about Japanese American soldiers themselves and about the 522nd Field Artillery Battalion. We found excellent information about the formation of 100th Battalion and the 442nd Regimental Combat Team in the War Department records compiled in *Raising American Troops, June 1942-November 1945*, volume 9 of *American Concentration Camps: A Documentary History of the Relocation and Incarceration of Japanese Americans, 1942-1945*, edited by Roger Daniels (New York, 1989). We also found an impressive number of works on Japanese American soldiers, although only Thomas Murphy's *Ambassadors in Arms* about the 100th Battalion (Honolulu, 1954; reprinted 1993), and to some extent *Unlikely Liberators: The Men of the 100th and 442nd* by Masayo Duus (Honolulu, 1987), can be characterized as scholarly. For our purposes we found two books written and published by Nisei veterans (neither was an interviewee) to be particularly useful, *Go For Broke* by Chet Tanaka (Richmond, California, 1982), and John Tsukano's *Bridge of Love* (Honolulu, 1985); both contain numerous photos of the men of the 100th Battalion and the 442nd

Regimental Combat Team. Tsukano's book contains a list of all the officers and men who served in both units. A series of articles written in 1944-45 for the *Honolulu Star-Bulletin* by Lyn Crost, the only war correspondent who covered the 100th and the 442nd exclusively, were available on microfilm. As might be expected, published information about the 522nd Field Artillery Battalion itself was limited. It consisted mainly of recent articles that had appeared in the *Hawaii Herald*, a Japanese American English-language newspaper, and issues of the battalion's 1945 mimeographed newspaper, *High Angle*, owned by several of the men. Copies of a few pages from the 522nd's military records that some of the men had saved over the years were also available.

An Unforeseen Research Issue

After consulting the sources described above, and talking to the Nisei veterans about military insignias, terminology, and rank, we decided it was time to put research aside, finalize our questionnaire, and begin interviewing. As we did so, it became apparent that none of the twelve 522nd "boys" (as the men still refer to each other) in our cohort could pinpoint the exact dates when he had been in the Dachau area in the late spring of 1945, or precisely where he had been. This is understandable in that the camps were not a major military objective and the men we interviewed moved in and out the area very quickly; some remember being there two or three days, others only overnight. Furthermore, as Robert Abzug explains in *Inside the Vicious Heart: Americans and the Liberation of Nazi Concentration Camps* (New York, 1991), Dachau was not only a major concentration camp, it was also the center of a system of many sub-camps spread out over a large geographic area. Despite the brevity of their time there, what the 522nd men witnessed at Dachau and its environs made a life-long impression on them. Their common memories included seeing the dead and the dying, dressed in what many of the men described as blue-and-white pajamas, along the roads of southern Germany; seeing people, probably released inmates, stripping and eating the raw flesh from dead horses or cows; and remembering, although it was late spring, that there was still snow on the ground. Several of the men described feeding ex-prisoners, although in some instances they had specifically been ordered not to.

One of the research issues that troubled the Hawaii Holocaust Project from its inception was whether or not the men of the 522nd Field Artillery Battalion, given the role they played at Dachau as described above, should be called "liberators." There are a few important sources on the subject of liberation, including Jon Bridgeman's *The End of the Holocaust: The Liberation of the* Camps (Portland, Oregon, 1990); *The Liberators: Eyewitness Accounts of the Liberation of Concentration Camps* (New York, 1981) by Yaffa Eliach and Brana Gurewitsch; and Brewster Chamberlin and Marcia Feldman, eds., *The Liberation of Nazi Concentration Camps 1945: Eyewitness Accounts of the Liberators* (Washington DC, 1987). Clearly the actions of the men we interviewed did not correspond with accounts of liberators preserved in these sources, or with the unforgettable images in Movietone newsreels and *Life* magazine. The use of the term "liberator" in stories about the 522nd in the local press provoked outraged responses from other veterans who insisted that the term should be reserved exclusively for the men from the 45th and 42nd divisions who liberated the main Dachau camp on April 29, 1945. We never doubted the veracity of the accounts the men we interviewed told us about their experiences at Dachau. Their truthfulness and our belief in it was fully vindicated. Declassified records from Record Group 407 that we examined at the National Archives indisputably document the presence of the 522nd in the Dachau area in late April and early May 1945, providing supporting fire for other military units. More detailed information on this and other research issues that still need to be addressed before a definitive history of the 522nd Field Artillery Battalion can be written can be found in my article, "Research Reports: Nisei Soldiers at Dachau Spring 1945," *Holocaust and Genocide Studies* 8 (Fall 1994): 258-274.

Preparing to Interview Jewish Interviewees

As in the case of the Nisei veterans, one of the first steps we took in preparing to interview Jewish interviewees was to contact other projects that had done similar work and request their interview questionnaires. These included the Center for Holocaust Studies in Brooklyn, New York and the Wisconsin Survivors of the Holocaust Documentation Project sponsored by the State Historical Society of

Wisconsin, Madison. Again, while these proved very helpful, we soon realized that we needed to design our own interview questions. In the process of doing so, we contacted the Fortunoff Video Archive for Holocaust Testimonies at Yale University, and consulted in person and by telephone with historians, archivists, and librarians at what is now the United States Holocaust Memorial Museum in Washington, DC. We were also very fortunate in being able to consult with Dr. Yehuda Bauer, the eminent Hebrew University Holocaust scholar, when he was in Hawaii.

Those involved in Holocaust-related research must, at a minimum, be conversant with a general history of the time period and with the Holocaust as a historical phenomenon. Initially, this can seem overwhelming because there has been such a proliferation of works on the Holocaust. Bibliographies, of course, provide a good means of gaining some control over this vast volume of material. The bibliography compiled and annotated by Abraham J. Edelheit and Hershel Edelheit, *Bibliography on Holocaust Literature* (Boulder, Colorado, Westview Press, 1986), is a good starting point because the volume is organized by subject, as is *The Holocaust: An Annotated Bibliography* by Harry James Cargas (Chicago, 1985). The four-volume *Encyclopedia of the Holocaust*, edited by Yisrael Gutman (New York, 1990), was also helpful because most entries include suggestions for additional works to consult on specific subjects. *The Index to Jewish Periodicals* describes journals that include articles on various aspects of the Holocaust. The journal *Holocaust and Genocide Studies*, for example, includes a bibliography of Holocaust-related literature based on a subject search of books cataloged by the On-Line Computer Library Center (OCLC).

Two collections of documents were especially valuable for primary research: *The Holocaust: Selected Documents in Eighteen Volumes*, edited by John Mendelsohn (New York, 1982), consists mainly of German documents but includes some American ones from the National Archives as well; and *Documents on the Holocaust*, edited by Yizhak Arad, Yisrael Gutman, and Abraham Margaliot (Jerusalem, 1981).

Of the many books available on the Holocaust, in my opinion, the following are especially valuable for initial research. The three-volume edition of Raul Hilberg's *The Destruction of the European*

Jews (New York, 1985); Nora Levin's *The Holocaust: The Destruction of European Jewry 1933-1945* (New York, 1968); and *The War Against the Jews, 1933-1945* by Lucy Dawidowicz (New York, 1975). Another excellent general source is the planning guide for commemorative programs published yearly under different titles by the United States Memorial Holocaust Council for the Days of Remembrance commemoration held each April. Although each volume focuses on a specific aspect of the Holocaust, the volumes also usually contain an extensive annotated bibliography, a glossary of Holocaust terminology, and a list of Holocaust-related programs and resource centers. Today information about other Holocaust-related projects may also be found on the Internet; this resource was not available when the Hawaii Holocaust Project was undertaken over a decade ago and is not included here.

Our fourteen Jewish interviewees, six men and eight women, were born in four different countries, Austria, Germany, Poland, and Lithuania; the oldest was born in 1908, the youngest in 1940. Although they initially appeared to be a more diverse group than the Nisei respondents, we soon found that despite individual differences in birthplace, class, education, or religious observance, in the context of Hitler's Third Reich, being a Jew transcended any and all other aspect of their identities.

As we listened to those from Germany or Austria, for example, we soon began to hear common themes. Depending on their ages, these interviewees often spoke either of being expelled from school because they were Jews, or of being forced to sell their companies, far below market value at best, in what was called the Aryanization of Jewish-owned businesses. This stranglehold on Jewish economic life, which became compulsory after *Kristallnacht*, also became a galvanizing force for emigration. By 1939, ten of the interviewees had managed to flee Austria or Germany, legally or illegally. Three of these left on children's transports, sponsored by the Quakers or the International Rotary Clubs. Two sources were useful in helping understand the increasingly repressive measures imposed on Jews beginning in 1933: *From Boycott to Annihilation: The Economic Struggle of German Jews, 1933-1943*, a scholarly work by Avraham Barkai (Hanover, New Hampshire, 1989), and a more personal account by Ingeborg Hecht, *Invisible Walls: A German Family Under the Nuremberg Laws* (New York, 1984).

Four of the fourteen Jewish interviewees were concentration camps survivors, two men and two women. One man was taken from the Vilna Ghetto in Lithuania in 1943. Somehow he managed to survive being moved to a succession of camps including Stutthof, Buchenwald, and Sachenshausen. Another man, originally from Poland, was picked up in a *razzia* or roundup of Jews on the streets of Nice, France in 1943. He was sent to Drancy, a transit camp near Paris, and then to Auschwitz-Birkenau where his musicianship as a violinist saved him from death. One interviewee was marched out of the Warsaw Ghetto as a twenty-year-old in the spring of 1943, after the famed uprising there failed. She was taken first to Majdanek and was later moved to a munitions factory where she was liberated by the Russians in January 1945. The youngest camp survivor was born in Berlin in 1940. Her earliest memories are of Theresienstadt in Czechoslovakia, where her mother died; she and her father were imprisoned until May 1945 when the camp was liberated by the Russians.

THE TRANSCRIPT REVIEW PROCESS

All interviews were video-taped and audio-taped simultaneously. At the completion of each interview, the audio-tape of the interview was transcribed. The interviewer then audio-reviewed each transcript, that is, compared it against the audio-tape and made corrections if needed, perhaps a word or phrase misunderstood by the transcriber. The transcript was returned to the Center for Oral History and corrected. The corrected transcript was then sent to the interviewee to review. Interviewees were encouraged to make any additions or deletions they considered necessary. In some instances they made only syntactic changes; others attached additions or explanations. The interviewee's corrections were incorporated into the transcripts and were indicated as such by parentheses. That corrected transcript was then sent to me for minor editing for clarity, verification of dates and place names, and for the addition of explanatory historical notes. Any additions I made were indicated by brackets.

This review process provided the interviewee the opportunity to decide what he or she wanted to leave for the public record. It permitted me to verify dates and place names, and to add explanatory notes to make the transcripts more understandable to the general reader. When the editing process was complete, the transcript was final-typed and proofed. All the interviewees received a bound copy of their transcript and a copy of their videotaped interview.

REFERENCE SOURCES USED
FOR EXPLANATORY NOTES

The purpose of adding historical information in explanatory notes to the interviewees' accounts was to make the transcripts as understandable as possible for the unknown person–historian, linguist, student, family member–who might use them in the future, without cluttering them with unneeded commentary. Doing so required using a variety of sources including dictionaries, maps, atlases and place name references, dictionaries or encyclopedias of history, biographical dictionaries, and dictionaries of terminology, including what might be referred to as Holocaust terminology. Sometimes the needed information might be found in more than one source. For instance, a particular German word might be found in a German-English dictionary and in a dictionary of terms about the Third Reich. Some of the sources used in the research phase of the project, such as the *Encyclopedia of the Holocaust* mentioned above, were consulted again in this phase.

Lexical Aides

All of our interviewees spoke English and all interviews were conducted in English. The Nisei respondents occasionally used words such as *Issei* [first-generation Japanese immigrants from Japan], *kibei* [children of Japanese immigrants born in the United States but educated in Japan], or *Sansei* [third-generation Japanese Americans] in their interviews. These words, as well as Nisei, can be found today in *Webster's Third New International Dictionary*. However, to make the transcripts more understandable to the general reader, these words were translated in the transcripts as were

Japanese words such as *on* [obligation] and *giri* [duty]. The Niseis' interviews also included words from the indigenous Hawaiian language that are commonly used in the islands. *The Hawaiian Dictionary* by Mary Kawena Pukui and Samuel Elbert (Honolulu, 1986 ed.) was the definitive reference for words such as *makai* [toward the ocean], *kanaka* [man], *make* [dead], and *puka* [hole].

As might be expected a variety of German, Polish, Lithuanian, and Yiddish words were found throughout the Jewish interviewees' transcripts. Most of the time a foreign language dictionary provided an adequate translation, although occasionally it was necessary to call and ask an interviewee the meaning of a word or to consult with another native speaker. Again translated words were bracketed, as in "My father was a *Schneider* [tailor]." Foreign language words in the transcripts included proper diacritical marks.

Place Names

As Deborah Lipstadt has described in *Denying the Holocaust: The Growing Assault on Truth and Memory* (New York, 1993), the denial of the Holocaust has become increasingly common. We believed that it was especially important to verify European place names in all our interviewees' transcripts, not because we doubted their accounts, but to preclude others from doing so. In the case of the 522nd interviewees, some of the men had copies of old typewritten military records listing where they had been in Germany in chronological order. However, some of the places listed do not appear on either current or wartime maps, or the spellings have changed or were not correct in the first place. Although we were able to confirm many of the place names mentioned in the men's accounts, using maps and gazetteers, the research needed to reconstruct the movements of the 522nd Field Artillery Battalion in Germany on a day-by-day basis remains to be done. It will require locating the unit's operational maps and then matching them with the many overlay maps that can be found with the 522nd's records at the National Archives.

For the most part, Jewish interviewees were familiar with the location and spellings of place names they mentioned and the location and spelling of concentration camp names. The most indispensable place name reference in this regard proved to be the *Macmillan*

Atlas of the Holocaust by Martin Gilbert (London, 1982). *A Dictionary of the Third Reich* by James Taylor and Warren Shaw (London, 1987), and the *Encyclopedia of the Holocaust*, cited earlier, were also useful in locating place names, in stating where specific camps were located, in identifying different kinds of camps, such as labor and transit camps, and in distinguishing concentration camps that were not explicitly extermination camps from those that were. Other terms used by our interviewees, such as the Sudentenland, the south German land, the section of Czechoslovakia ceded to Germany in 1938 as a result of the Munich Pact, and Ostland, the Baltic states of Estonia. Latvia, and Lithuania, and the western half of Belorussia, that were also occupied by the Nazis, were likewise found in these sources.

Biographical and Historical Dictionaries

General historical encyclopedias of world history, such as the *Macmillan Concise Dictionary of World History* compiled by Bruce Wetterau (New York, 1983), were useful in identifying historical personages or events that interviewees mentioned. Thus when an interviewee made reference to Chamberlain returning from meeting with Hitler in 1938 saying "Peace in our time," the note [Arthur Neville Chamberlain, Prime Minister of Britain 1937-40] was added, as shown here, after Chamberlain's name in the transcript. The biographical dictionary *Men and Women of Hawaii* (Honolulu, 1954 ed.) was useful in identifying the first names and occupations of prominent local residents mentioned in the Nisei veterans' transcripts, while John Tsukano's *Bridge of Love* (Honolulu, 1985) although not a biographical dictionary *per se*, nevertheless was particularly helpful in securing the ranks and names, usually the first names, of the Caucasian officers assigned to lead Japanese American units.

Another source that proved critical in annotating the Jewish interviewees transcripts was *A Dictionary of the Third Reich* mentioned earlier. In addition to place names and camps names, it also contains a wealth of other information about other terms used by the interviewees, including the name of the anti-Semitic newspaper *Der Sturmer* [The Attacker], more general terms like the Afrika Corps and the Wiemar Republic, and the names of various Nazi youth organizations such as the *Bund Deutscher Madel* [League of German Girls]. It also explained German military ranks and organizational names, including commonly used terms such as the SA (*Sturmabteilung*, the Storm Troopers or Brown Shirts), and the SS (*Schutzstaffel*, the Nazi military corps or Black Shirts). The *Dictionary of the Third Reich* also included many words that might be labeled "Holocaust terminology" words that recurred in interviewees' descriptions of life in the camps, such as *Appel* [roll call], *Samellager* [a camp where prisoners were collected before being send to a concentration camp], *Totenmarsch* [death march], *Kapo* [an inmate chosen to supervise other inmates] and many others. *The Terminology of the Third Reich* by Richard Wires (Muncie, Indiana, 1985) was also very helpful, especially in regard to German military organization and ranks.

Other Reference Sources

Occasionally an unfamiliar term would appear in the Nisei interviewees' transcripts, but for the most part American military ranks and language, such as AWOL, or GI, were familiar. In the case of the Jewish interviewees, however, it was sometimes necessary to consult sources such *The Encyclopedia of Judaism*, edited by Geoffrey Wigoder (New York, 1989), or Richard Kennedy's *International Dictionary of Religion* (New York, 1984) for definitions of religious terms such as *minyan* [the minimum number of Jewish males required for the public conduct of a Jewish service], *Kaddish* [in this usage the traditional Hebrew prayer for the dead recited by Jewish mourners], and *bar mitzvah* [the ceremony for admitting a Jewish male as an adult member of the community]. In respect for traditional religious beliefs, the word G-d was not spelled out in the Jewish interviewees' transcripts.

Finally, the interviewees themselves proved to be valuable sources of information. Their knowledge included not only a clear understanding of the complex historical events that had shaped their individual lives, but a grasp of words and meanings that may well become more elusive over time. Perhaps I would have eventually learned the meaning of the word "cosmoline" at some point from a standard source such as a dictionary. But it was much more interesting to learn, from a veteran who had spoken about spending a lot of his time in the early days of the war cleaning rifles that had been packed in the stuff, that cosmoline is a sticky tar-like substance used to prevent rust, and that must be removed with a solvent. It is unlikely that I would ever have figured out that another interviewee's references to "the joint" were not to a place but to the Joint Distribution Committee, an American Jewish welfare organization. The phone calls made to interviewees to clarify these pieces of information often yielded greater insights into their life stories than the facts and figures contained in conventional reference sources.

CONCLUSION

The sources of information described in this paper are not exhaustive. They do not include all the works consulted in preparing to interview our respondents, nor all those used later in verifying information or in adding explanatory notes to their transcripts. They are only a small fragment of the many resources available in one major research library, Hamilton Library at the University of Hawaii, where a keyword search of the word "Holocaust" results in over seven hundred entries. They are presented here as a representative sample of the kinds of resources that historians and reference librarians need to be familiar with as more and more books, articles, documentaries, and other projects about the Holocaust are undertaken.

NOTES

1. In this paper, the term concentration camp refers to the camps established by the Nazis for the confinement, persecution, and mass execution of prisoners. The term relocation camp refers to those camps in the United States established by the War Relocation Authority for Japanese Americans and those of Japanese ancestry under the authority of Executive Order 9066. The term Dachau includes the main Dachau concentration camp and its many subsidiary camps.

2. The Hawaii Holocaust Project was co-founded by Judy Weightman, an assistant professor of law at the University of Hawaii, and the author. The two-volume set of transcripts, *Days of Remembrance: Hawaii Witnesses to the Holocaust*, were published and distributed by the Project and the Center for Oral History at the University of Hawaii in 1991 and were reprinted by the Project in 1994. The transcripts are available at all University of Hawaii libraries and all

public libraries in Hawaii; at the Asian American Studies Center, University of California at Los Angeles; the Center for Holocaust Studies, Brooklyn, New York; the Simon Wiesenthal Center, Los Angeles (videotapes also available); the Library of Congress, Washington, D.C.; the United States Holocaust Memorial Museum, Washington, D.C. (videotapes also available); and at Hebrew University and the Yad Vashem Holocaust Memorial Museum, Jerusalem. Professor Weightman conducted many of the interviews described here. Nine of the interviews were edited and aired on public-access cable television. Professor Weightman also directed and produced a video documentary, *From Hawaii to the Holocaust: A Shared Moment in History* (Santa Monica, California: Direct Cinema Limited, 1993), that incorporates footage from the interviews with archival photos and the interviewees' personal photos, to recount a story that links the life stories of Jews and Japanese Americans in the context of the war.

REFERENCES

Abzug, Robert. *Inside the Vicious Heart: Americans and the Liberation of Nazi Concentration Camps.* New York: Oxford University Press, 1991.

Anthony, J. Garner. *Hawaii Under Army Rule.* Honolulu: University of Hawaii Press, reprint 1975.

Arad, Yizhak, Yisrael Gutman, and Abraham Margaliot, eds. *Documents on the Holocaust.* Jerusalem: Yad Vashem, 1981.

Barkai Avraham. *From Boycott to Annihilation: The Economic Struggle of German Jews, 1933-1943.* Translated by William Templer. Hanover, N.H. University Press of New England, 1989.

Bridgeman, Jon. *The End of the Holocaust: The Liberation of the Camps.* Portland, Oregon: Areopagitica Press, 1990.

Cargas, Harry James. *The Holocaust: An Annotated Bibliography.* 2nd. ed. Chicago: American Library Association, 1985.

Chamberlin, Brewster, and Marcia Feldman. eds. *The Liberation of Nazi Concentration Camps 1945: Eyewitness Accounts of the Liberators.* Washington DC: United States Holocaust Memorial Council, 1987.

Commission on Wartime Relocation and the Internment of Civilians. *Personal Justice Denied.* Washington, DC: Government Printing Office, 1982.

Daniels, Roger, ed. *Raising American Troops, June 1942-November 1945*, volume 9 of *American Concentration Camps: A Documentary History of the Relocation and Incarceration of Japanese Americans, 1942-1945.* New York: Garland Publishing, 1989.

Dawidowicz. Lucy. *The War Against the Jews, 1933-1945.* New York: Bantam Books, 1986.

Days of Remembrance: Planning Guide for Commemorative Programs. Annual; various titles. Washington, DC: United States Holocaust Memorial Holocaust Council.

Duus Masayo. *Unlikely Liberators: The Men of the 100th and 442nd.* Honolulu: University of Hawaii Press, 1983.

Edelheit, Abraham J., and Hershel Edelheit, eds. *Bibliography on Holocaust Literature*. Boulder, Colorado: Westview Press, 1986.

Eliach, Yaffa and Brana Gurewitsch. *The Liberators: Eyewitness Accounts of the Liberation of Concentration Camps*. New York: Center for Holocaust Studies 1981.

Gilbert, Martin. Macmillan. *Atlas of the Holocaust*. New York: Da Capo Press 1982.

Gutman, Yisrael, ed. *Encyclopedia of the Holocaust*. 4 vols. New York: Macmillan, 1990.

Hawaii Herald, 1912-.

Hawaii Holocaust Project. *Days of Remembrance: Hawaii Witnesses to the Holocaust*. 2 vols. Honolulu: Hawaii Holocaust Project and the Center for Oral History, University of Hawaii, 1991.

Hecht, Ingeborg. *Invisible Walls: A German Family Under the Nuremberg Laws*. San Diego: Harcourt Brace Jovanovich, 1984.

Hilberg, Raul. *The Destruction of the European Jews*, 3 vols. rev. ed. New York: Holmes and Meier, 1985.

Holocaust and Genocide Studies: An International Journal. 1986-.

Honolulu Star Bulletin. 1912-.

Index to Jewish Periodicals. 1963-.

Kennedy, Richard. *International Dictionary of Religion*. New York: Crossroads Publishing Co., 1984.

Levin, Nora. *The Holocaust: The Destruction of European Jewry 1933-1945*. New York: Crowell, 1968; Shocken Books, 1973.

Lipstadt, Deborah. *Denying the Holocaust: The Growing Assault on Truth and Memory*. New York: Free Press, 1993.

Men and Women of Hawaii. Honolulu: Star-Bulletin, 1954 ed.

Mendelsohn, John, ed. *The Holocaust: Selected Documents in Eighteen Volumes*. New York: Garland Publishing, 1982.

Menton, Linda K. "Research Report: Nisei Soldiers at Dachau, Spring 1945." *Holocaust and Genocide Studies* 8 Fall 1994, pp. 258-374.

Murphy, Thomas. *Ambassadors in Arms*. Honolulu: University of Hawaii Press, 1954; reprinted 1993.

Odo, Franklin, and Kazuko Sinoto. *A Pictorial History of the Japanese in Hawaii, 1885-1924*. Honolulu: Bishop Museum Press, 1985.

Ogawa Dennis. *Kodomo No Tame Ni (For the Sake of the Children)*. Honolulu: University of Hawaii Press, 1978.

Pukui, Mary Kawena, and Samuel Elbert. *Hawaiian Dictionary*. Honolulu: University of Hawaii Press, 1983 ed.

Takaki, Ronald. *Pau Hana: Plantation Life and Labor in Hawaii: 1835-1920*. Honolulu: University of Hawaii Press, 1983.

Tanaka, Chet. *Go For Broke*. Richmond, CA: Go For Broke Inc., 1982.

Taylor, James, and Warren Shaw. *Dictionary of the Third Reich*. London: Grafton Books, 1987.

Tsukano, John. *Bridge of Love*. Honolulu: Hawaii Hosts, 1985.

Wetterau, Bruce, comp *Concise Dictionary of World History*. New York: Macmillan, 1983.

Wigoder, Geoffrey, ed. *The Encyclopedia of Judaism*. New York: Macmillan, 1989.

Wires, Richard. *The Terminology of the Third Reich*. Muncie, IN: Ball State University, 1985.

Whose Holocaust Is It, Anyway?
The "H" Word
in Library Catalogs

Sanford Berman

On February 24, 1995, I sent this message and enclosures to the Chief of the Library of Congress Cataloging Policy and Support Office:

Dear Colleague,

Kindly explain why *The Story of Karl Stojka: A Childhood in Birkenau* (1992) was assigned the subject heading HOLOCAUST, JEWISH (1939-1945), IN ART when only the Jews can be clearly identified in the 20 reproduced paintings and the Preface unambiguously declares

This catalogue and the exhibition it documents tell the story of the Roma (Gypsy) survivor Karl Stojka and his immediate family through autobiographical art and reminiscences. Stojka's vivid art-as-memory canvases, painted since 1970, chronicle his childhood from 1939 to 1945. These documentary paintings recount his persecution as a Roma Gypsy growing

---

Sanford Berman is Head Cataloger, Hennepin County Library, Minnetonka, MN 55305-1909.

[Haworth co-indexing entry note]: "Whose Holocaust Is It, Anyway? The 'H' Word in Library Catalogs." Berman, Sanford. Co-published simultaneously in *The Reference Librarian* (The Haworth Press, Inc.) No. 61/62, 1998, pp. 213-225; and: *The Holocaust: Memories, Research, Reference* (ed: Robert Hauptman, and Susan Hubbs Motin) The Haworth Press, Inc., 1998, pp. 213-225. Single or multiple copies of this article are available for a fee from The Haworth Document Delivery Service [1-800-342-9678, 9:00 a.m. - 5:00 p.m. (EST). E-mail address: getinfo@haworth.com].

213

up in post-Anschluss Vienna after 1938 and his incarceration from 1943 to 1945 in three Nazi concentration camps . . .

Also, since material on what the Nazis deliberately did to Jews is consistently subject cataloged under HOLOCAUST, JEWISH (1939-1945), why is there no parallel form covering what the Nazis deliberately did to Roma at the same time and for precisely the same reason? Both peoples were regarded as Untermenschen, as dangerous vermin, as inferior species. And the firm policy to degrade and exterminate Jews and Romanies alike distinctly dates from the beginning of Third Reich itself, rather than being merely a consequence or byproduct of World War II. Therefore, the gloss for the "Jewish" and needed "Romani" description should be (1933-1945).

Can it be expected that as a long-overdue matter of accuracy and fairness

- HOLOCAUST, ROMANI (1933-1945) will be swiftly established and retrospectively assigned to all relevant works previously traced under WORLD WAR II–GYPSIES or manifestly miscataloged under some form of HOLOCAUST, JEWISH?
- HOLOCAUST, JEWISH (1939-1945) will be promptly converted to the historically-mandated HOLOCAUST, JEWISH (1933-1945)?

Enclosures: LC & HCL cataloging records
cc: United States Holocaust Memorial Council
   T. Sonneman (Romani-Jewish Alliance)
   I. F. Hancock (Romani-Jewish Alliance)
   MultiCultural Review
   S. Thomas, Director for Cataloging

LC/GPO CATALOGING RECORD

AUTHOR: Stojka, Karl, 1931-
   TITLE: The story of Karl Stojka: a childhood in Birkenau: exhibition at the embassy of Austria, April 30 to May 29, 1992: catalogue by the United States Holocaust Memorial Museum; a project of the United States Holocaust Memorial Council.

IMPRINT: The Council, copyright 1992.
COLLATION: 64 p.
SUBJECT: Stojka, Karl, 1931–Exhibitions.
SUBJECT: Brzezinka (Poland: Concentration camp) in art–Exhibitions.
SUBJECT: World War II–Gypsies–Exhibitions.
SUBJECT: Holocaust, Jewish (1939-1945), in art–Exhibitions.
ADDED ENTRY: U.S. Holocaust Memorial Museum.
ADDED ENTRY: United States Holocaust Memorial Council.

HCL CATALOGING RECORD

110 2 United States Holocaust Memorial Museum.
245 14 The story of Karl Stojka: a childhood in Birkenau.$cPrimary author: Sybil Milton.
260 0 $bUnited States Holocaust Memorial Museum,$c1992.
300   64p.
500   Catalog of the "exhibition at the Embassy of Austria, April 30 to May 29, 1992."
500   Features 20 paintings reproduced in color.
505   PARTIAL CONTENTS: Glossary. -Chronology. -Suggestions for teachers: use as a classroom resource.
590   UNISOKS99
591   1992
600   Stojka, Karl,$d1931-
650   Romani Holocaust (1993-1945) in art$xExhibitions.
650   Romani Holocaust survivors.
650   Concentration camps in art$xExhibitions.
650   Birkenau Extermination Camp in art$xExhibitions.
650   Prisoners' art$xExhibitions.
650   Painting, Romani$xExhibitions.
650   Romanies$zAustria.
650   Romani Holocaust (1933-1945)$xStudy and teaching.
650   Romani Holocaust (1933-1945)$xChronology.
650   Buchenwald (Concentration camp) in art$xExhibitions.
700   Milton, Sybil.

On March 17, 1995, Barbara B. Tillett, CPSO Chief, replied:

Dear Sandy,

I have received your letter regarding the cataloging for the book *The Story of Karl Stojka: A Childhood in Birkenau*. You raise a number of points in your letter and I will attempt to address them here.

First, we have traditionally brought out the subject of gypsies during the period 1939-1945 by using the heading World War, 1939-1945–Gypsies. I am not entirely convinced that this is the best way to bring out this topic. On the other hand, recent searches of the LC database, reference sources, and periodical literature do not offer justification for a heading like Holocaust, Romani (1933-1945). We recognize the fact that the term *Gypsy* is no longer acceptable in some circles, but we have found that it is still in widespread usage today. The third edition of *The American Heritage Dictionary* defines Romany as "a Gypsy." In addition, the *Washington Post* and *The New York Times* both still use the term Gypsy. We consulted with a reference librarian who specializes in this area, who informed us that there is very little consensus in the scholarly community as to which term to use.

With regard to the LCSH heading for the Holocaust, we can offer a bit more hope for a change. Current rules for creating headings in LCSH would force the heading to be entered in the direct form, Jewish Holocaust, rather than the inverted form. We have also been concerned about the dates chosen for the period. Our Hebraica catalogers and reference librarians in the Hebraica Section of the African and Middle Eastern Division did not have a problem with the dates chosen, nor were they aware of complaints from their colleagues outside of LC. I am sure that you are aware that changing this heading is a sensitive issue and one that we cannot approach lightly. We will be consulting with our colleagues at the United State Holocaust Museum and the Association of Jewish Libraries.

The Story of Karl Stojka: A Childhood in Birkenau received the following subject headings:

> Stojka, Karl, 1931- –Exhibitions.
> Brzezinka (Poland: Concentration camp) in art–Exhibitions.

World War, 1939-1945–Gypsies–Exhibitions.
Holocaust, Jewish (1939-1945), in art–Exhibitions.

With the preceding as background and information, I consider the subject cataloging of this book to be appropriate for now.

To summarize, we will be investigating the heading for the Holocaust. If we can find agreement on the form of the heading that would not include the word Jewish, we would then determine the best way to bring out subtopics including the fate of Gypsies and Gays during the period of the Holocaust.

Thank you for writing again on this topic.

On March 24th, I wrote:

Dear Barbara,

Many thanks for your March 17th letter concerning "Gypsy" and "Holocaust" headings. However, while pleased with the prompt reply, I am truly amazed and disturbed by the content:

- "Literary warrant" for a "Romani Holocaust" heading is abundant. The bimonthly HCL CATALOGING BULLETIN has been publishing such "authority" for years (examples enclosed). And some years ago I engaged in a lengthy, heavily-documented exchange on the topic with Mary Kay Pietris in TECHNICALITIES (which I'll forward next week).
- The same hold with respect to whether "Gypsies" or "Roma" (Romanies) is the authentic, self-preferred name. Although "Gypsies" is unquestionably the more familiar ethnonym, there's no doubt whatever that it's a corruption of "Egyptian," since Europeans some time ago believed the Rom to have originated in Egypt (instead of India!). It *HAS* been LC policy to replace well-known and widely-used ethnonyms with less-familiar but accurate forms (e.g., OROMO for GALLAS and WYANDOT for HURON, not to mention SAMI instead of LAPPS). This is an analogous situation. "Gypsies" is simply not their name. To determine precisely which variant of "Rom" to employ, why not consult with Ian Hancock, Professor of Linguistics and leading Romani advocate in the United States? . . .

- When researching the appropriate Holocaust dates, don't neglect the Simon Wiesenthal Center in Los Angeles. They explicitly favor the 1933-1945 period.
- Re Stojka's volume: The HOLOCAUST, JEWISH (1939-1945) IN ART heading has been grotesquely misassigned inasmuch as Stojka dealt almost wholly with Roma, *not* Jews. This bespeaks a serious failure to recognize that Romanies were not incidental victims of a *Jewish* "Holocaust," but rather were targeted by Nazis for degradation and extinction from the start of the Third Reich, as the Chronology compiled by Sybil Milton for the Stojka book amply testifies. In short, they were persecuted and annihilated at the same time and for the same reasons as Jews. So if there is a heading for HOLOCAUST, JEWISH there clearly needs to be a parallel descriptor to represent what happened to Romanies. WORLD WAR II–GYPSIES doesn't suffice. No more than WORLD WAR II–JEWS suffices to denote/express what happened to Jews.

Perhaps as a result of this correspondence, the *L.C. Subject Headings Weekly List* for May 31, 1995, contained the following entry:

> * 150 World War, 1939-1945–Gypsies CANCEL
>   150 Gypsies–Nazi persecution [May Subd Geog] [sp 85-148419]
>   450 UF Gypsy Holocaust
>   450 UF Nazi persecution of gypsies
>   450 UF World War, 1939-1945–Gipsies [EARLIER FORM OF HEADING]
>   450 UF World War, 1939-1945–Gypsies [EARLIER FORM OF HEADING]
>   550 BT Persecution

A few weeks earlier, *LCSHWL* No. 18 (May 3, 1995) reported two newly-introduced *see*-references under GYPSIES:

> *450 UF Romani
> *450 UF Roma (People)

Rather than belabor the point, suffice it to note that Roma are still not called by their own, self-preferred name, and their experience during the Third Reich–although comparable in most essential elements with what happened to Jews–remains "different," "other," and indisputably "less," a "persecution" rather than a deliberate and devastating genocide. In truth, the Nazi Holocaust targeted and decimated many groups, including Jews, Roma, gay men, Poles, and disabled people. To differentiate among the victims, assigning some a greater significance or suffering-quotient than others is to practice a repulsive and unjustified kind of moral mathematics. Indeed, it's playing the Nazis' own game of dehumanization and heartless number-crunching. Below are records from the Hennepin County Library Authority File that demonstrate a more even-handed approach to Holocaust victims:

150 Euthanasia Program (Third Reich)
450 Nazi Euthanasia Program.
450 Nazi Holocaust (1933-1945)
450 Third Reich Euthanasia Program.
550 Atrocities.
550 Disabled persons$xGovernment policy$zGermany.
550 Euthanasia$zGermany$xHistory$x20th century
551 Germany$xHistory$y1993-1945.
551 Germany$xPolitics and government$y1933-1945.
550 Nazism
550 Violence against disabled persons$zGermany$xHistory$y 1933-1945.
667 LC form: EUTHANASIA–GOVERNMENT POLICY-GERMA-NY–HISTORY–20TH CENTURY.
680 Here are entered materials on Nazi "eugenic measures to improve the quality of the German 'race'" that "culminated in enforced 'mercy' deaths for the incurably insane, permanently disabled, deformed, and 'superfluous.'" Ultimately, "three major classifications were developed: (1) euthanasia for incurables; (2) direct extermination by 'special treatment'; (3) experiments in mass sterilization."

150 Gay Holocaust (1933-1945)
450 Holocaust, Gay (1933-1945)
450 Homosexual Holocaust (1933-1945)
450 Nazi Holocaust (1993-1945)

550 Atrocities.
550 Crimes against humanity.
550 Gay men$zEurope$xHistory.
550 Homophobia$xEurope
550 Nazism.
550 Violence against gay men and lesbians.

667 LC form: GAYS–NAZI PERSECUTION.
150 Holocaust, Jewish (1933-1945)
450 Catastrophe, Jewish (1933-1945)
450 "The Final Solution" (1933-1945).
450 Hurban (1933-1945)
450 Hurban (1933-1945)
450 Holocaust, Jewish (1933-1945).
450 Jewish Catastrophe (1933-1945).
450 Jewish Holocaust (1933-1945).
450 Nazi Holocaust (1933-1945)
450 Shoah (1933-1945)
450 Shoah (1933-1945)
550 Antisemitism$zGermany
550 Antisemitism$xEurope
550 Atrocities.
550 Crimes against humanity.
550 Genocide
550 Jews, European$xPersecutions.
550 Jews, German$xHistory$y1933-1945.
550 Nazism
550 World War II$xJews.

667 LC form: HOLOCAUST, JEWISH (1939-1945).
150 Romani Holocaust (1933-1945)
450 "Gypsies"$xNazi persecution
450 "Gypsy" Genocide (1933-1945).
450 "Gypsy" holocaust (1933-1945).
450 Holocaust, "Gypsy" (1933-1945).
450 Holocaust, Romani (1933-1945).
450 Nazi Holocaust (1933-1945)
450 Porajmos (1933-1945).
450 Porajmos (1933-1945).

450 Porrajmos (1933-1945)
450 Romani genocide (1933-1945).
450 Romani Porajmos (1933-1945).
450 Romanies$xNazi persecution
450 Romany Holocaust (1933-1945).
450 Xaimos (1933-1945).
550 Atrocities.
550 Crimes against humanity.
550 Genocide.
550 Nazism.
550 Racism$zEurope.
550 Romanies$xDiscrimination.
667 LC form: GYPSIES–NAZI PERSECUTION.

And here are HCL Authority File entries for a variety of Holocaust-related topics warranted by the literature but not yet recognized by the Library of Congress–and thus not searchable in most LC-following libraries:

150 Canada and the Jewish Holocaust (1933-1945)
450 Canada and the Holocaust (1933-1945).
450 Holocaust, Jewish (1933-1945) and Canada.
667 HCL form.

150 Christian Church and the Jewish Holocaust (1933-1945)
450 Christian Church and the Holocaust (1933-1945)
450 Holocaust, Jewish (1933-1945), and Christian churches.
450 Holocaust, Jewish (1933-1945), and the Christian Church.
550 Antisemitism in Christianity
550 Christian church and Nazism.
550 Christianity$xRelations$xJudaism.
550 Jews$xRelations with Gentiles
550 Judaism$xRelations$xChristianity.
667 HCL form.

150 Finland and the Jewish Holocaust (1933-1945)
450 Finland and the Holocaust (1933-1945).
450 Holocaust, Jewish (1933-1945) and Finland.
667 HCL form.

150 Great Britain and the Jewish Holocaust (1933-1945)
450 Great Britain and the Holocaust (1933-1945)
450 Holocaust, Jewish (1933-1945) and Great Britain.
550 World War II$zGreat Britain.
667 HCL form.

150 Holocaust commemoration services.
450 Day of Remembrance services.
450 Yom HaShoah services.
550 Judaism$xRites and ceremonies.
667 HCL form.

150 Jewish-Americans and the Holocaust (1933-1945)
450 American Jews and Holocaust (1933-1945).
450 Holocaust, Jewish (1933-1945) and American Jews.
450 Holocaust, Jewish (1933-1945) and Jewish-Americans.
550 World War II$xJewish-Americans.
550 United States and the Jewish Holocaust (1933-1945)
667 HCL form.

150 Papacy and the Jewish Holocaust (1933-1945)
450 Jewish Holocaust (1933-1945) and the Papacy
450 Jewish Holocaust (1933-1945) and the Vatican
450 Vatican and the Jewish Holocaust (1933-1945).
550 Antisemitism in the Catholic Church.
550 Catholic Church and social problems.
510 Catholic Church$xRelations$xJudaism.
550 Christian Church and the Jewish Holocaust (1933-1945)
550 Judaism$xRelations$xCatholic Church.
667 HCL form.

150 Press and the Jewish Holocaust (1933-1945)
450 Holocaust, Jewish (1933-1945) and the press.
450 Jewish Holocaust (1933-1945) and the press.
667 HCL form.

150 Protestant churches and the Jewish Holocaust (1933-1945)
450 Holocaust, Jewish (1933-1945) and Protestant Churches
450 Jewish Holocaust (1933-1945) and Protestant churches.
550 Christian Church and the Jewish Holocaust (1933-1945)
667 HCL form.

150 Spain and the Jewish Holocaust (1933-1945)
450 Holocaust, Jewish (1933-1945) and Spain
450 Spain and the Holocaust (1933-1945)
667 HCL form.

150 United States and the Jewish Holocaust (1933-1945)
450 Holocaust, Jewish (1933-1945), and the United States.
450 United States and the Holocaust (1933-1945)
550 World War II$zUnited States.
667 HCL form.

Finally, there have been–regrettably–many "Holocausts" in history: tidal waves of atrocity and extermination visited upon "inconvenient," "inferior," or "socially undesirable" peoples. Not every such event has been dubbed a "holocaust" by historians, scholars, or the affected groups. But some have. And that should be reflected in library catalogs either by means of primary descriptors or cross-references. As examples, again from the HCL Authority File:

150 Armenian genocide, 1915-1923.
450 Armenian Holocaust, 1915-1923.
450 Armenian massacres, 1915-1923.
450 Genocide, Armenian, 1915-1923.
450 Holocaust, Armenian, 1915-1923.
550 Genocide
681 LC form: ARMENIAN MASSACRES, 1915-1923.

150 Middle passage (Atlantic slave trade)
450 African Holocaust (Atlantic slave trade)
450 Atlantic slave trade middle passage
450 Black Holocaust (Atlantic slave trade)
450 Holocaust, African (Atlantic slave trade)
550 Atrocities
550 Crimes against humanity
550 Slave-trade
667 HCL form.

150 Native American Holocaust (1492-1900)
450 American Indian Genocide (1492-1900)

450 American Indian Holocaust (1492-1900)
450 Amerindian Holocaust (1492-1900)
450 First Nations Holocaust (1492-1900)
450 Genocide, American Indian (1492-1900)
450 Genocide, Indian (1492-1900)
450 Genocide, Native American (1492-1900)
450 Holocaust, American Indian (1492-1900)
450 Holocaust, Indian (1492-1900)
450 Holocaust, Native American (1492-1900)
450 Indian Holocaust (1492-1900)
450 Indians of North America$xHolocaust (1492-1900)
450 Native American Genocide (1492-1900)
550 Atrocities
550 Crimes against humanity
550 Genocide
550 Indians of North America$xDiscrimination
550 Indians of North America$xGovernment relations
550 Indians of North America$xHistory
550 Indians of North America$xRelations with missionaries, trad-
    ers, etc.
667 HCL form.

So what does all this mean from the standpoints of both reference and technical services? First, the continuing reluctance at LC to specify "Holocaust" cross-references may frustrate searchers who reasonably approach a catalog expecting to find material, for instance, under NAZI HOLOCAUST. Or GAY HOLOCAUST. Finding nothing, not even a "see"-reference, they may wrongly conclude the library *has* nothing on those topics. Second, the relegation of Romani, Gay, and Polish experiences during the Third Reich to a mere "persecution" status unmistakably and unacceptably declares that these groups somehow suffered less or were no more than incidental victims of the Nazi madness. Third, colossal, historic events like the lethal Middle Passage and 400-year-long Native American tragedy are amply represented in most library collections, but not in most library catalogs. They appear not to have happened. And not to have generated any literature. Fourth, in this era of mindless "downsizing" and "outsourcing," such elementary acts as making "Holocaust" cross-references and correcting and amplifying an otherwise inaccurate and virtually useless bibliographic record like that for the Stojka book, much less creating and assigning needed headings for the Middle Passage, Native American Holocaust, and similar subjects, may become even less possible. After all, these catalog-enhancing things can't be done without catalogers. And if there's no cataloger *available* to establish a cross-reference or add a "500" note, and also *empowered* to do so, the catalog then progressively fails to do what it should: make the collection fully, quickly, and usefully accessible to reference staff and library users.

Overlooked Reference Tools
for Researching the Holocaust

Allan Mirwis

SUMMARY. General reference tools can be valuable sources of information for conducting research on the Holocaust. In addition to the articles in general encyclopedias, several specialized encyclopedias contain lengthy articles on this subject. Several sources for bibliographical essays are identified. Other publications discussed in this article are Gale's Literary Criticism Series and the *Biography Index*. *[Article copies available for a fee from The Haworth Document Delivery Service: 1-800-342-9678. E-mail address: getinfo@haworth.com]*

The reference librarian working with students who were assigned or have selected the Holocaust as a topic for a research paper may overlook a number of reference tools used to locate additional information on this subject. Most general encyclopedias include articles on the Holocaust that are an excellent place for students to start their research. Usually written by a noted authority, they provide background information for the subject, an overall perspective and a bibliography of the most important documents (see Appendix).

Allan Mirwis is Reader's Services Librarian, Robert J. Kibbee Library of Kingsborough Community College, 2001 Oriental Boulevard, Brooklyn, NY 11235. E-mail: AXMKB@CUNYVM.CUNY.EDU

[Haworth co-indexing entry note]: "Overlooked Reference Tools for Researching The Holocaust." Mirwis, Allan. Co-published simultaneously in *The Reference Librarian* (The Haworth Press, Inc.) No. 61/62, 1998, pp. 227-234; and: *The Holocaust: Memories, Research, Reference* (ed: Robert Hauptman, and Susan Hubbs Motin) The Haworth Press, Inc., 1998, pp. 227-234. Single or multiple copies of this article are available for a fee from The Haworth Document Delivery Service [1-800-342-9678, 9:00 a.m. - 5:00 p.m. (EST). E-mail address: getinfo@haworth.com].

SPECIALIZED ENCYCLOPEDIAS

In addition to general encyclopedias, a number of specialized encyclopedias have significant articles on the Holocaust. The most comprehensive coverage of the Holocaust can be found in *The Encyclopaedia Judaica* (New York: Macmillan, 1972) and its *Decennial Book 1983-1992: Events of 1982-1992* (New York: Macmillan/Simon & Schuster, 1994), *The Encyclopedia of the Holocaust* (New York: Macmillan, 1990), and the recently published *The World Reacts to the Holocaust* (Baltimore: The Johns Hopkins University Press, 1996).

The main set of *The Encyclopedia Judaica* contains an extensive 78 column article written in two parts by Jacob Robinson author of *Guide to Jewish History Under Nazi Impact* (New York: YIVO, 1960) and *The Holocaust and After: Sources and Literature in English* (Jerusalem: Israel Universities Press, 1973). The first part is a detailed history of the Holocaust and the second discusses the behavior of the victims as well as the literature of the Holocaust. There are articles entitled "Holocaust, Rescue from" and "Holocaust and the Christian Churches." Its index contains more than a page of citations to articles under the subject "Holocaust."

Israel Gutman, a noted Holocaust historian and Professor at the International Institute of Holocaust Studies of Yad Vashem, was the editor-in-chief of *The Encyclopedia of the Holocaust*. It was originally published in four volumes in 1990 and reissued as a two volume set in 1995.) Almost 1,000 articles investigate not only the central period of the Holocaust from 1933-1945 but also its antecedents in earlier times and its legacy to later ones. It is illustrated profusely with excellent photographs and maps. In most cases, this encyclopedia provides balanced presentations of controversial events and issues. Articles are signed and conclude with a short bibliography of materials primarily, but not exclusively, in English. A glossary, a chronology, and several useful appendices are also included.

Noted Holocaust historian, David S. Wyman, author of *The Abandonment of the Jews: America and the Holocaust, 1941-1945* (New York: Pantheon Books, 1984) and the thirteen volume *America and the Holocaust* (New York: Garland Publications, 1989-

1991), edited *The World Reacts to the Holocaust* that was sponsored by the Holocaust Memorial Center. Each essay chronicles the impact of the Holocaust on twenty-two countries and the United Nations.

Most specialized encyclopedias do not have any entries pertaining to the Holocaust. What treatment there is of the Holocaust in several major subject encyclopedias is altogether disappointing. For example, the article in *The New Catholic Encyclopedia* (New York: McGraw Hill, 1967-79) only discusses the Holocaust in its biblical context as a sacrifice performed at the Temple. There is no entry in either *The Encyclopedia of Sociology* (New York: Macmillan, 1992) or *The Encyclopedia of Philosophy* (New York: Macmillan, 1972). *The Encyclopedia of Psychology* (New York: Wiley, 1994) includes only one paragraph in an article, "Psychology in Israel," that mentions that the effect of the Holocaust on survivors and their children was the subject of research by Israeli psychologists. *The Encyclopedia of Human Behavior* (San Diego: Academic Press, 1994) discusses the Holocaust as part of an article on the subject of "Obedience and Conformity."

A pleasant surprise is *The Encyclopedia of Religion* (New York: Macmillan, 1989) that contains two excellent articles. The first is a three page history of the Holocaust written by Christopher R. Browning, author of *The Path to Genocide* (New York: Cambridge University Press, 1992), and several other books on the Final Solution. The second is a nine page article, "Jewish Theological Responses to the Holocaust," written by Steven Katz, author of *The Holocaust in Historical Context* (New York: Oxford University Press) and several other important books on the Holocaust. This is a unique essay exploring and criticizing eleven different responses to the theological complexities emerging from the Holocaust.

The Encyclopedia of the Third Reich (New York: Collier Macmillan, 1991), originally published in German in 1985, covers the principal characters, organizations and crucial events from Hitler's birth through the Nuremberg trials. Although it contains no article on the Holocaust, it does contain more than 3,000 entries and 27 longer signed essays on such central topics as Anti-semitism, the Final Solution and persecution of Jews.

BIBLIOGRAPHIES

A number of bibliographies on the Holocaust have been published, most notably Abraham and Hershel Edelheit's *Bibliography on Holocaust Literature* (Boulder: Westview Press, 1986) and its supplement (Boulder: Westview, 1990). Many bibliographies have also appeared in professional library journals. Especially useful are those prepared by George M. Kren, Professor of History at Kansas State University ("The Literature of the Holocaust," *Choice*, January 1979, 1479-1490) and its update ("The Literature of the Holocaust: The Last Decade," *Choice*, July/August 1992, 1641-1648). Another well done bibliographic essay was written by Rahel Musleah ("The Holocaust Bookshelf 50 Years After Liberation," *Publishers Weekly*, May 8, 1995, 37-45) published to mark the anniversary of the ending of World War II.

GALE'S LITERARY CRITICISM SERIES

An especially valuable resource is the Gale Literary Criticism Series. Every fourth volume of *Literature Criticism From 1400 to 1800, Nineteenth-Century Literary Criticism, Contemporary Literary Criticism*, and *Twentieth-Century Literary Criticism* is devoted to literary topics that cannot be covered under the author approach used in the rest of these series. "Holocaust Literature" is one of the topics covered in Volume 42 of *Twentieth-Century Literary Criticism*. Almost one hundred pages in length, it contains excerpts of critical literature for over eighty authors arranged under the headings, "Historical Overview," "Critical Overview," "Diaries and Memoirs," "Novels and Short Stories," "Poetry," and "Drama." Also provided is an annotated bibliography for further reading. A second essay, "Holocaust Denial Literature," was published in Volume 58 and is arranged under the headings, "Overviews," "Robert Faurisson and Noam Chomsky," "Holocaust Denial Literature in America," "Library Access to Holocaust Denial Literature," "The Authenticity of Anne Frank's Diary," "David Irving and the 'Normalization' of Hitler," and "Further Reading."

Additional excerpted critical literature or biographical information for almost all of the authors included in these two volumes appear in other volumes of Gale's Literary Criticism Series. These references can be easily located by using the cumulative index to *Contemporary Authors*. The table below indicates citations to entries for each of the authors included in the "Holocaust Literature" essay for four titles in the Literary Criticism Series–*Contemporary Authors*, Volumes 1-154 (CA) and *Contemporary Authors New Revision Series*, Volumes 1-55 (CANR), *Contemporary Literary Criticism*, Volumes 1-96 (CLC), *Dictionary of Literary Biography*, Volumes 1-174 (DLB), and *Twentieth-Century Literary Criticism*, Volumes 1-66 (TCLC).

	CA	CANR	CLC	DLB	TCLC
Aichinger, Ilse	85-88			85	
Amichai, Yehuda	85-88	42	9, 22, 57		
Anderson, Alfred					
Barkai, Meyer					
Becker, Jurek	85-88		7, 19	75	
Bellow, Saul	5-8R	29, 53	1, 2, 3, 6, 8, 10, 13,15, 25, 33, 34, 63,79	82	
Berg, Mary					
Bettelheim, Bruno	81-84	23, 131	79		
Bor, Josef		115			
Borowski, Tadeusz		106, 154			9
Bryks, Rachmil	97-100				
Celan, Paul	85-88	33	10, 19 53, 82	69	
Delbo, Charlotte					
Des Pres, Terrence	73-76	124			
Donat, Alexander					
Eliach, Yaffa		110			
Epstein, Leslie	73-76	23	27		
Feldman, Irving	1-4R	1	7	169	
Flinker, Moses					
Frank, Anne		113, 133			17
Frankl, Viktor	65-68		93		
Friedlander, Saul		117, 130	90		
Gary, Romain		138	25	83	
Gershon, Karen	53-56	47, 141			
Glatstein, Jacob	33-36R				
Goldstein, Charles					
Gray, Martin	77-80	14			
Green, Gerald	13-16R	8		28	
Hecht, Anthony	9-12R	6	8, 13, 19	5, 169	
Heimler, Eugene	13-16R	8			

Semprun, Jorge		111		
Shapell, Nathan	49-52			
Shaw, Robert	81-84	4	5	13, 14
Singer, Isaac B.	1-4R	1, 134	1, 3, 6, 9, 11, 15, 23, 38, 69	6, 28, 52
Singer, Israel J.				33
Sobol, Joshua				60
Steiner, George	73-76	31	24	67
Styron, William	5-8R	6, 33	1, 3, 5, 11, 15, 60	2, 143
Tabori, George	49-52	4	19	
Thomas, D. M.				
Urin, Leon	1-4R	1, 40	7, 32	
von Kardoff, Ursula				
Wells, Leon W.	17-20R			
Wiesel, Elie	5-8R	8, 40	3, 5, 11, 37	83
Wincelberg, Shimon	45-48	46		

There is a title index for each of these four volumes which can be used to locate critical literature for specific titles. For example, there are nine references to criticism of Primo Levi's *Survival in Auschwitz: The Nazi Assault on Humanity* in the title index for the volumes in *Contemporary Literary Criticism*.

> *Se questo e un uomo (Survival in Auschwitz: The Nazi Assault on Humanity)* (Levi)
> **37**:220, 223, 225, 227; **50**:323-26, 332, 334, 336-37, 340

BIOGRAPHY INDEX

A periodical index that is a useful source of information on the Holocaust is the *Biography Index*. It includes the heading "Holocaust Survivors" in its "Index to Professions and Occupations." These citations direct the reader to biographical or autobiographical sources that were published either in periodicals or books. Each volume contains approximately one hundred entries.

Reference collections in most college libraries include hidden gems of superb resource material for researching the Holocaust. These treasures are often overlooked and librarians should be aware of their availability and usefulness for students and faculty interested in investigating this topic.

APPENDIX

Articles on the Holocaust in Major General Encyclopedias

1. *Collier's Encyclopedia*
    A half page article written by John Weiss, author of the recently published *Ideology of Death: Why the Holocaust Happened in Germany* (Chicago: I. R. Dee, 1996).

2. *Compton's Interactive Encyclopedia*
    A one page unsigned entry.

3. *Encarta '95*
    A computerized encyclopedia, it provides a four page article written by Raul Hilberg, noted author of *The Destruction of the European Jews* (Chicago: Quadrangle Books, 1961) and several other important books on the Holocaust.

4. *The Encyclopedia Americana*
    A half page article written by Seymour Rossel, author of *The Holocaust: The Fire That Raged* (New York: F. Watts, 1989).

5. *The Grolier International Encyclopedia*
    Also available as a computerized encyclopedia, it provides a half page article written by Saul S. Friedman, author of *Holocaust Literature: A Handbook of Critical, Historical, and Literary Writings* (Westport, Conn., Greenwood Press, 1993), and several other books on the Holocaust.

6. *The New Encyclopedia Britannica*
    Also available as a comprised encyclopedia, it provides a full page unsigned article.

7. *The World Book Encyclopedia*
    A half page article written by Leon A. Jick, author of *Teaching of Judaica in American Universities* (Waltham, Mass., Brandeis University, 1969).

Closing Circles, Opening Pathways:
The Reference Librarian
and the Holocaust

Paul Howard Hamburg

SUMMARY. The reference librarian in the setting of a Holocaust library serves several unique functions. Together with survivors and their families the librarian assists in reaching closure in their search for information about relatives who perished in the Holocaust. The reference librarian also serves as facilitator for future generations in learning about the Holocaust and coming to terms with the past. The paper also describes the tools and sources that enable these processes to be accomplished. *[Article copies available for a fee from The Haworth Document Delivery Service: 1-800-342-9678. E-mail address: getinfo@haworth.com]*

In 1982, I attended a piano recital at Bar-Ilan University in Israel given by Edit Steiner-Kraus, a survivor of the Terezin Concentration Camp in Czechoslovakia. The program was in itself not unusual–works from the standard repertoire, Beethoven, Chopin, Smetena et al.–but the impact of the recital was overwhelming. It was at this recital Edith Steiner-Kraus replicated her first recital performed in Terezin in 1942. When I attended that concert I knew little about Terezin, or the Holocaust for that matter. Most of the older members

---

Paul Howard Hamburg is Reference Librarian, Simon Wiesenthal Center Library & Archives, 9760 West Pico Boulevard, Los Angeles, CA 90035.

[Haworth co-indexing entry note]: "Closing Circles, Opening Pathways: The Reference Librarian and the Holocaust." Hamburg, Paul Howard. Co-published simultaneously in *The Reference Librarian* (The Haworth Press, Inc.) No. 61/62, 1998, pp. 235-243; and: *The Holocaust: Memories, Research, Reference* (ed: Robert Hauptman, and Susan Hubbs Motin) The Haworth Press, Inc., 1998, pp. 235-243. Single or multiple copies of this article are available for a fee from The Haworth Document Delivery Service [1-800-342-9678, 9:00 a.m. - 5:00 p.m. (EST). E-mail address: getinfo@haworth.com].

of the kibbutz where I then lived had managed to immigrate to Palestine in the 1930s and were more interested in recalling stories about the establishment of the kibbutz and the events surrounding the rise of the State of Israel than to remember life in Germany after the rise of Hitler and Nazis. The subject of the Holocaust was rarely discussed outside the annual commemorations during Yom Hashoah (Holocaust Remembrance Day).[1] In the United States in the 1950s and 1960s, as I was growing up, the subject of the Holocaust was also rarely, if ever, spoken about. At the recital I was confronted for the first time with the role of memory in the reconstruction of the Holocaust and with the raw courage of a survivor in confronting the past. In my role as reference librarian at the Simon Wiesenthal Center Library & Archives this confrontation with reconstruction and memory takes place daily, both in encounters with survivors who repeatedly reveal their courage, with their relatives, as well as with students and teachers who seek to learn about the Holocaust.

What is most comprehensible about the Holocaust is its incomprehensibility. Despite the prodigious literature that has developed, the student of the Holocaust must ultimately submit to silence. As more and more details of the Holocaust are researched in the form of newly accessible archives and historical studies, the ultimate questions of the Holocaust remain unanswered. In my work at the Library I am confronted with the memory of the Holocaust as an ongoing emotional and intellectual process, and I act as a guide to a wide variety of patrons who seek out my expertise. On a daily basis I am reminded of the profound impact I can have on other people's lives. In assisting survivors, children of survivors and their relatives, in closing the circle of uncertainty with regard to loved ones who perished at the hands of the Nazis and their collaborators, I am present at moments of intense pain. As they discover, one line in a deportation list can seal forever the ultimate fate of a father, mother, brother, or sister. On a rare occasion I am also present in assisting family members in making connections with long-lost relatives. The library also serves as a unique resource center for future generations to confront the Holocaust, opening up pathways for understanding to what has become an international clientele of patrons. This paper will describe the nature of this unique work, the range of seekers of information and some of the sources and tools that aid the reference librarian in this process.

The Simon Wiesenthal Center Library & Archives, where I have served as reference librarian since 1992, was established in 1978 and serves as the primary repository of books, periodicals and archival materials for the Simon Wiesenthal Center, an international organization devoted to Holocaust remembrance, human rights and the Jewish people. Since 1993, the Beit Hashoah Museum of Tolerance of the Simon Wiesenthal Center has attracted over one million visitors, many of who seek the assistance of the reference librarian, the institution's primary information provider. The library serves as the primary resource center on the West Coast with over 30,000 volumes, 400 periodicals and numerous other resources.

The scope of Holocaust studies is vast and a comprehensive collection of materials, such as the materials found at the Simon Wiesenthal Center Library, runs the gamut of the Library of Congress classification system. The wide range of disciplines related to Holocaust studies as well as the constantly growing literature in all these fields presents a continuing challenge to the reference librarian. The following are samples of subjects about which patrons frequently seek resources: the philosophical and theological implications of the Holocaust; the psychological effects of the Holocaust on survivors and children of survivors; the history of the Holocaust; the American and world response to the Holocaust; the ideological precedents of the eugenics movement in the development of Nazi ideology; the post-war prosecution of Nazi war criminals; the role of educators, jurists, doctors and scientists in the perpetration of the Holocaust. This wide range of queries necessitates familiarity with a broad spectrum of subjects from philosophy, psychology and history to literature, music and science. While a library of Holocaust studies is specialized, it is also thoroughly multidisciplinary.

That technology has changed the modus operandi of reference librarianship is now a commonplace fact. In the setting of the Simon Wiesenthal Center these changes have opened up access to the resources of the center to patrons worldwide. Queries now derive not only from patrons who visit the library, but from visitors to the Museum of Tolerance as well as via letters, telephone and electronic mail. In June 1992, the center established its own home page on the World Wide Web (www.wiesenthal.com). Since that time over 300,000 visitors have accessed our site and some 5,000 electronic mail messages have been forwarded to the reference librarian. The information resources available on the site include more than forty bibliographies on a variety of Holocaust-related subjects, a Holocaust timeline, glossary and series of frequently asked questions about the Holocaust. Growing familiarity with the resources on the site will provide for electronic distribution of materials to a wide spectrum of users of the electronic media.

The reference librarian in the setting of a Holocaust studies library will serve a wide, but unique spectrum of patrons. Each class of patrons has special needs which need to be addressed. Survivors and relatives of survivors represents a significant groups of users. More than fifty years after the end of the war, many reach the library seeking information about lost relatives. In the past they may have appealed unsuccessfully to various agencies in the hope of finding at least a trace of a lost parent, sibling, or other relative. Others have never really known where to search for information. Several factors influence the librarian's ability to provide information and in many instances it is unfortunately not possible to provide the information that is being sought. In general, people seeking information about survivors and victims from Western Europe have a much greater possibility of finding information that those seeking information about relatives in Eastern Europe. Deportation lists to Auschwitz have been compiled for Jews from France and Belgium.[2] In addition the German Bundesarchiv has compiled a two-volume memorial book of victims from the former West Germany.[3] A complete list of victims from Holland[4] was recently published as were the complete deportation lists to the Terezin concentration camp.[5] Victims of Hungarian forced labor battalions are also now available.[6]

Finding information about Jews from Eastern Europe is substantially more difficult. There are several explanations for this difficulty. First and foremost, the circumstances surrounding the destruction of the Jewish communities in Poland the the Soviet Union differed from the Jews in Western Europe. The participants at the Wannsee conference that took place near Berlin in January, 1942 determined that Polish Jewry and Jews living in Soviet controlled territories would be destroyed before the Jews of Western Europe. Before the convening of the conference the Jews of Estonia had already been exterminated. It was in Eastern Europe that the Nazis experimented with a variety of methods of mass destruction. Before the implementation of Zyklon B gas in the extermination camps, many people were murdered in incidents of mass shooting and with the use of mobile killing units (Einsatzgruppen) who used gas asphyxiation vans. Many of these murders took place in the villages and surrounding forests where the Jewish population had lived for generations. No lists were compiled as entire communities were systematically and brutally murdered. Residents of many small villages were consolidated into ghettos in larger towns. Many perished in the ghettos from disease resulting from the poor sanitary conditions or from the effects of starvation. Others were murdered at the hands of the SS and their collaborators. Again no record exists for these victims. As the ghettos were liquidated, many were deported to the killing centers at Treblinka, Sobibor and Belzec under Operation Reinhard. These centers, having completed that sinister task of mass destruction, were systematically dismantled by the Nazis again leaving no written trace of their victims. In the case of Auschwitz-Birkenau, the story is far more complicated. Upon arrival a selection process took place where the vast majority were sent immediately to the gas chambers. These victims included nearly all of the children under the age of fourteen and adults over the age of forty-five. Only those deemed capable to work were given the chance of survival. However, most of those selected for forced labor also were subjected to the brutalities of the camp including poor nutrition, disease and indiscriminate beatings meted out by camp guards and many were subsequently sent to the gas chambers as their usefulness as workers diminished. Only a limited number of records are extant in recording the slave labor system in Auschwitz-Birkenau. In addition, it must be remembered that the camp was liberated by the Soviets who subsequently transported records to archives which have remained closed to scholars. The entire history of post-World War II Europe and the history of the Cold War has profoundly affected our ability to document the fate of individual victims of the Holocaust. Only recently has the museum at Auschwitz begun to compile a computerized database of inmates and victims.

While it is often impossible to provide information about specific individuals, more general information about communities in Eastern Europe is often available. Since 1991 the reference librarian has been assisted by an important resource, *Where Once We Walked: A Guide to the Jewish Communities Destroyed in the Holocaust.*[7] This essential resource in invaluable in providing access to resources on more that twenty thousand communities. In addition to providing essential demographic and geographic information about these communities, this volume also serves as a guide to a wide variety of resources that provide detailed historical information. Not the least of these resources are the memorial volumes or Yizkor books.[8] To date more than eight hundred Yizkor books have been compiled, primarily by survivors of individual communities. These volumes describe the history of the community, the various religious, social, political and educational institutions that existed before the war, the events that occurred in the community during the Holocaust. Many of the volumes include a wealth of photographs of the community taken before the war including those of many who perished in the Holocaust. In a small number of instances, the volumes contain necrologies giving lists of community member who perished. For many seeking information about the lost world of their relatives these volumes exist as the sole link to that past. Considerable difficulties, however, limit the accessibility of these volumes to the general public. In addition to the limited number of volumes printed for each community, the primary barrier lies in the fact that most of these volumes were written in either Yiddish or Hebrew with only a very short English language section in rare instances. Currently efforts are being made to create translations of these volumes. At present only a handful of memorial books are available in an English language edition.[9]

There are rare occasions when the process of closing the circle in the tragedy of the Holocaust can have, as it were, a happy ending. The following anecdote also serves to illustrate the power of the Internet and the World Wide Web as a vehicle capable of creating bridges between people. Recently, a letter came across my desk from a lawyer in Denmark who had visited our web site. Mounted on the site are the photographs and short biographies of over one hundred children. The vast majority of these children perished in the Holocaust. However, a handful survived, including the cousin of the Danish lawyer who wrote asking for our assistance in tracing her lost relative. Going back to the records in our archive of the donation of this photograph I was able to find the lost relative and to establish a renewed connection between them.

While the interaction between the reference librarian and survivors and their families is a significant aspect of the kind of service provided by a Holocaust library reference librarian it is by all means not the only class of patrons who require such services. The ability to communicate with our web site has also created an international net of patrons for the reference librarian. As was previously mentioned, since the establishment of the web site nearly two years ago over 5,000 e-mail requests have arrived via the web site alone. In addition, electronic mail has become the preferred means of communication between the reference librarian and patrons, allowing an efficient means for transferring bibliographic citations and other documents. Two other main sources of queries should be mentioned in reviewing the type of patrons that regularly seek assistance. The Simon Wiesenthal Center as an international organization frequently interacts with a wide range of sources in the various communications media who seek our assistance. This assistance can be provided both for information regarding breaking stories and for projects of a more documentary nature. Typical users of reference services include television and radio stations, newspaper and magazine feature writer, documentary film makers and screenwriters. Such patrons often provide the reference librarian with the privilege of collaborating on significant projects that reach wide audiences, including such films as *Schindler's List* and the Emmy award winning screenplay for the children's program "Children Remember the Holocaust."

An equally significant sector of interaction between the reference librarian and patrons includes the various levels of the educational system. Of growing significance is the interaction between the librarian and students participating the national History Day competition. Each year a broad theme is selected as a framework for the competition. Such themes as Conflict and Compromise or Triumph and Tragedy lend themselves readily to projects relating to the Holocaust. Students from all levels and from many regions of the United States contact the library requesting assistance with their projects. As more and more states incorporate the study of the Holocaust into their language arts and social studies curricula requests from teachers for appropriate material grows more frequent. The reference librarian serves a significant role in opening up resources to students and teachers. Mention must be made of the role of the reference librarian in dealing with the trauma of the Holocaust. While not trained in therapy, the reference librarian is very often called upon to listen to the experiences of survivors and their relatives. Moreover, the teaching of the Holocaust requires confrontation with the realities of the Holocaust and both teachers and students must be prepared to read emotionally difficult materials, view disturbing footage and photographs. I am often asked how it is possible to continue to deal with this difficult material on a daily basis and not "burn out." Perhaps the answer lies in the realization that there remains a significant triumph in the tragedy of the Holocaust. That despite the devastation perpetrated during that period, the human spirit was not vanquished. Poetry was written and music was composed. Despite overwhelming odds there were those who resisted, physically and spiritually in ghettos, forests and concentration camps and in hiding. As a reference librarian I have the privilege of disseminating the legacy of the Holocaust to future generations. It is truly sacred work.

NOTES

1. For an excellent discussion of the role of the Holocaust in Israeli society see Segev, Tom. The Seventh million: the Israelis and the Holocaust; translated by Haim Watzman. 1st ed. New York: Hill and Wang, 1993.

2. Klarsfeld, Serge. Le memorial de la deportation des juifs de France. Pris: Klarsfeld, [1978] and Klarsfeld, Serge and Maxime Steinberg. Memorial de la deportation des juifs de Belgique. Bruxelles: Union des deportes juifs en Belgique et filles et fils de la deportation; New York, NY: Beate Klarsfeld Foundation, [1982].

3. Gedenkbuch: Opfer der Verfolgung der Juden unter der nationalsozialistischen Gewaltherrschaft in Deutschland 1933-1945. Koblenz: Bundesarchiv, 1986. Recently lists have been published for victims from Berlin and Hamburg.

4. In Memoriam; Le-Zekher. Den Haag: Sdu Uitgeverij Koninginnegracht, 1995.

5. Kárny, Miroslav, [et al.], eds. Terezinska Pametni Kniha: zidovské obeti nacistickych deportací z Cech a Moravy 1941-1945. Praha: Terezínská iniciativa; Melantrich, 1995.

6. Names of Jewish Victims of Hungarian Labour Battalions. New York: Beate and Serge Klarsfeld Foundation, 1991-.

7. Mokotoff, Gary and Sallyann Amdur Sack. Where Once We Walked: A guide to the Jewish Communities Destroyed in the Holocaust. Teaneck, NJ: Avoteynu, 1991.

8. For an introduction to the genre of Yizkor books: Kugelmass, Jack and Jonathan Boyarin. From a Ruined Garden: The Memorial Books of Polish Jewry. New York: Schocken Books, 1983.

9. Baker, Zachary M., comp. Bibliography of Eastern European Memorial (Yizkor) Books; edited by Steven W. Siegel. New York (P.O. Box 6398, New York 10128): Jewish Genealogical Society Inc., 1992.

Expand Reference Resources:
Research the Holocaust
Through the Internet

Judy Anderson

SUMMARY. The Internet opens a wide range of possibilities for accessing materials from both traditional sources and more volatile areas—personal homepages, e-mail and discussion groups archives. Though the role of reference librarians to find the most relevant information for our users seems monumental in this medium, it is an area that needs the objective, ethical expertise of the librarian and archivist. In this 50th year of remembrance of the Holocaust, the Internet is especially active with information on that historic tragedy. Excerpts from accounts by one Hungarian and one Norwegian political prisoner interned in the camps are included as illustrations of material which may not have been found using more traditional research tools. *[Article copies available for a fee from The Haworth Document Delivery Service: 1-800-342-9678. E-mail address: getinfo@haworth.com]*

INTRODUCTION

Traditional facilities have been the gatekeepers of information about the Holocaust for five decades. Historians, librarians, archivists, and others interested in conserving and preserving information about the personal and societal tragedies of the World War II

Judy Anderson is Automated Services Librarian, Del Mar College, 101 Baldwin, Corpus Christi, TX 78404-3897.

[Haworth co-indexing entry note]: "Expand Reference Resources: Research the Holocaust Through the Internet." Anderson, Judy. Co-published simultaneously in *The Reference Librarian* (The Haworth Press, Inc.) No. 61/62, 1998, pp. 245-254; and: *The Holocaust: Memories, Research, Reference* (ed: Robert Hauptman, and Susan Hubbs Motin) The Haworth Press, Inc., 1998, pp. 245-254. Single or multiple copies of this article are available for a fee from The Haworth Document Delivery Service [1-800-342-9678, 9:00 a.m. - 5:00 p.m. (EST). E-mail address: getinfo@haworth.com].

Nazi concentration camps have given their contributions. In the past, it was difficult for those living outside major urban areas to access this information. Often material could only be used by special permission or viewed in person. In this 50th year of remembrance, many reference departments and private homes have electronic tools at their disposal. These afford access to a wide range of information without requiring the patron to travel to reach special sites, or request that fragile materials be loaned or copied. I speak, of course, of the Internet, that democratic international medium which opens the archives of history and the discussions of today to users worldwide.

Having such a wide variety of information available does make the job of deciphering accurately and indexing efficiently more difficult. The traditional role of reference to find the most relevant documents are at times monumental given the amount of data and the archaic computer indexing available. But the World Wide Web has opened new avenues which afford our clientele access to, not just the traditional scholarly information and published statistics seen by those researching 20 years ago, but ideas from thousands of people with personal experiences or an intellectual interest in the occurrence. We are already seeing a trend to move data to this electronic medium.

As resources and access to Internet sites become more prevalent, those who have traditional skills in indexing and preserving materials are bringing their expertise in information collection and retrieval to the Web. Library, museum, archive and Holocaust organization[1] sites are already building databanks containing digital versions of original documents, diaries, photographs, etc., for any to view. The Internet also opens doors for personal communications that link interested parties to fresh accounts of the horrific times. Correspondence through e-mail to families around the world requesting information about family experiences may unearth personal accounts that have never made their way to formal archives or publications. With the advent of personal Web pages, organizations and individuals may provide information to the public concerning the devastation which occurred in the camps, information which, for political or personal reasons, has not been seen until today.

Reference has become more complex, but with the new challenge comes the knowledge that the public is best served when information covering many views is available for analysis. The traditional role of selection of the most relevant and "best" material is needed now more than ever. The Internet is in its infancy as far as organizing resources for storage and retrieval. As more patrons become familiar with the difficulties of searching for material, library reference services take on a new value. Clients ask library staff to help them develop effective search strategies, find data and target appropriate sites.

ETHICS AND OBJECTIVITY IN REFERENCE SERVICES

It is imperative that librarians sell more than basic service. In this information age, libraries must maintain high ethical standards and a credibility that reflects a responsible, impartial viewpoint. Whether the service involves gathering information for a patron, suggested readings or subject headings in the area of a client's interest, or teaching a person to use library resources more effectively, it is the librarian's responsibility to present materials and sites that give a comprehensive view of the information sought. Topics which carry a high profile of social interest or perhaps a personal bias must be approached with the knowledge that libraries do not exist to be society's censors. They are established to ensure that information is not lost or altered to reflect a current political environment. At times this might mean offering cautions or disclaimers about the context of a site to help the user make selections appropriate for their sensibilities. But librarians are ethically bound to maintain an objective, moral view. They are under an obligation to their clientele to present information that reflects perceptions from many sides on a given topic.

RESOURCE BASES AND TIMELY MATERIAL

We are fortunate to be living in a time when many persons who went through the ordeals of the concentration camps are still alive and willing to contribute their knowledge of the time to the general body of information. Many in recent times have documented their experiences. Materials–photographs, films, letters, official reports, diaries and journals–are being found and archived. An interest in reminding people of the horrors that one part of society forced on another has been rejuvenated in this 50th year of remembrance.

Since World War II was an international experience, the topic continues to have global implications. The Internet lends itself to gathering materials globally in an efficient time frame. Topics such as the Holocaust present an especially challenging situation. Each person who has knowledge of World War II in Europe has emotional reactions to the subject based on personal and familial beliefs and experiences, cultural circumstances or perhaps political, philosophical or religious preferences. Patrons requesting information in this area have various reasons for asking for reference assistance in finding the information. For this reason it is particularly important that reference assistance is given in a professional, objective setting.

As has been the tradition, the reference interview is the best starting point. Realistically, the interview may not always be as complete or precise as is written in the textbooks, but having a clear understanding of the type of information being requested is extremely helpful for narrowing the search time and finding the most appropriate materials.

PERSONAL ACCOUNTS FROM HOLOCAUST SURVIVORS

My experience with a researcher interested in the Holocaust took an unexpected turn. Information needed was not in the tragedy of the 6 million "undesirables" traced, but in the impressions of those who were interned with them. What of the Jews and Protestants, Catholics and atheists "legitimately" incarcerated as political prisoners? What were their experiences, their impressions of the horror around them? Traditional resources available brought up information on Jewish survivors, resistance fighters, condemnation for the praise given the resistance fighters, descriptions of experiments done in the camps, and studies done on the survivors. Personal accounts were located but did not meet the client's needs. Queries also returned opinions of those who believe the Holocaust is propaganda and fiction in much the same way as some persons believe the moon landing images projected in 1969 were done in the deserts of the Southwest.

The Internet, more specifically e-mail and the Web, was used to find accounts of persons who may or may not have formally published information about their experiences. Accounts by Peter A. Zuckerman, Hungarian, and Sverre Landöy, Norwegian, indicate the types of material found through the Internet channels. Although their backgrounds and circumstances differed, their accounts have a similar quality, a triumph of the human spirit. Mr. Zuckerman's account[2] is posted on his Web homepage at the time of this writing. E-mail to family members in Norway uncovered Mr. Landöy's personal account in manuscript. The family sent a copy of the work for our use. Mr. Landöy and his father were taken prisoner when they were assisting the resistance in gun smuggling off the shores of Bergen, Norway. Mr. Zuckerman was among those collected for the camps when his community in Hungary was destroyed. He was fifteen years old and a learned typesetter when he became part of the conscripted labor force—first stop Auschwitz.

In Peter Zuckerman's account, he speaks of the confusion, depersonalization, and threat of unprovoked violence. Peter's own method of survival was to be sensitive to the suffering of those around him, but detached. "As horror piled up on horror, Peter had to become an observer, if only to retain his sanity."[3]

He spoke with respect for the orthodox Jews, who, in the face of being clubbed by guards, started to say the *Kaddish*, the final prayer for the dead. Peter recounts the horror he and fellow prisoners felt at the realization that the furnaces were burning members of their families and communities, not just old clothes and other refuse.

> Now he became a nameless cog, identified only with his number. The thousands of prisoners represented every country in Europe. There were Catholics, Protestants, Jews and atheists. They were there for many reasons . . . [but t]hey had one thing in common. They were declared unilaterally enemies of Germany . . . [and t]hey were exploited for their labor.[4]

He also tells of being shipped to many camps and of how through good fortune his life was spared. He relates memories of the extra ration provided by a sympathetic guard or fellow prisoner, the charity of a German woman who requested laborers and then quietly provided them with extra food to help them survive. His bout with typhus left him near death, but he awakened in an unguarded prison abandoned by the Germans in the face of advancing Allied troops and eventual safety.

After the war, Mr. Zuckerman had to make a decision. Where should he resettle? He had no ties; family and friends had died or been killed. Native Hungary was no longer a place he trusted. Post-holocaust Germany and Palestine with its Arab and Jewish tensions were hostile environments. He chose America and now fights to establish an awareness of the need for all to protect the environment and build a global community free of the hostilities of the past.

Mr. Landöy's internment began alongside his father in German camps in Norway, the first being Ulven. They had hidden weapons coming from the Shetland Bus, a resistance operation that ran guns from Scotland to Norway. At Ulven, conditions were poor, and food was scarce, but there was still contact with those outside the camps. When he was moved to Grini, conditions grew worse and the fear of beatings heightened. Little food and extreme physical labor reduced their numbers daily. In 1942 they were put on a transport for Germany.

> The gang waiting to receive us at Rothau station must surely have been Satan's most loyal servants on earth . . . We marched through the gate [Natzweiler] and lined up outside the shower block . . . I was absolutely stunned by the sight of these men—or creatures, to find a better word. They were walking skeletons in rags.[5]

Natzweiler was a *Nacht und Nebel* camp, a camp were prisoners were sent to stay until they died. Freezing cold, exhausting labor and little food made illness and death a part of daily existence. Fear of being beaten or killed was constant.

> The next day, Sunday, the Germans decided to find out what kind of stuff we were made of. A squad of SD soldiers with dogs, whips and revolvers appeared. The jailbird gangleaders were also there to get the tempo up. We were herded into a

sandpit. Half of us were given heavy wheelbarrows and the other half picks and shovels to fill them. We were made to run about 50 meters with the wheelbarrows full of sand and run back again to the sandpit. There was no time to straighten our backs . . . If we stopped, even for a few seconds, they hit us.[6]

One incident involved a Polish prisoner. After solitary confinement, the guards stripped him, threw him in the snow and beat him with sticks. The image of steam rising from his back remained a clear memory for Mr. Landöy. Three weeks later the man walked to the gallows unassisted, stood on the trap door and was hanged.

> Nobody can ever know how much that man suffered–unless it was Christ himself. Whatever else he was thinking of, he looked relieved that it was all nearly over . . . Could we have done anything to prevent it? The question still haunts me.[7]

Despondency was more dangerous than hunger or fear. The fellow prisoners from Norway united to keep each other alive. With stories and plans for after the war they managed to keep each other interested in living no matter how bad the conditions around them.

> Harald, Asbjørn and I tried to stick together . . . During the autumn Harald got the notion that we were going to freeze to death as soon as winter came. I disagreed but he argued strongly. "How can we expect to survive in these rags?" . . . We had several disputes about this during the autumn until one day we walked by a puddle with a thin layer of ice on top . . . "Look, I told you. It strikes me that we are both still alive . . ." Here was proof that we had a chance to survive the winter . . . To work in that wet cold slush in our rags and poor shoes was a severe drain on our courage. Prisoners began to look for a purpose–any purpose–to keep themselves alive through the winter . . .
>
> Hans Cappelen . . . could persuade anybody that the war would be over in a month . . . Every scrap of information he had been able to glean about the conduct of the war he worked upon and changed until it became to our advantage . . . I am convinced that Cappelen saved lives by his blessed chatter, but

he did not know how good he was at holding up the courage of others.[8]

Shortly before Mr. Landöy and his fellow prisoners were transported from Natzweiler, the Germans began experimenting with gas chambers. Using groups of 4 prisoners, they calibrated the amount of gas needed to kill. When the experiments were successful, many prisoners were quickly relocated to a different camp. Mr. Landöy and his fellow prisoners were moved to Allach. As he marched, he thought of fellow members of the prison community who had gone "up the chimney." Some were friends and neighbors from the past, whose ashes had been spread over icy stairs to keep steps safe in the freezing snow. He thought of how they would have wanted to be leaving alive.

At Allach, among criminal supervisors trying to outdo each other in kicking and butting prisoners, he found a camp segregated with Jews on one side and all nationalities on the other.

> It was bad on our side, but on the other side it must have been horrific. Punishment exercises were constantly going on, not in a dry land, but in a wet clay swamp . . . Now and then a raging lion in the shape of a guard would appear. He raved and struck people with no apparent rhyme or reason.[9]

He was at Dachau as the fall of Germany approached. Conditions there were not as harsh. His luck had held. A supervisor selected a few Norwegians to share his quarters. The fairness of the man amazed the selected prisoners. Although not safe, the situation was less fearful, and the food was rationed fairly. But the fear of uncertainty never left. When rumors said that Scandinavians were being rounded up to be shipped out, the first thoughts were NN, e.g., *Nacht und Nebel*, prisoners marked to be killed. Instead they were to be transported to Sweden. Only 2 of the 11 captured in the smuggling and sent to Natzweiller had survived.

Through the telling was the occasional reference to the even greater maltreatment of Jews. Despite his trials, he retained pride in being a Norwegian–respected by their captors for their honesty–and belief in the power of God and the human spirit.

ADDITIONAL RESOURCES

These were not the only accounts of political prisoners. These are just two samples of the types of information and links to information accessible through the less traditional resources of the Internet. Archives of on-line discussion groups[10] also proved valuable in showing the multifaceted interpretations of facts and beliefs surrounding the Holocaust. The Internet discussion groups[11] recorded people bringing up instances and having those ideas challenged by others. They reflect personal accounts from all nationalities and ideological beliefs, a pool of democratic debate from all over the world.

CONCLUSION

The wealth of possibilities for using this medium for reference work is just beginning to surface. Professional organizations, personal contacts, listservs, on-line discussion groups and community resources are valuable caches available to the reference professional. The challenge to locate and identify the information most relevant for our clients is just beginning, but the resource has great potential. The possibilities posed by such controversial topics as the Holocaust lend themselves to this rising medium. Users require assistance now more than ever to find relevant information on topics of interest. The challenge remains, as always, to locate resources not easily found by our users, and to link that data for retrieval.

REFERENCES

1. Jim Blackaby <jblackaby@ushmm.org> *United States Holocaust Research Institute Reading Room/Information Access* <http://www.ushmm.org/ushmm_ia.html> (15 April 1997). Their Information Access system searches multiple databases. Matches display with abstracts. Resources are in many formats.

2. Peter Zuckerman <pazpax@apn.org> *Auschwitz and Other Concentration Camps* <http://www.aprn.org/pazpax/pazholocaust.html> (15 April 1997). Mr. Zuckerman titles himself and "Activist for Human Progress and Survival." His page includes a disclaimer which states the information may be disturbing for those unprepared. It is for the serious websurfer.

3. *ibid.*

4. *ibid.*

5. Sverre Landöy, *untitled*, MTS, 1994.

6. *ibid.*

7. *ibid.*

8. *Ibid.*

9. *ibid.*

10. Edward <edward@Cent.com> *Forty Questions on the Holocaust* <news:alt. politics.correct> (8 April 1997). Questions are posed on such topics as faked photographs, the disputed authenticity for the *Diary of Anne Frank* and other topics which challenge the accuracy of the Holocaust. For our search for discussion groups, we used the *Deja News* and *Liszt* search sites. There are many others which also index archives of on-line discussions.

11. Daniel Faigin <faigin@pacific.net> *FAQ: Holocaust, Anti-Semitism, Missionaries* <news:soc.culture.jewish> (8 April 1997). In a question and answer style, the author gives information on places to find information on the Holocaust, disputes claims that only Jewish casualties are given attention and explains fallacies about the Jewish culture.

Locating Holocaust Information
on the Internet

Jackie C. Shane

SUMMARY. The Internet, being a global tool capable of supporting multi-media format, can provide a venue for information in ways that traditional resources cannot. There is an abundance of information on the Internet regarding various aspects of the Holocaust. Responding to the broad disparity of the quality of information, political agendas of information providers, and the multi-disciplinary nature of the topic, this article is designed to provide an overview of available resources, and a spring-board for further research using the Internet as a medium. *[Article copies available for a fee from The Haworth Document Delivery Service: 1-800-342-9678. E-mail address: getinfo@haworth.com]*

There exists a wide variety of World Wide Web pages devoted entirely to the discussion of the Holocaust. Searching the term "holocaust" with any popular Web search engine generally produces over 30,000 hits. As is to be expected, the quality and focus of Internet resources varies immensely, from a national museum exhibit to Nazi propaganda uploaded to a personal Web page. The resources in this bibliography were selected for their value and presumed reliability. Some sites provide digitized text online; oth-

---

Jackie C. Shane is Assistant Professor and Science/Government Information Librarian, Centennial Science & Engineering Library, University of New Mexico, Albuquerque, NM 87311. E-mail: jshane@unm.edu

[Haworth co-indexing entry note]: "Locating Holocaust Informaton on the Internet." Shane, Jackie C. Co-published simultaneously in *The Reference Librarian* (The Haworth Press, Inc.) No. 61/62, 1998, pp. 255-264; and: *The Holocaust: Memories, Research, Reference* (ed: Robert Hauptman, and Susan Hubbs Motin) The Haworth Press, Inc., 1998, pp. 255-264. Single or multiple copies of this article are available for a fee from The Haworth Document Delivery Service [1-800-342-9678, 9:00 a.m. - 5:00 p.m. (EST). E-mail address: getinfo@haworth.com].

ers are more administrative in nature, offering such things as library catalogs or exhibit information. Undoubtedly the trend will be for research centers to upload increasing amounts of archival information online as historians rush to preserve oral histories of the last aging generation of survivors coupled with the declining cost of computer memory. In the meantime, between privacy issues and the tedium of digitizing historical text, secondary information is much more prevalent.

It is important to keep in mind that the Holocaust is not only multi-disciplinary but also international. Searching with English vocabulary retrieves sites which are either produced in English or have been linked to a translation. The good news is that many sites, particularly those in Western Europe, do translate at least an introductory page of their Web sites into English. Shoah, the Hebrew term, is often used alternately for the English word, Holocaust. The content of available Internet resources is extremely varied, and spans the areas of political science, sociology, history, literature, the arts, science, education, religion, and ethics.

SEARCH ENGINES

Yahoo!

www.yahoo.com

Most search engines will retrieve anywhere from four to over fifty thousand hits in response to the query "holocaust," so quantity is not the challenge. The vast majority of Web sites examined use *Excite, Alta Vista,* or *Yahoo!* as an internal search engine. For multiple site searching, and overall, only *Yahoo!* has a comprehensive search category devoted strictly to Holocaust sites, this being *20th Century: Holocaust, The. Yahoo!* further divides this area into five different sub-categories of Holocaust search engines covering the arts and humanities, society and culture, history, religion, and the news media, with arts and humanities being the richest category. Each of these sub-categories may in turn be sub-divided into specific topics, such as concentration camps, conferences, memorials, and Yom HaShoah (Holocaust Remembrance Day).

FOREIGN COUNTRIES

Yahoo! allows the user to limit a search by country for Germany, France, Canada, Japan, and the UK. The easiest way to locate foreign Web sites is to limit by country, further limit to a Holocaust category, and create a search term in the native language of that country. Since *Yahoo!* consistently organizes their subjects across languages, one can refer to *Yahoo, Deutschland*, for example beginning with the category (kategorie): *Geistes- und Sozialwissenschaft: Geisteswissenschaften: Geschichte: 20. Jahrhundert: Dritte Reich, Das: Holocaust, Der.*

Major museums and research centers (such as the Simon Wiesenthal Center) generally create multilingual Web pages, but there are local treasures which would not be retrieved without a refined search query. One such example is:

Die Geschichte der Juden in Kaisersesch (The History of the Jews in Kaisersesch)

http://titan.informatik.uni-bonn.de/~wagener/inhalt.html

This is an html narrative which documents the Jewish population and lifestyle in one particular German town, before and after the war.

Nizkor Search Engine

http://www.almanac.bc.ca/search.html

The Nizkor Project is one of the few Holocaust Web sites which has its own internal search engine. This provides access to their Web pages, ftp archives, and the discussion group *alt.revisionism* archives.

MUSEUMS AND RESEARCH CENTERS

Yad Vashem

http://www.yad-vashem.org.il/

Located in Jerusalem, Israel, Yad Vashem is probably the oldest and most famous Holocaust museum in the world. It is a complex of museums, monuments, research centers, a library, teaching facilities, and a resource center. Two exhibits are currently online via their Web page. These are entitled "The Anguish of Liberation" and "Eleventh Hour Rescue Campaign." This site provides an excellent overview of the museum staff and functions, but offers very few full-text documents online.

United States Holocaust Memorial Museum

http://www.ushmm.org/index.html

Located in Washington, D.C. this museum is dedicated not only to Jews, but to all who perished in the Holocaust. The museum, in addition to its formidable exhibits, is also a research institute consisting of academic programs, publications, a library, archives including photo-archives and oral histories, a multi-media center, and a survivor's registry. The Web site contains a calendar of research center events and a listing of public programs.

The Library, although young, is building some of the world's most specialized collections on the Holocaust and its historical context. There are currently more than 22,200 books and journals in this multi-language collection. In light of the aging community the library has been actively collecting personal narratives.

Simon Wiesenthal Center

http://www.wiesenthal.com/

Named after the world's most famous Nazi hunter, the Center (centre) concerns itself with documenting the Holocaust and fighting the Holocaust deniers. It also focuses on racial hatred and all types of bigotry no matter at whom it is directed. The site has a strong emphasis on current events more than most Holocaust Web sites. With the software package TrueSpeech, one can listen to audio programs on contemporary Jewish events and political newsmakers. A recent feature is a database of frozen Swiss bank accounts containing money confiscated from Jews during the Holocaust.

The Ghetto Fighters' House Museum of the Holocaust and Resistance

http://www.amfriendsgfh.org/Docs/gfh.html

Located in Israel, this museum focuses on the uprisings and resistance that took place within the Jewish ghetto. The Web site has an online gallery and a list of the museum's publications and films.

LIBRARIES

All of the museums mentioned above are affiliated with a library and a research center for that institution. In addition, there is one autonomous Web library that must be noted:

Cybrary of the Holocaust

http://remember.org/

This is possibly the richest site in terms of digitized full text and graphics. What at first sight appears commercial or superficial is actually a very moving collection of books, photographs, children's artwork, bibliographies for genealogy, history, and education in general.

ARCHIVES

The Internet may be used to contact research centers that register Holocaust victims and survivors. One should never assume, however, that the World Wide Web is necessarily representative of all available resources. Archival information in general is something that is still much more pervasive in print. Probably the biggest clearinghouse for locating records of victims or survivors of the Holocaust are the Arolson Archives[1] in Arolson, Germany. Mormon Centers are another good source for locating people, as the Mormons have very rich archives of birth records in Salt Lake City.

Finally, the Red Cross, upon request, will search records of war victims.

Yad Vashem Archives

http://www.yad-vashem.org.il/ARCHIVE.HTM

The Yad Vashem Archives contain approximately 50 million pages of international documentation including a large collection of documentation from the postwar trials against Nazi war criminals. The collection is comprised of original documents, photocopied documents, and microfilm. Very little is online at present, but plans are underway to automate.

PHOTOGRAPHIC ARCHIVES

Most museums generally have at least a small portion of their paintings, photographs, or sculpture works online. The following sites are autonomous archives of photography and artwork meant to illustrate a story and to be downloaded.

Holocaust Pictures Exhibition

http://modb.oce.ulg.ac.be/schmitz/holocaust.htm

This site features 37 photographs in their re-scaled and original versions, accompanied with text in English and French. Although the gallery is small, these world-famous photographs represent a wide variety of countries and circumstances.

The Holocaust Album

http://www.hooked.net/users/rgreene/index.html

A small collection of contemporary and historical photographs predominantly about people who made a positive difference either during or after the war, such as the story of the Japanese Consul-General Chiune Sugihara who, with his wife, saved more than 6,000 Jews.

ART

The Miami Beach Holocaust Memorial

http://wahoo.netrunner.net/~holomem/index.html

Located in Florida this sculpture garden was designed to express Jewish culture and those that lost their lives in the Holocaust. The site provides high quality photographic renditions of poignant sculpture pieces. The design of the Web site is as creative as the sculpture. Expect the unexpected. This is not just a page; it is a journey.

ORGANIZATIONS

Members of the Association of Holocaust Organizations

http://www.ushmm.org/related.htm

The United States Holocaust Memorial Museum has compiled an alphabetically arranged, hyper-linked list of nearly 100 local North American organizations, dedicated in a variety of ways to remembering the Holocaust. A separate list of directors is available as well.

EDUCATION
(K-12)

Holocaust Resources Materials

http://www.socialstudies.com/holo.html

Social Studies School Service has dedicated an entire Web site to educational materials on the Holocaust. This site is a veritable catalog of curricula, texts, posters, CD-ROMs, and audio-visual materials targeted primarily for children and teenagers.

EDUCATION
(ACADEMIC)

Responses to the Holocaust: A Hypermedia Sourcebook for the Humanities

http://jefferson.village.virginia.edu/holocaust/response.html

The University of Virginia has been a front-runner in digitizing and networking full text. Robert S. Leventhal, Department of German, created this hypermedia full text work in order to introduce various discourses, disciplines, media and institutions that have produced significant critical and theoretical positions and discussions concerning the Nazi Genocide of the Jews of Europe. This provocative compendium of works encompasses various media and institutions, including literature, philosophy, literary criticism and theory, sociology, psychoanalysis, history and historiography, religious studies, film, art and architecture, political theory, informatics and the history of technology, and popular culture or cultural studies.

HOLOCAUST DENIAL

Responses to Revisionist Arguments

http://www.wiesenthal.com/resource/revision.htm

Weisenthal Center Researcher Aaron Breitbart prepared referenced responses to common allegations of "Holocaust Revisionists," such as the claim that six million Jewish losses is a gross exaggeration. The responses give an appreciation to the painstaking research that has gone into uncovering evidence after the war.

The Nizkor Project

http://www1.us.nizkor.org/

Often incorrectly referred to as "Holocaust Revisionism" this site addresses the notion that the Holocaust never happened. Besides being the home of the *Auschwitz Alphabet*, which defines Holocaust terminology and documents arguments, this site contains well-organized answers to *FAQs* (these are not so much *frequently asked questions* as they are *frequent accusations* of denial). *Revisionism* is rejected as a term since history is continually *revised*, as opposed to an adamant *denial* that six million Jews were murdered under Hitler's final solution. (Nizkor is Hebrew for "we will remember.")

INTERVIEWS WITH HOLOCAUST SURVIVORS

Survivors of the Shoah Visual History Foundation

http://www.vhf.org/home.html

Founded by Steven Spielberg in 1994, this is a collaborative project to videotape eyewitness accounts of the Holocaust. Over the next several years, tens-of-thousands of testimonies will be videotaped, catalogued, and made available to educational institutions via state-of-the-art interactive network technology, and through books, CD-ROMs, and documentaries. To date nearly 24,000 interviews have been conducted in twenty-two languages. By the end of 1997, *Survivors of the Shoah Visual History Foundation* plans to make its complete archive available via secure on-line computer networks to the following five initial repositories:

- The U.S. Holocaust Memorial Museum, Washington, D.C.
- The Simon Wiesenthal Center, Los Angeles, CA
- Yad Vashem, Jerusalem, Israel
- The Fortunoff Video Archive for Holocaust Testimonies, Yale University, New Haven
- The Museum of Jewish Heritage, New York

In the future, the archive will be available to additional repositories throughout the world. Selected interviews at Yale University are already available online. The Registry at the *Benjamin and Vladka Meed Registry of Jewish Holocaust Survivors* in Washington, D.C. defines a survivor as a person who was displaced, persecuted, and/

or discriminated against by the racial, religious, ethnic, and political policies of the Nazis and their allies.

BIBLIOGRAPHIES

L'Chaim: A Holocaust Web Project

http://www.charm.net/~rbennett/l'chaim.html

This site is the home of the *Virtual Tour of Dachau*, and a Holocaust glossary. Watch out for some technical errors in the html tags within the essay "A Survivor Speaks." This site is most valuable for its links to other Holocaust Web pages.

USENET NEWS GROUPS

Newsgroups, although the epitome of serendipity, can often provide an avenue for positing questions, and referral to further resources, such as academic papers and preprints. Two popular, moderated news groups are *soc.culture.jewish.holocaust* and *soc.history.war.world-war-ii.*

REFERENCE

1. Information provided by the Benjamin and Vladka Meed Registry of Jewish Holocaust Survivors, Washington, D.C.

Holocaust Resources on the Internet:
A Presence and Usage Survey

Scott A. Mellendorf

SUMMARY. Due to the wealth of information available on the Internet, using it for research is often difficult and time consuming. These barriers can be traced to the Internet's mystic appeal. This misplaced focus often leads users away from the very thought process that directed them to this resource tool. The following article stresses a research process rather than the delivering technology. It details the use of an established evaluation criteria that helps identify quality Net resources. The process also involves locating Net information based on resource type (museums, research centers, oral testimonies, library catalogs, etc.). Although this survey focuses on the Holocaust, the process is universal. *[Article copies available for a fee from The Haworth Document Delivery Service: 1-800-342-9678. E-mail address: getinfo@haworth.com]*

INTRODUCTION

The horrifying persecution of the Jews, Poles, Slavs, and any other group considered "anti-social" by the Nazi regime will al-

---

Scott A. Mellendorf is Reference and Internet Librarian, Saginaw Valley State University. He is a member of the American Library Association and the Michigan Library Association.

Address correspondence to: Scott A. Mellendorf, Zahnow Library, Saginaw Valley State University, University Center, MI 48710. E-mail: mel@tardis.svsu.edu

The author expresses sincere thanks to colleagues Anita Dey, Monica Carr, John Mauch, and Janice Kimmel of Zahnow Library, Saginaw Valley State University for their assistance. A special thanks to Mary and David Mellendorf for their support with the completion of this project.

[Haworth co-indexing entry note]: "Holocaust Resources on the Internet: A Presence and Usage Survey." Mellendorf, Scott A. Co-published simultaneously in *The Reference Librarian* (The Haworth Press, Inc.) No. 61/62, 1998, pp. 265-285; and: *The Holocaust: Memories, Research, Reference* (ed: Robert Hauptman, and Susan Hubbs Motin) The Haworth Press, Inc., 1998, pp. 265-285. Single or multiple copies of this article are available for a fee from The Haworth Document Delivery Service [1-800-342-9678, 9:00 a.m. - 5:00 p.m. (EST). E-mail address: getinfo@haworth.com].

ways be a definitive example of humankind at its worst. Tragic death based on individual beliefs, behavior, and nationality should never occur in a civilized world. It is hard to accept that just over fifty years ago it did. The Holocaust has left an ominous scar that cuts deep into the soul of humankind. The following annotated list of Holocaust Internet resources is done in honor of the six million Jews, nearly two million Poles and Slavs, more than three million Soviet prisoners, and thousands of other Holocaust victims.[1]

RESOURCE CRITERIA

The Internet's nature (wealth of resources, heavy use, open publishing, varying formats, changing URLs) makes it difficult to compile an authoritative and comprehensive subject specific list. Thus the following Holocaust resource list is not meant to be one. Not being a scholar on Holocaust study, the list was compiled with an established criteria that would produce resources to assist those conducting Holocaust research. Please accept an apology if a major resource was not included in this very important field of study.

The enormous amount of Holocaust sites on the Internet make it nearly impossible to survey and analyze each one. Specific criteria must be established in order to compile a list that will assist with effective research. This does not mean that they are the best, just that they meet a rigid criteria that should ensure their usefulness. The following criteria applies to only Web resources in the list. Each site must adhere to:

1. Presence

Refers to the number of other sites on the World-Wide Web that offer a link to the selected resource. This form of flattery provides a debatable measure of the resource's importance on the Web. Although this number should be carefully scrutinized (flaws include duplicate entries in search engine database, sub-linked within own organization, different link to numbers among search engines), it still can give an idea of the site's significance on the Web. All Web, Gopher, and Library Catalog sites surveyed are listed in descending order based on their presence average between two search engines (used link: search command in Alta Vista and Infoseek Ultra).

2. Content

How much content is provided and in what format? The content should be more than just site information. It should include "real data" such as articles, essays, testimonies, etc. Included sites must contain at least five distinct data sets.

3. Purpose

What is the site's mission and/or goals? The site must also have a contact person clearly stated and made available either by email or phone.

4. Updates

Each site should be updated at a regular basis. This ensures accurate links and new information. All Web sites had to meet a no later than six month since last update policy.

In addition to these four evaluation criteria, the Holocaust research sites were divided into five tools/categories most used to gather information from the Internet. These include the World-Wide Web, Gopher sites, Library Catalogs, FTP sites, and Listservs/Newsgroups. This gives a complete survey of the major methods for storing information on the Net. Within the World-Wide Web, the resources are divided into four distinct types. These include Museums/Organizations, Research Centers, Oral Testimonies and Libraries/Special Collections.

WORLD-WIDE WEB/MUSEUMS-ORGANIZATIONS

United States Holocaust Memorial Museum (www.ushmm.org)

Presence: 4/12/97–AltaVista = 2,000 and InfoSeek Ultra = 1,725 Average = 1,863,
   Content: Full text articles, excerpts, lists, audio, and images.
   Purpose: "To advance and disseminate knowledge about the Holocaust."
   Summary: This web site combines information about the mu-

seum and provides access to some of its holdings. Online exhibits and full text educational documents (i.e., "The Holocaust: An Historical Summary"–six pages in length) are just two online examples. This site's Research Institute (www.ushmm.org/ushmm_ia.html provides online access to the library, archives, or any museum department.

Cybrary of the Holocaust (remember.org)

Presence: 4/12/97–AltaVista = 300 and InfoSeek Ultra = 512, Avg = 406.

Content: Full text articles, poetry, witness accounts, bookstore, lesson plans and other educational material for teachers, bibliographies, paintings, and images.

Purpose: To remember the Holocaust through Holocaust Survivors. "Dedicated to the memories of the Survivors."

Summary: One of the best multi-purpose sites on the Web. Researchers can use the witness accounts for primary sources and use the historical studies for secondary analysis. The image collection is large and well organized. One very useful component is the "Education" section. It contains many materials and is a must for Holocaust educators to examine. This site is impressive and serves as a model for what can be done on the Web for disseminating information in various formats.

Museum of Tolerance (www.wiesenthal.com/mot)

Presence: 4/12/97–AltaVista = 100 and InfoSeek Ultra = 204, Avg = 152.

Content: Full text articles, Children of the Holocaust biographies, and an on-line museum tour.

Purpose: "To educate the public about the importance of tolerance in our society."

Summary: The "On-Line Tour" gives Web users at least an idea of what this interactive, hands-on, experimental museum has to offer. Full text articles about the Holocaust are found under the "Holocaust Section" of the "On-Line Tour." Another valuable use for this site is the "Children of the Holocaust" stories.

Holocaust Pictures Exhibition (modb.oce.ulg.ac.be/schmitz/ holocaust.html)

Presence: 4/12/97–AltaVista = 100 and InfoSeek Ultra = 170, Avg = 135.

Content: Images and supportive comments.

Purpose: Francois Schmitz wanted to display the photos and supportive comments from the Daniel Keren Gopher site collection on the Web. The original photos and comments are also available in files on the Nysernet Gopher.

Summary: Thirty seven images depict the suffering endured and senselessness of the Holocaust. Image comments describe the photos that are also translated in French by Francois Schmitz. This is an excellent image resource and is linked often by others.

L'Chaim (www.charm.net/~rbennett/l'chaim.html)

Presence: 4/12/97–AltaVista = 100 and InfoSeek Ultra = 138, Avg = 119

Content: Images and text.

Purpose: "This web site stands to remind us all that the death of just one human being at the hands of another is one too many."

Summary: Nice combination of images, links to other Holocaust resources, and a "Virtual Tour of Dachau." The "Holocaust Glossary" is an excellent tool for the beginning Holocaust researcher. Another unique and useful feature is the update notification option. Users can submit their email address and receive site page update notification via email.

Miami Beach Holocaust Memorial (netrunner.net/~holomem)

Presence: 4/12/97–AltaVista = 51 and InfoSeek Ultra = 50, Avg = 51.

Content: Virtual image tour of Ken Treister's sculpture memorial.

Purpose: "A memorial to the Jewish Culture and the individuals killed in the Holocaust. It expresses in photographs and sculpture the history of the Holocaust so future generations will never forget."

Summary: A very moving Web resource that captures the suffering and annihilation experienced by Holocaust victims. Serves as a fine example of utilizing the Web's technology via the arts.

WWW RESEARCH CENTERS

Simon Wiesenthal Center (www.wiesenthal.com)

Presence: 4/16/97–AltaVista = 800 and InfoSeek Ultra = 961, Average = 880.

Content: Full text articles, live audio events, archived audio events, topical news, and bookstore.

Purpose: Cited as "an international center for Holocaust remembrance and the defense of human rights and the Jewish people." This is done through "social action, public outreach, scholarship, education and media projects."

Summary: As its presence ratings indicate, the Simon Wiesenthal Center has an established online reputation. It offers a variety of multimedia information tools for Holocaust researchers. The "36 questions about the Holocaust" and the "Glossary of the Holocaust" are just two features that assist basic research needs. The live audio events and "CyberWatch" section are two interactive features unique among Holocaust web sites.

The Nizkor Project (www.nizkor.org)

Presence: 4/16/97–AltaVista = 1,000 and InfoSeek Ultra = 730, Avg = 865.

Content: Full text information. Audio and images to be added soon.

Purpose: Site states it is "a collage of projects focused on the Holocaust and its denial."

Summary: Extensive FTP archive of nearly 11,000 files now being made available in html form through "The Holocaust Web Project." This archive of information "will include hundreds of thousands of pages from the National Archives of the United States, Canada, Germany, France, and the United Kingdom." The Nizkor Project's specific focus, denial of the Holocaust, makes it an excellent research tool for that aspect of Holocaust research. Its high presence rating reinforces that assessment.

The Anti-Defamation League Home Page (www.adl.org)

Presence: 4/16/97–AltaVista = 100 and InfoSeek Ultra = 161, Avg = 131.

Content: Full text articles, news stories, and newsletter.

Purpose: "To stop the defamation of the Jewish people and to secure justice and fair treatment of all citizens alike."

Summary: Serves as an excellent source for identifying current stories, programs, and services that the ADL is conducting to counteract anti-semitism. Also provides access to "Frontline," the organization's newsletter. Site has a very useful search engine and quick links to press releases and other material.

Response to the Holocaust: A Hypermedia Sourcebook for the Humanities (jefferson.village.virginia.edu/holocaust/response.html)

Presence: 4/16/97–AltaVista = 97 and InfoSeek Ultra = 128, Avg = 113.

Content: Full text, images, film, audio.

Purpose: "To offer the navigator of this hypermedia archive a way to access important information regarding the study and critical discourse concerning the Holocaust, and to provide a research, teaching, and learning resource for the student, teacher and scholar of the Holocaust."

Summary: Robert S. Leventhal, Department of German, University of Virginia, has put together a multi-discipline study site. It provides researchers, educators, and students with in-depth multimedia Holocaust information. There are currently twelve disciplines/media categories (some under construction) that are easy to use and the page states that all will eventually include bibliographies and further reading options.

YAD VASHEM (yad-vashem.org.il)

Presence: 4/16/97–AltaVista = 83 and InfoSeek Ultra = 61, Avg = 72.

Content: Currently text information about YAD VASHEM.

Purpose: "YAD VASHEM is the Holocaust Memorial of the

Jewish People. Located on the Har Hazikaron, the Mount of Rememberence, in Jerusalem, Israel, it is a complex of museums, monuments, research, and teaching and resource center. Its library's aim is to be a repository of all published material about the Holocaust and related subjects."

Summary: The YAD VASHEM Holocaust memorial has the largest collection of Holocaust material in the world. Currently, the library catalog is not available online. When it is, watch this site's presence rates increase.

SICSA (www2.huji.ac.il/www_jcd)
Vidal Sassoon International Center for the Study of Antisemitism

Presence: 4/16/97–AltaVista = 46 and InfoSeek Ultra = 60, Avg = 53.

Content: Full text articles, online bibliographic database.

Purpose: SICSA is "dedicated to an independent, non-political approach to the accumulation and dissemination of knowledge necessary for understanding the phenomenon of antisemitism."

Summary: Researchers will find the "Felix Posen Bibliographic Project on Antisemitism" a very effective tool for Holocaust study. This online and annotated bibliographic database includes works on the Holocaust as part of the history of antisemitism in the twentieth century. Researchers without online access may contact SICSA for a search request.

ORAL TESTIMONIES

Survivors of the Shoah Visual History Foundation (www.vhf.org)

Presence: 4/16/97–AltaVista = 100 and InfoSeek Ultra = 100, Average = 100.

Content: Full text organization information.

Purpose: "The Survivors of the Shoah Visual History Foundation is a nonprofit organization dedicated to videotaping and archiving interviews of Holocaust survivors all over the world. Its archive will be used as a tool for global education about the Holocaust and to teach racial, ethnic, and cultural tolerance."

Summary: Although this site has no interviews available online, it does provide links to repository sites that do. The organization information is very detailed and lists how and where to contact the foundation. Founded by Steven Spielberg in 1994, the foundation is obtaining its goal to "compile the most comprehensive library of survivor testimony ever assembled" (as of March 3, 1997, 25,402 interviews were completed).

Fortunoff Video Archive for Holocaust Testimonies (www.library. yale.edu/testimonies/homepage.html)

Presence: 4/16/97–AltaVista = 69 and InfoSeek Ultra = 59, Avg = 64.

Content: Audio/video excerpts, full text essays, newsletter.

Purpose: "The videotaped testimonies were given by Holocaust survivors and witnesses motivated by the desire to counteract forgetfulness, ignorance, and malicious denial."

Summary: The Fortunoff Video Archive, part of the Manuscripts and Archives collection at Sterling Memorial Library, Yale University, is a Shoah foundation repository. Video and archive excerpts are available online and are very well done. The online newsletter offers more personal insight with articles by participants about the interviewing experience. This resource provides researchers with valuable primary resources.

The Frances and Jacob Hiatt Collection of Holocaust Materials (webster.holycross.edu/crossway/library/hiatt)

Presence: 4/16/97–AltaVista = 7 and InfoSeek Ultra = 55, Avg = 31.

Content: Full text articles, biographies, images, audio clips.

Purpose: Sponsored by the College of Holy Cross, the site strives "to preserve in memory the six million Jews put to death by the Nazis as it strives to educate continually about the Holocaust that such atrocities might never again occur."

Summary: Although the audio clips "Local Oral Histories" section is currently under construction, this is a definite site to bookmark for future visits. It has many other valuable research components. These include an image collection (very clear photos), speeches from the collection dedication ceremony and a biographical/name listing of "Catholic Martyrs of the Holocaust." The site also includes a search engine for users to search the entire Holocaust collection.

Holocaust Survivor Oral History Project (holocaust.umd.umich. edu)

Presence: 4/16/97–AltaVista = 2 and InfoSeek Ultra = 3, Avg = 3.
Content: Full text transcripts, audio clips.
Purpose: To transcribe recorded interviews from Holocaust survivors and enter them into the online catalog of the Mardigian Library, University of Michigan-Dearborn, and OCLC, the Online Computer Library Catalog.
Summary: This site, explains Dr. Sid Bolkosky, Professor of History at the University of Michigan-Dearborn, efforts to interview Holocaust survivors and have the tapes become part of the library collection. He has interviewed "over 150 survivors and compiled about 330 hours of audio tapes and 60 hours of video tapes." The Web site also provides online interview excerpts. They are well explained, and offered in both text (html or Adobe Acrobat) and audio ("au" or "Real Audio") media. With this easy to use format, this primary resource site's presence ratings are sure to increase as it becomes more known on the Net.

GOPHER SITES

Jerusalem One Gopher/Virtual Jerusalem (gopher://jer1.co.il)

Presence: Web version–4/16/97–AltaVista = 2,000 and InfoSeek Ultra = 2,170, Average = 2,085.
Content: Text headline news, weekly poll, lists of related links.
Purpose: To provide "a user-friendly, regularly updated index of "neighborhoods" covering the full spectrum of Jewish and Israeli life, including the arts and entertainment, science and technology, business and finance, religion, politics, travel, children and education."
Summary: At date of visit, the Gopher version was down but

cited as "Back soon" on the Web site. Although this site has a Jewish culture focus, it would still play a prominent role in Holocaust research. It can be used for Jewish culture education and the headline news component will keep visitors updated on current events (some of which could include the Holocaust).

Global Jewish Information Network (http://jewishnet.net/gopher.html)

Presence checked using (http://jewishnet.net): 4/16/97–AltaVista = 300 and InfoSeek Ultra = 348, Avg = 324.

Content: Lists other Jewish Gophers.

Purpose: Strictly lists other Jewish/Holocaust Gopher sites.

Summary: Although this site offers only the list of Jewish Gophers, it still serves a valuable purpose. Gopher sites are difficult to locate as many have given way to the Web. Gophers remain useful for text-only browsing and therefore can assist in that way. This site currently lists over 40 gophers that could provide Holocaust research assistance. These include gophers at Israeli Universities, the Library of Congress, and some online electronic journal sites.

Nysernet: Shamash Gopher (gopher://israel.nysernet.org)

Presence: 4/16/97–AltaVista = 100 and InfoSeek Ultra = 451, Avg = 276.

Content: Full text documents, information, and graphic files.

Purpose: Serves as an online source for Jewish information.

Summary: This gopher is linked often on the Web and for good reason. It has many full text documents about the holocaust that provides information and offers a framework for learning. Nysernet also focuses on Jewish culture.

Literature of the Holocaust (gopher://dept.english.upenn.edu:70/11/Courses/Holocaust)

Presence: 4/16/97–AltaVista = 3 and InfoSeek Ultra = 73, Avg = 38.

Content: Full text documents, testimony excerpts, bibliographies, book reviews, Holocaust news reports, online journal links, newsgroup selections, and other Holocaust links.

Purpose: "These pages are about hope."

Summary: Mr. Al Filreis, Professor of English at the University of Pennsylvania, has put together an extensive list called "Literature of the Holocaust." This list contains 108 files and 11 directory links that lead researchers to an immense amount of information about varying Holocaust topics. These include "Bystanders: Did they know about the camps?," "Compensation to those who hid them," "Disowning & Denial," "Henry Ford & Anti-semitism," and "Silence on Holocaust in the 50s and 60s." Professor Filreis also provides access to an annotated list of Holocaust sites (see list of links section for url).

I*EARN Holocaust/Genocide Project (gopher://gopher.igc.apc. org:7009 also www.igc.apc.org/iearn/hgp)

Presence: 4/16/97–AltaVista = 23 and InfoSeek Ultra = 1, Avg = 12.

Content: Full text articles, Holocaust bibliography, historic time line.

Purpose: "The Holocaust/Genocide Project (HGP) is an international, nonprofit, telecommunications project focusing on the study of the Holocaust and other genocides. Its purpose is to promote education and awareness and to encourage the application of this knowledge in a way which makes a positive difference in the world. The HGP welcomes all students, age 12-17, and teachers, internationally."

Summary: The unique focus and participation group (students and teachers-internationally) makes this site worth a visit for their perspective alone. It gives insight from an age group that needs to be aware of the Holocaust and other genocides so they can assist to make positive change in the world. The Student Magazine title says it all: "An End To Intolerance." This site also has a Web version that includes nine pages of other Holocaust links (see list of links section for url).

WWW/TELNET LIBRARY
CATALOGS-HOLOCAUST COLLECTIONS

Jewish Theological Seminary (telnet://jtsa.edu)

Presence: 4/12/97–AltaVista = 900 and InfoSeek Ultra = 685, Avg = 793.
Content: Judaism, Torah commentaries, one-half of library on-line.

Isser & Rae Price Library of Judaica, Univ. of Florida (www.uflib.ufl.edu)

Presence: 4/12/97–AltaVista = 700 and InfoSeek Ultra = 842, Avg = 771.
Content: Judica, Historical and Current.

University of Haifa (www-lib.haifa.ac.il/www)

Presence: 4/12/97–AltaVista = 400 and InfoSeek Ultra = 539, Avg = 470.
Content: Centre for Holocaust Studies.

UCLA, Univ. of Judaism Library (www.library.ucla.edu)

Presence: 4/12/97–AltaVista = 400 and InfoSeek Ultra = 449, Avg = 425.
Content: Judaica and Hebraica studies.

Ohio State University–Jewish Studies Library (aleph.lib.ohio-state.edu)

Presence: 4/12/97–AltaVista = 100 and InfoSeek Ultra = 89, Avg = 95.
Content: Jewish Studies, LCSH in Jewish Studies, access to the Association of Jewish Libraries Home Page, links to related sites.

Chabad/Lubavitch (telnet://lubavitch.chabad.org)

Presence: 4/12/97–AltaVista = 100 and InfoSeek Ultra = 78, Avg = 89.
Content: Judaica Studies.

Brandeis University Library (louis.brandeis.edu)

Presence: 4/12/97–AltaVista = 37 and InfoSeek Ultra = 26, Avg = 32.

Content: Holocaust Survivors Collection, Resistance Collection, and Theresienstadt Concentration Camp Documents Collection.

George Washington University (www.aladin.wrlc.org)

Presence: 4/12/97–AltaVista = 36 and InfoSeek Ultra = 17, Avg = 27.

Content: Yiddish books from the National Yiddish Book Center that include Holocaust Studies and social and political history.

University of Pennsylvania Center for Judaic Studies Library (www.cjs.upenn.edu/library/aleph.html)

Presence: 4/12/97–AltaVista = 7 and InfoSeek Ultra = 12, Avg = 10.

Content: Judaic Studies, Multilingual on-line catalog (Hebrew and English). 96,000 titles, more than 75% of collection online.

FTP SITES

FTP sites offer a unique way to use the Internet to obtain documents, images, and other remote files. Recent Net search advancements have made file transfer much easier than it was a few years ago (pre-Web). Three current and high-powered FTP search engines include:

- Filez (www.filez.com)
- FTP Search (www.ftpsearch.ntnu.no/ftpsearch)
- Snoopie (www.snoopie.com)

Each search engine employs many features that enable users to refine and customize both the search and search results. All three are available and can be searched simultaneously with the multi-search engine called *Dogpile (www.dogpile.com)*.

Utilizing these search tools provide researchers with the exact link to a document file or directory of files. This is useful but makes it difficult to determine the actual size of the FTP archive site. Therefore, the following list of five FTP sites are provided because they appear (according to the results obtained using Dogpile-FTP search) to have the largest set of total files from the conducted search. Please note that many of the Internet sites previously mentioned also have archived FTP files as a site option.

Holocaust FTP Sites

Obtained from Dogpile-FTP search (4/19/97) Search=Holocaust.

- ftp://ftp.argonet.co.uk
- ftp://ftp.doc.ic.ac.uk
- ftp://ftp.crl.go.jp
- ftp://ftp.almanac.bc.ca
- ftp://ftp.belnet.be

LISTSERVS/NEWSGROUPS

Listservs and Newsgroups are another form of Internet information that can assist Holocaust researchers. They provide focused discussions on varying topics within the Holocaust field of study. The following list of discussion groups was generated by a search using the *Liszt (www.liszt.com)* discussion group search engine.

H-ANTIS (h-net2.msu.edu/~antis)

Focus: Antisemitism discussion group.
Moderated: Yes

H-German (h-net2.msu.edu/~german)

Focus: Scholarly topics in German history.
Moderated: Yes–restricted to professors, lecturers, librarians, archivists, and graduate students.

H-Holocaust (listserv@h-net.msu.edu)

Focus: Holocaust studies, Anti-Semitism, Jewish history.
Moderated: Yes

Hlist (server@nizkor.almanac.bc.ca)

Focus: "Dedicated to research and the development of material related to Holocaust denial."
Moderated: Yes–private and invitational participation.

I*EARN (apc.iearn.hgp)

Focus: Student/Teacher International Holocaust Study Project.
Moderated: ?

Nizkor-L (listserv@veritas.nizkor.org)

Focus: Holocaust denial.
Moderated: No

Rev-psych (majordomo@list.pitt.edu)

Focus: Psychology of Holocaust Revisionism.
Moderated: ?

2nd gen (listproc@jer1.co.il)

Focus: Holocaust survivors' children and grandchildren discussion.
Moderated: No

SHOAH (soc.culture.jewish.holocaust)

World War II (soc.history.war.world-war-ii)

LIST OF LINKS

The list of related links on many Web pages provide a great service to Holocaust researchers. It allows them to continue searching Internet sites by specific topic. Users can then bookmark the larger sites and have an immediate collection. The following "List of Links" are listed in descending order by the number of links offered. Keeping these lists accurate is a dutiful job and all those involved with any such list are to be commended for creating and maintaining it.

Holocaust/Shoah links by David M. Dickerson (www.igc.org/ddickerson/holocaust.html)

Focus: Holocaust.
Number of links: 160+ (includes duplicates across categories).

Al Filreis–Literature of the Holocaust, Links section (dept.english.upenn.edu/~afilreis/Holocaust/holhome.html)

Focus: Holocaust—many aspects of.
Number of links: 150.

Hillel, Links to Jewish Resources on the Internet (www.site.gmu.edu/~hillel/links.html)

Focus: Holocaust, Jewish resources, Jewish periodicals.
Number of links: 101.

Ohio State University, Jewish Studies Library (aleph.lib.ohio-state.edu)

Focus: Holocaust-many aspects of.
Number of links: 95.

I*EARN Holocaust/Genocide Project, Other Sites of Interest (www.igc.apc.org/iearn/hgp/other-sites.html)

Focus: Holocaust, Anti-semitism and Racism, Genocide, Human Rights.
Number of links: 75.

One Stop Research Spot, Tulane University, Southern Institute (www.tulane.edu/~so-inst/holjud.html)

Focus: Holocaust and Judaism.
Number of links: 71.

Holocaust Information, Other Sites
(www.almanac.bc.ca/other-sites/holocaust-information.html)

Focus: Holocaust–many aspects of.
Number of links: 62.

Maven, Jewish/Israel Index (Holocaust & Antisemitism)
(www.maven.co.il/subjects/idx178.htm)

Focus: Holocaust and Anti-semitism.
Number of links: 57.

Holocaust Resources on the Web
(www-stud.uni-essen.de/~sg0047/shoah.hmtl)

Focus: Holocaust resources–annotated.
Number of links: 37.

SEARCH TOOLS

Conducting Holocaust research on the Internet and the World-Wide Web is possible because of the current search engines available. Sites listed in this survey were mostly located with the search tools listed below. They make the difficult task of locating quality sites somewhat easier. Their developers and owners have done a great service by providing free access.

Holocaust Specific Search Engines

- JC Navigate, Jewish Communication Network (www.jcn18.com/jhot00.htm)
- Nizkor Project Holocaust Archives (search.nizkor.org/search.html)

General Search Engines

- Alta Vista (altavista.digital.com)
- Dogpile (www.dogpile.com)
- Infoseek Ultra (ultra.infoseek.com)

Discussion List Search Engine

- LISZT (www.liszt.com)

REFERENCE

1. "The Holocaust: An Historical Summary." *United States Holocaust Memorial Museum-Education Document.* http://www.ushmm.org/misc-bin/add_goback/education/history.html (28 Jan. 1997).

APPENDIX

List of URLs Cited

Museums

- United States Holocaust Memorial Museum (www.ushmm.org)
- Cybrary of the Holocaust (remember.org)
- Museum Of Tolerance (www.wiesenthal.com/mot)
- Holocaust Pictures Exhibition (modb.oce.ulg.ac.be/schmitz/holocaust.html)
- L'Chaim (www.charm.net/~rbennett/l'chaim.html)
- Miami Beach Holocaust Memorial (netrunner.net/~holomem)

Research Centers

- Simon Wiesenthal Center (www.wiesenthal.com)
- The Nizkor Project (www.nizkor.org)
- The Anti-Defamation League Home Page (www.adl.org)
- Response to the Holocaust: A Hypermedia Sourcebook . . . (jefferson.village.virginia.edu/holocaust/response.html)
- YAD VASHEM (yad-vashem.org.il)
- SICSA (www2.huji.ac.il/www_jcd)

Oral Testimonies

- Survivors of the Shoah Visual History Foundation (www.vhf.org)

- Fortunoff Video Archive for Holocaust Testimonies (www. library.yale.edu/testimonies/homepage.html)
- The Frances and Jacob Hiatt Collection of Holocaust Materials (webster.holycross.edu/crossway/library/hiatt)
- Holocaust Survivor Oral History Project (holocaust.umd.umich. edu)

Gophers

- Jerusalem One Gopher/Virtual Jerusalem (gopher://jer1.co.il)
- Global Jewish Information Network (http://jewishnet.net/gopher. html)
- Nysernet: Shamash Gopher (gopher://israel.nysernet.org)
- Literature of the Holocaust (gopher://dept.english.upenn.edu: 70/ 11/Courses/Holocaust)
- I*EARN Holocaust/Genocide Project (gopher://gopher.igc.apc.org: 7009 *also* www.igc.apc.org/iearn/hgp)

Library Catalogs

- Jewish Theological Seminary (telnet://jtsa.edu)
- Isser & Rae Price Library of Judaica (www.uflib.ufl.edu)
- University of Haifa (www-lib.haifa.ac.il/www)
- UCLA, Univ. of Judaism Library (www.library.ucla.edu)
- Ohio State University–Jewish Studies Library (aleph.lib.ohio-state.edu)
- Chabad/Lubavitch (telnet://lubavitch.chabad.org)
- Brandeis University Library (louis.brandeis.edu)
- George Washington University (www.aladin.wrlc.org)
- University of Pennsylvania Center for Judaic Studies Library (www.cjs.upenn.edu/library/aleph.html)

FTP Sites

- ftp://ftp.argonet.co.uk
- ftp://ftp.doc.ic.ac.uk
- ftp://ftp.crl.go.jp
- ftp://ftp.almanac.bc.ca
- ftp://ftp.belnet.be

Listservs/Newsgroups

- H-ANTIS (h-net2.msu.edu/~antis)
- H-German (h-net2.msu.edu/~german)
- H-Holocaust (listserv@h-net.msu.edu)
- Hlist (server@nizkor.almanac.bc.ca)
- I*EARN (apc.iearn.hgp)
- Nizkor-L (listserv@veritas.nizkor.org)
- Rev-psych (majordomo@list.pitt.edu)
- 2nd gen (listproc@jer1.co.il)
- SHOAH (soc.culture.jewish.holocaust)
- World War II (soc.history.war.world-war-ii)

List of Links

- Holocaust/Shoah links by David M. Dickerson (www.igc.org/ddickerson/holocaust.html)
- Al Filreis–Literature of the Holocaust, Links section (dept. english. upenn.edu/~afilreis/Holocaust/holhome.html)
- Hillel, Links to Jewish Resources on the Internet (www.site.gmu. edu/~hillel/links.html)
- Ohio State University, Jewish Studies Library (aleph.lib.ohio-state.edu)
- I*EARN Holocaust/Genocide Project, Other Sites of Interest (www.igc.apc.org/iearn/hgp/other-sites.html)
- One Stop Research Spot, Tulane University, Southern Institute (www.tulane.edu/~so-inst/holjud.html)
- Holocaust Information, Other Sites (www.almanac.bc.ca/other-sites/holocaust-information.html)

Search Engines

- JC Navigate, Jewish Communication Network (www.jcn18.com/jhot00.htm)
- Nizkor Project Holocaust Archives (search.nizkor.org/search.html)
- AltaVista (altavista.digital.com)
- Dogpile (www.dogpile.com)
- Infoseek Ultra (ultra.infoseek.com)
- LISZT (www.liszt.com)

Holocaust Denial and the Internet

Betty Landesman

SUMMARY. The Holocaust denial movement began with Nazi officials and continues today. The term revisionism rather than denial is used by the movement's proponents. They do not deny the Holocaust, but are skeptical of the claims of six million dead, gas chambers, and an extermination policy. The Internet has made revisionist ideas and research more widely available than ever before. This article examines the major revisionist and refutation sites and documents available on the Internet today. *[Article copies available for a fee from The Haworth Document Delivery Service: 1-800-342-9678. E-mail address: getinfo@haworth.com]*

With the Holocaust came its denial. The movement began with Nazi officials themselves, saw a growth spurt in the 1970s and 1980s, and continues to this day. Denial takes many forms. The number of deaths was far fewer than six million. There was no extermination policy behind the deaths that occurred; they resulted from the prevailing bad wartime conditions. Jews died in no greater numbers than other people. The gas chambers that existed were used for delousing clothing, not for murder. Any intentional killings in the camps were planned by Himmler and SS officers, not by

Betty Landesman is Systems Training Librarian and Subject Specialist for Judaic Studies, Religion, Classics, Music, Telecommunication, and Forensic Sciences at The George Washington University.

Address correspondence to: Betty Landesman, Gelman Library, George Washington University, 2130 H Street NW, Washington, DC 20052. E-mail: betty@gwis2.circ.gwu.edu

[Haworth co-indexing entry note]: "Holocaust Denial and the Internet." Landesman, Betty. Co-published simultaneously in *The Reference Librarian* (The Haworth Press, Inc.) No. 61/62, 1998, pp. 287-299; and: *The Holocaust: Memories, Research, Reference* (ed: Robert Hauptman and Susan Hubbs Motin) The Haworth Press, Inc., 1998, pp. 287-299. Single or multiple copies of this article are available for a fee from The Haworth Document Delivery Service [1-800-342-9678, 9:00 a.m. - 5:00 p.m. (EST). E-mail address: getinfo@haworth.com].

287

Hitler. The real enemies were Stalin and the Soviet Union. The Holocaust "story" is a hoax, a propaganda attempt to gain sympathy for Zionist ideals.

The term revisionism rather than denial is used by the movement's proponents. They do not deny that there was a "Holocaust," but wish to revise the meaning assigned to the word. They are skeptical of the claims of six million dead, of deadly gas chambers, of an extermination policy. Since critical thinking should always be applied to history in order to bring it into accordance with actual facts, revisionists are pursuing normal historical investigatory techniques. They are also exercising their freedom of expression in publishing the results of these investigations.

With the advent of the Internet as an international publishing tool, revisionist ideas and research are becoming even more widely available than before. People using the Internet to do research on the Holocaust will find revisionist documents in response to searches on "Auschwitz" and "gas chambers." Some sites are specifically focused on Holocaust revisionism, others have a broader anti-Semitic or anti-Zionist focus. Some sites are well organized and reasonable in tone; others are somewhat hysterical, using the term "exterminationist" to refer to organizations such as the Simon Wiesenthal Center and the Anti-Defamation League of B'Nai B'rith. Revisionist sites often include statements on freedom of expression and the necessity to avoid censorship on the Internet, and have links to other sites that promote these goals. In response, there are also Internet sites aimed not only to provide information about the Holocaust itself but also to counter the revisionists' arguments.

An extensive overview of Holocaust denial literature will be found in *Twentieth-Century Literary Criticism*, Vol. 58, ed. Jennifer Gariepy (Detroit: Gale Research, 1995), pp. 1-110. This article will focus on the aspects of the subject that can be found on the Internet. As the publishers of the HateWatch home page (http://hatewatch. org/) state, "The information found here may be offensive to some but we believe the best way to fight this cultural poison is to face to [sic] head on."

INTRODUCTORY MATERIAL

Users of *Yahoo!* can take the following path to find some of the major revisionist sites:

Arts → Humanities → History → 20th Century → Holocaust,
The → Holocaust Revisionists

There is another subcategory beyond this one, called *Refutation*. As of this writing, it contains links to some counter-revisionist documents and one of the major sites, the Nizkor Project, which is described in more detail below. *Yahoo!* does not include a comprehensive listing of Internet resources on the topic, but it does provide a useful starting point for research, and its use of subject headings such as *Revisionists* and *Refutation* is very clear.

There is a Usenet newsgroup called alt.revisionism. The archives from April 1996 are maintained on the Nizkor Project site (ftp://ftp1.us.nizkor.org/pub/usenet/alt.revisionism/(archives)) and are searchable back to 10/1/96 (http://www.nizkor.org/search.html).

Some Internet-accessible documents that provide an overview or introduction to the topic are as follows:

- Austin, Ben S. "A Brief History of Holocaust Denial." 1997. URL: http://www.mtsu.edu/~baustin/denhist.htm

- Collette, Lin. "Encountering Holocaust Denial." This is a version without footnotes of an article that originally appeared in *The Public Eye*, September 1994. URL: http://www.publiceye.org/magazine/holodeni.html

- Fresco, Nadine. "The Denial of the Dead: On the Faurisson Affair." From *Dissent*, fall 1981. URL: http://mediatheque.ircam.fr/~mf/anti-rev/textes/Fresco81a/nobody.html

- Miele, Frank. "Giving the Devil His Due: Holocaust Revisionism as a Test Case for Free Speech and the Skeptical Ethic." Electronically "reprinted" from *Skeptic*, vol. 2, no. 4, 1994, pp. 58-70. URL: http://www.skeptic.com/02.4.miele-holocaust.html

- Vidal-Naquet, Pierre. "Assassins of Memory." 1987; translated by Jeffrey Mehlman in *Assassins of Memory: Essays on the Denial of the Holocaust*, Columbia University Press, 1992.
  URL: http://mediatheque.ircam.fr/~mf/anti-rev/textes/Vidal Naquet92b/ body.html

- _____ . "Theses on Revisionism." 1985; translated by Jeffrey Mehlman in *Assassins of Memory: Essays on the Denial of the Holocaust*, Columbia University Press, 1992.
  URL: http://mediatheque.ircam.fr/~mf/anti-rev/textes/Vidal Naquet85a/ body.html

REVISIONIST INTERNET SITES

- Adelaide Institute.
  URL: http://www.adam.com.au/~fredadin/rev.html

This site states that "we are not deniers of the Jewish-Nazi Holocaust. We affirm that to date there is no proof that millions of people were gassed by Germans in homicidal gas chambers. Dare you join us in this final intellectual adventure of the 20th Century?" They provide links to many of other revisionist sites which are described below, including the Zündelsite, Greg Raven's page, CODOH, Radio Islam, AAARGH, and Hoffman, as well as HateWatch.

- L'Association des Anciens Amateurs de Récits de Guerre et d'Holocauste (AAARGH).
  URL: http://www.abbc.com/aaargh/engl/engl.html

This site explains that revisionists "request the application of the routine objective historical methods to analyze the events which led to the end of the War, because it is a crucial part of our common history." AAARGH hosts the largest collection of Internet texts by the major French revisionists Robert Faurisson and Serge Thion, many in English translation and more in the original French (see Archive Faurisson and Archive Thion under *Revisionist Authors*, below). Here is also found the Archive La Vieille Taupe, the publisher of many revisionist works including *les Annales d'Histoire Révisionniste*.

- The Campaign for Radical Truth in History.
  URL: http://www.hoffman-info.com/

  Michael Hoffman, "activist historian," is the author of *The Great Holocaust Trial: The Landmark Battle for Freedom of Speech*, about Ernst Zündel. He states that Jewish Communists caused Russian genocide, that there is racist hatred of Germans, and that the Holocaust is propaganda to expand Jewish power. There are links to sites on World War Two Revisionism as well as on Black Heritage and Separatism, White Heritage and Separatism, Palestine, Judaica, Conspiracy, and Inappropriate Technology.

- Committee for Open Debate on the Holocaust (CODOH).
  URL: http://www.codoh.com

  Bradley R. Smith, the publisher of this site, states that its purpose is "to promote intellectual freedom with regard to this one historical event, which in turn will promote intellectual freedom toward all historical events (thus all other issues) . . . We're focused on American culture, on the American ideal that liberty has the power to wash a people clean and that there is no liberty without intellectual freedom." Smith was responsible for placing ads questioning the Holocaust in college newspapers, setting off discussion on free speech. The Historical Revisionism page (http://www.codoh.com/revision.html) is organized by topics such as Gas Chambers and Vans, War Crimes Trials, Zionism-Stalinism and the Holocaust, and New Revisionist Voices. There are also sections devoted to revisionist authors such as Robert Faurisson and Roger Garaudy as well as links to other revisionist sites. There are site indexes by subject and title and by author, and an extensive graphics listing. Note: I found this site to be well organized, updated frequently, professionally presented, and containing a fair amount of content on the topics. It can't therefore be dismissed as easily as some of the other sites.

- Greg Raven's Web site for revisionist materials from the Institute for Historical Review (and elsewhere).
  URL: http://www.kaiwan.com/~ihrgreg/

Raven is the associate editor of the *Journal of Historical Review*. This site contains an index to the entire run of that journal, as well as a lengthy Holocaust Revisionism FAQ, articles by Butz and Faurisson (see below), the author's "Sixty-Six Questions and Answers on the Holocaust," and a series of pamphlets published by the Institute for Historical Review. While Raven states that this web site is his own personal project, he posts the text of many IHR publications and includes a section describing its mission. The IHR is a "research, educational and publishing center devoted to truth and accuracy in history." There are links to other revisionist sites as well as the "Blacks and Jews Newspage" and many Zündelsite mirrors including his own.

Magellan (http://www.mckinley.com/) described this site as follows: "An associate editor for the Institute for Historical Review posts a sampling of their infamous articles, most of which attempt to prove that the Holocaust didn't happen, but was invented by Jews for political gain. A terribly sad site; Greg thoughtfully suggests that if you're offended, 'browse elsewhere.' "

- Radio Islam.
  URL: http://www.flashback.se/~rislam
  U.S. mirror site: http://abbc.com/islam

According to their home page, "Radio Islam is against racisms of all kinds and forms, against all kinds of discrimination of people based on their colour of skin, fatih [sic], ethnical bakground [sic]. Consequently, Radio Islam is against Jewish racism towards non-Jews, and the political aims of World Zionism." In addition to the revisionism page, this site contains pages on Zionism and the Palestine Question and on Judaism, Jewish Power and Jewish Racism. The revisionism page (http://abbc.com/islam/english/english.htm#revision) contains a substantial list of articles by major and not-so-major revisionist authors as well as an alphabetical library of revisionist authors and their works.

- Zündelsite.
  URL: http://www.webcom.com/ezundel/english
  Mirror sites: http://www.eskimo.com/~kay/
  http://www.wsu.edu:8080/~lpauling/zundel.
  html

This site was founded by Ernst Zündel, the Canadian publisher of "Did Six Million Really Die?" who was prosecuted under a "false news" statute (see Harwood under *Revisionist Authors*, below). The site contains the text of that pamphlet as well as the text of the Leuchter report (see Leuchter, below) and an extensive dialogue with and about the Nizkor Project, to whose site Zundel links "for relentless Holocaust promotion." He states that his publication of Harwood's pamphlet on the site caused the German government to censor his server, "the first-time-ever censorship ban on the Net." The site's mission statement is as follows: "The Zündelsite has as its mission the rehabilitation of the honor and reputation of the German nation and people." Greg Raven charges that the Canadian Human Rights Commission is attempting to shut the Zündelsite down. Other sites have taken up support of this server by acting as mirror sites. In preparing this article, I was unable to connect to the Zündelsite at its regular address, only through the mirror sites.

REFUTATION INTERNET SITES

- HateWatch.
  URL: http://hatewatch.org

HateWatch began in 1996, and provides "an online resource for concerned individuals, academics, organizations and the media to keep abreast of and to combat hate activity on the Internet." They classify hate by category: white supremacy, music, racist skinheads, neo-Nazism, Holocaust denial, Christian identity, foreign, nationalism, black racism, anti-gay, anti-Christian, anti-Arab. The Holocaust Denial page (http://hatewatch.org/revision.html) contains introductory articles on the subject and links to the major revisionist sites. More than just listings, the links include the sites' graphics and paragraph-length excerpts from the home pages, to give the flavor of what the site is about.

- The Nizkor Project.
  URL: http://www.nizkor.org/index.html

  "Nizkor is not a single collection of Web pages, but a collage of projects focused on the Holocaust and its denial, often incorrectly referred to as Holocaust 'revisionism.'" The word "Nizkor" means "We will remember." This site contains four extensive FAQs (http://www1.us.nizkor.org/faqs/) that "have served as "a layman's guide" to issues surrounding Holocaust-denial since 1993." It also contains replies to IHR's "Sixty-six Questions & Answers about the Holocaust," an essay on "Revision or Denial?", and an open letter to Zündelsite visitors. The Nizkor site hosts the Shofar FTP Archive with over 11,000 files on antisemitism, camps, the Holocaust, the Trial of the Major War Criminals Before the International Military Tribunal, organizations, people, and places. It also hosts the archives of the alt.revisionism newsgroup. The ftp documents are searchable by keyword and concept using the Excite search engine. The Nizkor site provides links to other refutation sites and documents as well as Holocaust sites.

- Ressources documentaires sur le genocide nazi et sa négation/ Documentary Resources on the Nazi Genocide and its Negation.
  URL: http://mediatheque.ircam.fr/~mf/anti-rev/

  This site is on the personal web pages of Michel Fingerhut, a staff member at the Médiathèque de l'Ircam, Institute de Recherche et Coodination Acoustique/Musique, the multimedia library of the Centre Georges Pompidou in Paris. It contains articles and essays (some in English, more in French) including the Vidal-Naquet and Fresco introductory articles (see *Introductory Material*, above), poems, a bibliography with some items hot-linked, and links to other Internet resources. There is a full-text search of the site available.

REVISIONIST AUTHORS

- Ball, John. "Air Photo Evidence."
  URL: http://www.air-photo.com

These are studies of World War II air photos and 3-D color maps of Auschwitz, Treblinka, Belzec, and Majdanek, obtained from the National Archives. The author states that "It is physically impossible mass gassings occurred in the alleged buildings, and it is irrational to believe mass murders could have been conducted for even one day in the visible corners of busy work camps." He also says that physical evidence on site as well as the air photos were tampered with. This study is often cited in revisionist writings.

- Butz, Arthur R. "A Short Introduction to the Study of Holocaust Revisionism."
  URL: http://pubweb.nwu.edu/~abutz/di/intro.html

Butz is an associate professor of Electrical Engineering and Computer Sciences at Northwestern University. He is the author of *The Hoax of the Twentieth Century: The case against the presumed extermination of European Jewry*, published in 1976. This article was published in 1991 in the *Daily Northwestern*.

- Faurisson, Robert. "Elie Wiesel: A Prominent False Witness."
  URL: http://abbc.com/islam/english/revision/wiesel.htm

- _____. "How Many Deaths at Auschwitz?" December 19, 1995.
  URL: http://abbc.com/islam/english/revision/faurdeat.htm

- _____. "The U.S. Holocaust Memorial Museum: A Challenge."
  URL: http://abbc.com/islam/english/revision/faurvict.htm

Faurisson was a professor of literary criticism at the University of Lyons. In 1979 he wrote *The "Problem of the Gas Chambers," or "The Rumor of Auschwitz."* His 1980 work, *Mémoire en défense contre ceux qui m'accusent de falsifier l'histoire: la question des chambres à gaz*, contained a preface by Noam Chomsky, who defended scholars' rights to freely publish their ideas. Faurisson was prosecuted under French laws against questioning the existence of crimes against humanity. The Internet-accessible articles listed above are those that have been translated into English. For those who read French, a more extensive list is available at the Archive Faurisson (URL: http://www.abbc.com/aaargh/fran/archFaur/archFaur.html).

- Garaudy, Roger. "The Founding Myths of Israeli Politics." 1996.
  URL: http://www.codoh.com/zionweb/zionmythgar.html

- Harwood, Richard E. "Did Six Million Really Die: Truth At Last—Exposed."
  URL: http://www.sinet.it/Islam/judaism/0003.txt

Richard Harwood is a pseudonym of Richard Verrall, a member of the British National Front. This pamphlet was originally published in 1974. It was republished in Canada with a new introduction by Ernst Zündel, who was subsequently prosecuted for publishing "false news." Zündel's trial generated controversy over freedom of expression.

- Irving, David. "Hitler's War: An Introduction to the New Edition." 1989.
  URL: http://www.codoh.com/irving/irvhitwar.html

- _____. "On Contemporary History and Historiography." Remarks delivered at the 1983 International Revisionist Conference.
  URL: http://www.codoh.com/irving/irvcontem.html

David Irving is a British historian. His book, *Hitler's War*, was published in 1977. It stated that Himmler, not Hitler, was responsible for planning and carrying out the "final solution."

- Leuchter, Fred. "The Leuchter Report: The End of a Myth: A Report on the Alleged Execution Gas Chambers at Auschwitz, Birkenau and Majdanek, Poland by an Execution Equipment Expert." Samisdat Publishers Ltd., 1988.
  URL: http://www.kaiwan.com/~ihrgreg/zundel/english/leuchter/
  report1/leuchtertoc.html

This report, commissioned by Zündel and used as evidence at his trial, stated that there were not and could not have been execution gas chambers at these camps.

- Rassinier, Paul. "Debunking the Genocide Myth: A Study of the Nazi Concentration Camps and the Alleged Extermination of European Jewry." 1978.
  URL: http://www.abbc.com/aaargh/engl/PRdebunkIntro.html
  http://www.abbc.com/aaargh/engl/PRdebunk1.html
  http://www.abbc.com/aaargh/engl/PRdebunk2.html

In addition to this work, Rassinier (a former Buchenwald inmate) wrote *The Drama of the European Jews* in 1975 and *The Real Eichmann Trial, or, the Incorrigible Victors* in 1979. He claims that at most one million Jews died, but as a result of bad conditions and often at the hands of Jewish *kapos* in the camps, not of policy. He also holds the Communists rather than the Nazis responsible for any atrocities that occurred.

- Raven, Greg. "Sixty-Six Questions and Answers on the Holocaust." Last updated 1/95.
  URL: http://www.kaiwan.com/~ihrgreg/pamphlets/66questions.
  html

Raven is the associate editor of the *Journal of Historical Review*. This journal, which began in 1980, is published by the Institute for Historical Review. The IHR sponsors a great deal of revisionist research and publication. This particular document is often cited on revisionist and counter-revisionist Internet sites.

- Thion, Serge. "European History and the Arab World." 1993.
  URL: http://www.codoh.com/zionweb/zionthion1.html

- _____ . "On Pressac: History by Night or in Fog?" 1994.
  URL: http://www.abbc.com/aaargh/engl/nightfog.html

  Thion's major revisionist work is *Vérité historique ou vérité politique? Le dossier de l'affaire Faurisson. La question des chambres à gaz.* The Internet-accessible articles listed above are those that have been translated into English. For those who read French, a more extensive list is available at the Archive Thion (URL: http://www.abbc.com/aaargh/fran/histo/SF1.html).

- Weber, Charles E. "The 'Holocaust': 120 Questions and Answers." Institute for Historical Review, 1983.
  URL: http://abbc.com/islam/english/revision/holo-120.htm

- Zündel, Ernst. "Holocaust Myth 101." January 1996.
  URL: http://www.eskimo.com/~kay/english/101/101toc.html

  This document, by the publisher of "Did Six Million Really Die?", summarizes eight broad revisionist claims.

REFUTATION AUTHORS

- Breitbart, Aaron. "Responses to Revisionist Arguments." Simon Wiesenthal Center, 1995.
  URL: http://www.wiesenthal.com/resource/revision.htm

- McVay, Kenneth. "Holocaust FAQ: Willis Carto & The Institute for Historical Review." 1996.
  URL: ftp://rtfm.mit.edu/pub/usenet/news.answers/holocaust/
      ihr/part01
      ftp://rtfm.mit.edu/pub/usenet/news.answers/holocaust/
      ihr/part02

- McVay, Kenneth and Daniel Keren. "Holocaust Denial & The Big Lie." 1993.
  URL: http://shamash.org/holocaust/denial/answers.txt

- Nizkor Project. "QAR Index: A Reply to the IHR/Zündel's '66 Q&A.' "
  URL: http://www2.ca.nizkor.org/features/qar/

Index

Haworth
DOCUMENT DELIVERY
SERVICE

This valuable service provides a single-article order form for any article from a Haworth journal.

- *Time Saving:* No running around from library to library to find a specific article.
- *Cost Effective:* All costs are kept down to a minimum.
- *Fast Delivery:* Choose from several options, including same-day FAX.
- *No Copyright Hassles:* You will be supplied by the original publisher.
- *Easy Payment:* Choose from several easy payment methods.

Open Accounts Welcome for . . .
- Library Interlibrary Loan Departments
- Library Network/Consortia Wishing to Provide Single-Article Services
- Indexing/Abstracting Services with Single Article Provision Services
- Document Provision Brokers and Freelance Information Service Providers

---

MAIL or *FAX* THIS ENTIRE ORDER FORM TO:

Haworth Document Delivery Service
The Haworth Press, Inc.
10 Alice Street
Binghamton, NY 13904-1580

or FAX: 1-800-895-0582
or CALL: 1-800-342-9678
9am-5pm EST

PLEASE SEND ME PHOTOCOPIES OF THE FOLLOWING SINGLE ARTICLES:

1) Journal Title: _____
   Vol/Issue/Year: _____ Starting & Ending Pages: _____
   Article Title: _____
   _____

2) Journal Title: _____
   Vol/Issue/Year: _____ Starting & Ending Pages: _____
   Article Title: _____
   _____

3) Journal Title: _____
   Vol/Issue/Year: _____ Starting & Ending Pages: _____
   Article Title: _____
   _____

4) Journal Title: _____
   Vol/Issue/Year: _____ Starting & Ending Pages: _____
   Article Title: _____

(See other side for Costs and Payment Information)

COSTS: Please figure your cost to order quality copies of an article.

1. Set-up charge per article: $8.00
   ($8.00 × number of separate articles) _____

2. Photocopying charge for each article:
   - 1-10 pages: $1.00 _____
   - 11-19 pages: $3.00 _____
   - 20-29 pages: $5.00 _____
   - 30+ pages: $2.00/10 pages _____

3. Flexicover (optional): $2.00/article _____

4. Postage & Handling: US: $1.00 for the first article/
   $.50 each additional article _____

   Federal Express: $25.00 _____

   Outside US: $2.00 for first article/
   $.50 each additional article _____

5. Same-day FAX service: $.35 per page _____

   GRAND TOTAL: _____

METHOD OF PAYMENT: (please check one)

❏ Check enclosed   ❏ Please ship and bill. PO # _____
   (sorry we can ship and bill to bookstores only! All others must pre-pay)

❏ Charge to my credit card: ❏ Visa; ❏ MasterCard; ❏ Discover;
   ❏ American Express;

Account Number:_____ Expiration date:_____

Signature: **X**_____

Name: _____ Institution: _____

Address: _____

_____

City: _____ State:_____ Zip:_____

Phone Number: _____ FAX Number: _____

MAIL or *FAX* THIS ENTIRE ORDER FORM TO:

Haworth Document Delivery Service
The Haworth Press, Inc.
10 Alice Street
Binghamton, NY 13904-1580

or FAX: 1-800-895-0582
or CALL: 1-800-342-9678
9am-5pm EST)